George T. Ferris

Great Musical Composers

German, French and Italian

George T. Ferris

Great Musical Composers
German, French and Italian

ISBN/EAN: 9783337237103

Printed in Europe, USA, Canada, Australia, Japan

Cover: Foto ©Thomas Meinert / pixelio.de

More available books at **www.hansebooks.com**

GREAT MUSICAL COMPOSERS

GERMAN, FRENCH, AND ITALIAN

By GEORGE T. FERRIS

EDITED, WITH AN INTRODUCTION
BY
MRS. WILLIAM SHARP

LONDON
WALTER SCOTT, 24 WARWICK LANE
PATERNOSTER ROW
1887

CONTENTS.

	PAGE
INTRODUCTION	vii
BACH	1
HANDEL	7
GLUCK	36
HAYDN	46
MOZART	59
BEETHOVEN	70
SCHUBERT AND SCHUMANN	87
CHOPIN	103
WEBER	115
MENDELSSOHN	124
WAGNER	131
PALESTRINA	147
PICCINI, PAISIELLO, AND CIMAROSA	154
ROSSINI	175
DONIZETTI AND BELLINI	200
VERDI	213
CHERUBINI AND HIS PREDECESSORS	226
MEHUL, SPONTINI, AND HALEVY	260
BOIELDIEU AND AUBER	273
MEYERBEER	281
GOUNOD	297
BERLIOZ	310
APPENDIX: CHRONOLOGICAL TABLE	335

Introduction.

THE following biographical sketches were originally published in America by Mr. George T. Ferris, in two volumes, separately entitled *The Great German Composers* and *The Great Italian and French Composers*. They have achieved the success they deserved: for while we have whole libraries of books upon the history and technicalities of music in general, upon musical theories and schools, and upon the exponents thereof in their artistic capacity, there has been a distinct dearth of treatises dealing in a brief and popular fashion with the lives of eminent composers themselves. Now, when music is "mastered and murdered" in almost every house throughout the length and breadth of the land, there can be no doubt that compilations of this kind must be welcome to a very large number—we will not say of musical students, but of lovers of music. There are, it would be needless to attempt to prove, great numbers of the music-loving public, who practically have no facilities towards making acquaintance with the leading facts in the lives of those men whose compositions they have such a genuine delight in rendering: to these mainly is such a book as *Great Composers* addressed. But, indeed, to every one interested in music and musicians the volume can hardly fail to be of interest. In his preface to *The Great Italian and French Composers*, Mr

Ferris explained that—as was very manifest—"the task of compressing into one small volume suitable sketches of the more famous Italian and French composers was, in view of the extent of field and the wealth of material, a somewhat embarrassing one, especially as the purpose was to make the sketches of interest to the general music-loving public, and not merely to the critic and scholar. The plan pursued has been to devote the bulk of space to composers of the higher rank, and to pass over those less known with such brief mention as sufficed to outline their lives, and fix their place in the history of music."

To *The Great German Composers* he prefaces a few words which may be quoted—"The sketches of composers contained in this volume may seem arbitrary in the space allotted to them. The special attention given to certain names has been prompted as much by their association with great art epochs, as by the consideration of their absolute rank as composers. The introduction of Chopin, born a Pole, and for a large part of his life a resident of France, among German composers, may require an explanatory word. Chopin's whole early training was in the German school, and he may be looked on as one of the founders of the latest school of pianoforte composition, whose highest development is in contemporary Germany. He represents German music by his affinities and his influences in art, and bears too close a relation to important changes in musical forms to be omitted from this series."

Various important events have occurred since the publication of these volumes in America: *inter alia*, the performance of Wagner's last great work "Parsifal," and the death of the great German musician; the production of new works by Gounod and Verdi; and so forth. The editor has endeavoured, as briefly as practicable, to supplement Mr. Ferris's *causeries* with the addenda necessary to bring *Great Composers* down to date. Mr. Ferris further acknowledges his obligation to the following authorities for the facts embodied in these sketches:—Hullah's *History of Modern Music;* Fetis' *Biographie Universelle des Musiciens;* Clementi's *Biographie des Musiciens;* Hogarth's *History of the Opera;* Sutherland Edwards' *History of the Opera;* Schlüter's *History of Music;* Chorley's *Thirty Years' Musical Reminiscences;* Stendhall's *Vie de Rossini;* Bellasy's *Memorials of Cherubini;* Grove's *Musical Dictionary;* Crowestl's *Musical Anecdotes;* Schœlcher's *Life of Handel;* Liszt's *Life of Chopin;* Elsie Polko's *Reminiscences;* Lampadius' *Life of Mendelssohn;* Urbino's *Musical Composers;* Franz Hueffer's *Wagner and the Music of the Future;* Haweis'

INTRODUCTION.

Music and Morals; and the various articles in the leading cyclopædias.

To this volume the present editor has appended a chronological table of the musicians referred to in the following sketches.

In reading the lives of these great musical composers, we can trace the gradual development of music from its earliest days as an art and as a science. Unlike the other arts which have flourished, decayed, and had rebirth, music, as we now understand it, sprang into being out of the ferment of the Renaissance, and therefore is the youngest of the arts—a modern growth belonging particularly to the later phases of civilisation. Music in a rude, undeveloped condition has existed doubtless "since the world began." In all nations, and in the records of past civilisations, indications of music are to be found; martial strains for the encouragement of warriors on the march; sacred hymns and sacrificial chants in religious ceremonials; and song accompanied by some rude instrument—we find to have been known and practised among remote tribes as well as among potent races. The bards of divers peoples and many countries in ancient days played upon the harp not merely for delight, but for the exorcism of evil spirits, the dispersion of melancholy, the soothing and cure of mental and physical disorders. Here we find music as the direct expression of feeling, but not as a science. The Greeks made further use of music by incorporating it into their dramas, but it was chiefly declamatory, and was used solely in the choruses. To modern ears such music would sound very inefficient, more especially as the antique instruments were of the crudest—and although musical sounds, to a limited extent, could be produced from them, all attempts at *expression* must have been unsuccessful.

In Europe in the early middle ages there existed two kinds of music: that of the people, spontaneous, impulsive, the song of the Troubadour, unwritten and orally transmitted from father to son; that of the Church, which had been greatly encouraged since the days of Constantine, and especially owed much to St. Ambrose and St. Gregory. For a time music became the handmaid of the Church, but it thereby, to a certain extent, also gave voice to the lyrical feelings of the people; for the chorister and composer not only embodied popular songs into the chants, but in many instances interpolated the words themselves. This incongruity at length necessitated the reform, brought about by Palestrina—the father of sacred music as we now know it —whose *Missa Papae Marcelli*, performed in 1565, established a type which has been more or less adhered to ever since. The services of the Church gave rise to the oratorio, which, however, chiefly owes its development to Protestant genius, more especially to Handel. In 1540 San Filippo Neri formed in Milan a Society called "Le congregazione dei Padri dell' Oratorio" (from *orare* to pray), and we are told by Crescembini that "The oratorio, a poetical composition, formerly a commixture of the dramatic and narrative styles, but now entirely a musical drama, had its origin from San Filippo Neri, who in his chapel, after sermons and other devotions, in order to allure young people to pious offices, and to detain them from earthly pleasures, had hymns, psalms, and such like prayers sung by one or more voices." " Among these spiritual songs were dialogues; and these entertainments, becoming more frequent and improving every year, were the occasion that, in the seventeenth century, oratorios were invented, so called from their origin."*

Then came the fulness of the Renaissance, quickening dead forms into new life, laying its vivifying touch on the new-born art, music, and making it its nursling. At first the change was hardly perceptible. It was church music out of church, fine, stately, what may with seeming parodox be called statuesque, which came to bear the name of *L'Opera*, signifying *The Work:*—but, though born to a heritage of good aims, possessed of very inadequate means for their fulfilment. Once liberated from its presumed function of expressing religious feeling, and thus subjected to other impelling forces, music could not long remain in the old forms. It began to feel its way into new channels, and in the form of the opera became a national institution. Its growth at first was weak and faulty; but finally it developed into a perfect art. It was as the novice, who, freed from the sanctity of the convent with its calm lights and shadows, enters at last the portals of the life of the world—a varied world full of turmoil, passion, and strife. A greater world, after all, than that quitted, because composed of so many possibilities in so many directions, and comprising the sufferings, the joys, the aspirations of such innumerably differentiated beings; a world wherein the novice learns to widen her sympathies, to feel with and for the people, and to express for them the never-ceasing craving for something beyond the fleeting moment. At first, therefore, the stately art and the musical needs of the people were dissimilar and apart; but little by little each gave to and took from the other, till at length, out of the marriage of these elementaries, a third arose to become the expression of the life of the people,

* Hawkin's *Musical History*, vol. iii., p. 441.

partaking in likeness of both, having lost certain qualities, having gained many more, becoming richer, broader, more eclectic—in short, developing into the more fitting expression of the manifold aspirations of modern days, when life is varied and intense, and the mind gropes blindly in every direction.

This development is traceable in all art, and in the sphere of music it is most manifest in the opera. Like all great movements the opera began humbly. Towards the end of the sixteenth century a number of amateurs in Florence, dissatisfied with the polyphonic school of music, combined "to revive the musical declamation of the Greeks," to wed poetry and music—so long dissevered—to make the music follow the inflexion of the voice and the sense of the words. The first opera was "Il Conte Ugolino," composed by Vicenzio Galileo—father of the famous astronomer—and it was followed by various others, the titles of which need not here be recorded. At first, such performances took place in the palaces of nobles on grand occasions, when frequently both performers and musicians were of high rank. At length, however, in 1637 a famous theorbo player, Benedetto Farrari, and Francesco Manetti, the composer, opened in Venice an opera-house at their own risk, and a little later brought out with great success "Le nozzi di Peleo e di Telide" by Cavalli, a disciple of Monteverde, and it was henceforth that the opera became, as we have said, a national institution. Schools for singing were opened in Rome, Naples, and Venice—the science of music made rapid strides—instruments for orchestral purposes naturally likewise improved in quality and in variety; and the opera developed continuously in breadth of treatment and form in the hands of Scarlatti, Leo Jommelli, and Cimarosa.

About the beginning of the eighteenth century a rival to the *serious* opera sprang up in Naples—the *comic* opera, the direct offspring of the people, and of lower artistic standing. But as the serious opera became more stately, more scientific, more purely formal, less human, less the expression of direct feeling, cultivated more for art's sake solely, the comic opera throve on the very qualities that its elder sister rejected, till at length the greatest musicians of the day, Pergolesi, Cimarosa, Mozart, wrote their masterpieces for it. Ultimately the two were fused into one, that is, into the modern Italian opera. The comic opera, as we now understand it, is of French origin.

From Italy the opera found its way into other countries with varying results. In England it took early root, and assimilated itself with the earlier *masques* which were played at Whitehall and at Inns of Court. In the early productions in this country, however, the music was merely incidental. During the Commonwealth, an opera entitled "The Siege of Rhodes," composed by Dr. Charles Colman, Captain Henry Cook, Henry Lawes, and George Hudson, was performed in 1655, under the express license of Cromwell. Purcell seems, however, to have been the first to see the possibility of a national English opera;—his music to Dryden's "King Arthur," and to the "Indian Queen," is considered very beautiful; "his recitative was as rhetorically perfect as Lulli's, but infinitely more natural, and frequently impassioned to the last degree; his airs are not in the Italian form, but breathe rather the spirit of unfettered natural melody, and stand forth as models of refinement and freedom." "The Beggar's Opera," set to music by Dr. Pepusch, and Dr. Arne's "Artaxerxes," a translation from Metastasia's libretto, adapted to melodious music, were deservedly popular, and long retained a place on the stage. Nevertheless, when the Italian opera became an institution in England, the national opera made no further progress. During the last few years the former seems to have practically died out in England, and it remains to be seen in what form the English opera will revive and flourish once more as a national product. We have good promise in the works of such musicians as Balfe, Wallace, Sterndale Bennet, Sir G. A. Macfarren, Dr. A. C. Mackenzie, Sir Arthur Sullivan, Mr. C. V. Stanford, and others.

The end of the sixteenth and end of the seventeenth centuries form what has been called "the golden age of English music—aye for all musical Europe—of the madrigal. Nowhere was the cultivation of that noble form of pure vocal music, whether in composition or in performance, followed with more zeal or success than in England." The Hon. Roger North, Attorney-General to James II., in his *Memories of Musick*, speaks thus of the state of music in the first half of the seventeenth century—"Afterwards these (Italian *fantazias*) were imitated by the English, who, working more elaborately, improved upon their patterne, which gave occasion to an observation, that in vocall the Italians, and in instrumental music the English excelled." Again he alludes to "those authors whose performance gained the nation the credit in excelling the Italians in all but vocall." In instrumental music, then, in the madrigal, the cantata, and in ecclesiastical music, England prospered. Among her most important composers were John Dowland, Ford, Henry Lawes, John Jenkens, Pelham Humphreys, Wise, Blow, Henry Purcell—great in secular and ecclesiastical works, in instrumental and in vocal—Croft and Weldon; all were predecessors of Handel, who, though one of the greatest of German composers, lived nearly fifty years in England, composed several operas and all his famous oratorios for England, and is therefore not unjustifiably added to the list of English composers.

The opera was first introduced into France by Cardinal Mazarin early in the seventeenth century, but the lyrical drama owes its origin in that country to Lulli, who also introduced into it the ballet, which was a favourite pastime of the young king Louis XIV. The ballet has since become an integral part of the French and also of the later Italian operas. It was Lulli, again, who extended the "meagre prelude" of the Italian opera into the overture as we now know it. But as the rise and progress of the French opera is fully portrayed in the following musical sketches, it is needless to trace it further here.

Germany—equally with Italy the land of music, but of harmonious in contra-distinction to melodic music, which belongs most properly to Italy, well named the land of song—was much later in developing her musical powers than Italy, but she cultivated them to grander and nobler proportions; for to Germany we owe the magnificent development of instrumental music, which culminates in the form of the sonata for the piano, and in that of the symphony for the orchestra, in the hands of such masters as Bach, Haydn, Mozart, Beethoven. In Germany the opera took root by means of a translation of Rinaccini's "Dafne," set to music by Henry Schütz in 1627, with Italian airs and German recitative. The first German opera or *singspiel*, "Adam und Eva," by Johann Theil, was performed in 1678, but it became national through the works of Reinhard Keiser, whose opera "Basilino" was performed in 1693. "His style was purely German, less remarkable for its rhetorical perfection than that of Lulli, but exhibiting far greater variety of expression, and more earnest endeavour to attain that spirit of Dramatic Truth which alone can render such music worthy of its intended purpose." He was worthily followed by Hasse, Grann, by Mozart's "Le Nozze di Figaro," "Die Zauberflöte.," "Don Giovanni," and by Beethoven's one opera "Fidelio."

The growth of a national opera in Germany and France, competing with that of Italy, induced also the rise of party quarrels between the adherents of the several schools; and the history of music demonstrates the fact, often seen in the history of politics, that in such contentions the real point at issue—the *excellence* of the subject in question—is lost sight of in the fierce strife of opponents; the broader issues are obscured in the narrowing influences of mere partizanship, wherein each side on principle shuts its eyes equally to the merits of its adversary and to its own faults. Thus in the following sketches are recorded the quarrels between the adherents of Lulli and Rameau, Handel and Bonacini, Piccini and Gluck, Mozart and Salieri, Weber and Rossini, and in the present day between the advocates of Wagner's "Music of the Future" and those of the "Music of the Past." "The old order changes, giving place to new," but only after a long protracted struggle, a struggle that will not be productive of good as long as the bitterness of partizanship exists, whose aim is wholly to annihilate its adversary, though thereby much that is good and fine be lost. This is not, however, the place to discuss the importance of such strife, nor the comparative advantages and disadvantages of its existence or non-existence—but it is as well to draw attention to it in order to point out that in the history of music the belligerents are usually blind to the important fact that, inasmuch as nations differ essentially in ways of thought and action, in character, temperament, and fundamental nature, so also must the various phases of art differ which are their mediums of expression.

The history of the art of music is divisible into two great epochs—the first dating from its birth about three centuries ago under the impelling influences of the Renaissance, to the end of the eighteenth century, when psuedo-classicism had given all it had to give; the second dating from the rise of Romanticism in the beginning of the nineteenth century to the present day. The revival of the "forgotten world of old romance—that world of wonder and mystery and spiritual beauty," no longer crippled by lack of science, and fettered by asceticism, was to music, that youngest of the arts, a novel influence, which pushed it vigorously in a new direction, towards the more direct expression of the cravings of humanity—making it more *human*, more the fitting medium expression of this democratic age. The true romantic feeling has been described as "the ever present apprehension of the spiritual world, and of that struggle of the soul with earthly conditions." This later period gave "new seeing to our eyes, which were once more opened to the mysteries and the wonder of the universe, and the romance of man's destiny; it revived, in short, the romantic spirit enriched by the clarity and sanity that the renascence was able to lend."

In the opera Gluck was one of the earliest masters who came under the influence of the new movement, and he anticipated

Wagner in many of his reforms. He decreased the importance of the singer, and increased that of the orchestra, elaborated the recitative, and made the music to follow the rhythm of the words, and he also gave importance to the dramatic expression of the human emotions. In Germany Weber is styled the Father of the Romantic opera, as in France the most noteworthy figure is Berlioz, and the new method was further developed in the instrumental music by Schumann, and demonstrated by other musicians, dead and living, who, from the limited space of this volume, have not been specially noticed—Liszt, Franz, Thomas, Brahm, Rubenstein, Dvorák, Massinet, Bizet, Jensen, Grieg, and others. Gounod, is, of course, unmistakably under the same influence, and may be considered as the direct descendant of Gluck, and there is every reason to suppose that he is the last great composer of the grand opera of France, as Verdi is undeniably that of the Italian opera. The most remarkable figure of the movement, he who has carried it to its utmost limits, is Richard Wagner. At first he refused for his compositions the name of "Music of the Future," and desired for them the more comprehensive term of "Work of Art of the Future." It is impossible to predict to what extent his theories will be followed: it is not desirable that they should be blindly worked out by musicians of power inferior to his; but they are in the right direction, and may ultimately bring about a new art mode in music. The resources of art are endless, being, as the Abbé Lamennais tells us, to man what creation is to God; and music may safely be trusted to develop in such a way as to ever be the most fitting expression of the inarticulate cravings and aspirations of the human soul. Wagner has attempted to unite the three arts of Painting, Poetry, and Music: and of his work a competent judge has writen—"The musical drama is undoubtedly the highest manifestation of which men are capable. All the most refined arts are called in to contribute to the idea. The author of a musical drama is no more a musician, or a poet, or a painter; he is the supreme *artist*, not fettered by the limits of one art, but able to step over the boundaries of all the different branches of æsthetic composition, and find the proper means for rendering his thought wherever he wants it. This was Wagner's aim. His latter works, "Tristram and Isolde," the "Niebelungen Ring," and "Parsifal," are the actuation of the theory, or at least are works showing what is the way towards the aim." Another eminent critic, Mr. Walter Pater, writing upon the fine arts, tells us that "*All art constantly aspires towards the condition of music*. . . . It is the art of music which most completely realises this artistic ideal, this perfect identification of form and matter. In its ideal consummate moments, the end is not distinct from the means, the form from the matter, the subject from the expression; they inhere in and completely saturate each other; and to it, therefore, to the condition of its perfect moments, all the arts may be supposed constantly to tend and aspire. Music, then, and not poetry, as is so often supposed, is the true type or measure of consummate art. Therefore, although each art has its incommunicable element, its untranslatable order of impressions, its unique mode of reaching the 'imaginative reason,' yet the arts may be represented as continually struggling after the law or principle of music, to a condition which music alone completely realises."

We may rest assured—as assured as Emerson or Matthew Arnold concerning the illimitable possibilities of poetry—that the future has great riches in store for all lovers of music. Giants, indeed, are they who are no longer among us, but it is not derogatory to these great ones to believe and hope that—life being "moving music" according to the definition of the Syrian Gnostics—the world will yet be electrified by the genius of successors worthy of such royal ancestry as Handel and Mozart, Beethoven and Wagner.

ELIZABETH A. SHARP.

THE GREAT COMPOSERS.

[GERMAN.]

BACH.

I.

HE growth and development of German music are eminently noteworthy facts in the history of the fine arts. In little more than a century and a-half it reached its present high and brilliant place, its progress being so consecutive and regular that the composers who illustrated its well-defined epochs might fairly have linked hands in one connected series.

To JOHANN SEBASTIAN BACH must be accorded the title of "father of modern music." All succeeding composers have bowed with reverence before his name, and acknowledged in him the creative mind which not only placed music on a deep scientific basis, but perfected the form from which have been developed the wonderfully rich and varied phases of orchestral composition. Handel, who was his contemporary, having been born the same year, spoke of him with sincere admiration, and called him the giant of music. Haydn wrote—" Whoever understands me knows that I owe much to Sebastian Bach, that I have studied him thoroughly and well, and that I acknowledge him only as my model." Mozart's unceasing research brought to light many of his unpublished manuscripts, and helped Germany to a full appreciation of this great master. In like manner have the other luminaries of music placed on record their sense of obligation to one whose name is obscure to the general public in comparison with many of his brother composers.

Sebastian Bach was born at Eisenach on the 21st of March 1685, the son of one of the court musicians. Left in the care of his elder brother, who was an organist, his brilliant powers displayed themselves at an early period. He was the descendant of a race of musicians, and even at that date the wide-spread branches of the family held annual gatherings of a musical character. Young Bach mastered for himself, without much assistance, a thorough musical education at Lüneburg, where he studied in the gymnasium and sang in the cathedral choir; and at the age of eighteen we find him court musician at Weimar, where a few years later he became organist and director of concerts. He had in the meantime studied the organ at Lübeck under the celebrated Buxtehude, and made himself thoroughly a master of the great Italian composers of sacred music—Palestrina, Lotti, Vivaldi, and others.

At this period Germany was beginning to experience its musical *renaissance*. The various German courts felt that throb of life and enthusiasm which had distinguished the Italian principalities in the preceding century in the direction of painting and sculpture. Every little capital was a focus of artistic rays, and there was a general spirit of rivalry among the princes, who aspired to cultivate the arts of peace as well as those of war. Bach had become known as a gifted musician, not only by his wonderful powers as an organist, but by two of his earlier masterpieces—"Gott ist mein König" and "Ich hatte viel Bekümmerniss." Under the influence of an atmosphere so artistic, Bach's ardour for study increased with his success, and his rapid advancement in musical power met with warm appreciation.

While Bach held the position of director of the chapel of

Prince Leopold of Anhalt-Köthen, which he assumed about the year 1720, he went to Hamburg on a pilgrimage to see old Reinke, then nearly a centenarian, whose fame as an organist was national, and had long been the object of Bach's enthusiasm. The aged man listened while his youthful rival improvised on the old choral, "Upon the Rivers of Babylon." He shed tears of joy while he tenderly embraced Bach, and said—"I did think that this art would die with me; but I see that you will keep it alive."

Our musician rapidly became known far and wide throughout the musical centres of Germany as a learned and recondite composer, as a brilliant improviser, and as an organist beyond rivalry. Yet it was in these last two capacities that his reputation among his contemporaries was the most marked. It was left to a succeeding generation to fully enlighten the world in regard to his creative powers as a musical thinker.

II.

Though Bach's life was mostly spent at Weimar and Leipsic, he was at successive periods chapel-master and concert-director at several of the German courts, which aspired to shape public taste in matters of musical culture and enthusiasm. But he was by nature singularly retiring and unobtrusive, and recoiled from several brilliant offers which would have brought him too much in contact with the gay world of fashion, apparently dreading any diversion from a severe and exclusive art-life; for within these limits all his hopes, energies, and wishes were focalised. Yet he was not without that keen spirit of rivalry, that love of combat, which seems to be native to spirits of the more robust and energetic type.

In the days of the old Minnesingers, tournaments of music shared the public taste with tournaments of arms. In Bach's time these public competitions were still in vogue. One of these was held by Augustus II., Elector of Saxony and King of Poland, one of the most munificent art-patrons of Europe, but best known to fame from his intimate part in the wars of Charles XII. of Sweden and Peter the Great of Russia. Here Bach's principal rival was a French *virtuoso*, Marchand, who, an exile from Paris, had delighted the king by the lightness and brilliancy of his execution. They were both to improvise on the same theme. Marchand heard Bach's performance and signalised his own inferiority by declining to play, and secretly leaving the city of Dresden. Augustus sent Bach a hundred louis d'or, but this splendid *douceur* never reached him, as it was appropriated by one of the court officials.

In Bach's half-century of a studious musical life there is but little of stirring incident to record. The significance of his career was interior, not exterior. Twice married, and the father of twenty children, his income was always small even for that age. Yet, by frugality, the simple wants of himself and his family never overstepped the limit of supply; for he seems to have been happily mated with wives who sympathised with his exclusive devotion to art, and united with this the virtues of old-fashioned German thrift.

Three years before his death, Bach, who had a son in the service of the King of Prussia, yielded to the urgent invitation of that monarch to go to Berlin. Frederick II., the conqueror of Rossbach, and one of the greatest of modern soldiers, was a passionate lover of literature and art, and it was his pride to collect at his court all the leading lights of European culture. He was not only the patron of Voltaire, whose connection with the Prussian monarch has furnished such rich material to the anecdote-history of literature, but of all the distinguished painters, poets, and musicians whom he could persuade by his munificent offers (but rarely fulfilled) to suffer the burden of his eccentricities. Frederick was not content with playing the part of patron, but must himself also be poet, philosopher, painter, and composer.

On the night of Bach's arrival Frederick was taking part in a concert at his palace, and, on hearing that the great musician whose name was in the mouths of all Germany had come, immediately sent for him without allowing him to don a court dress, interrupting his concert with the enthusiastic announcement, "Gentlemen, Bach is here." The cordial hospitality and admiration of Frederick was gratefully acknowledged by Bach, who dedicated to him a three-part fugue on a theme composed by the king, known under the name of "A Musical Offering." But he could not be persuaded to remain long from his Leipsic home.

Shortly before Bach's death, he was seized with blindness, brought on by incessant labour; and his end was supposed to have been hastened by the severe inflammation consequent on two operations performed by an English oculist. He departed this life July 30, 1750, and was buried in St. John's churchyard, universally mourned by musical Germany, though his real title to exceptional greatness was not to be read until the next generation.

III.

Sebastian Bach was not only the descendant of a widely-known musical family, but was himself the direct ancestor of about sixty of the best-known organists and church composers of Germany. As a master of organ-playing, tradition tells us that no one has been his equal, with the possible exception of Handel. He was also an able performer on various stringed instruments, and his preference for the clavichord* led him to write a method for that instrument, which has been the basis of all succeeding methods for the piano. Bach's teachings and influence may be said to have educated a large number of excellent composers and organ and piano players, among whom were Emanuel Bach, Cramer, Hummel, and Clementi; and on his school of theory and practice the best results in music have been built.

That Bach's glory as a composer should be largely posthumous is probably the result of his exceeding simplicity

* An old instrument, which may be called the nearest prototype of the modern square piano.

and diffidence, for he always shrank from popular applause; therefore we may believe his compositions were not placed in the proper light during his life. It was through Mozart, Haydn, and Beethoven, that the musical world learned what a master-spirit had wrought in the person of John Sebastian Bach. The first time Mozart heard one of Bach's hymns, he said, "Thank God! I learn something absolutely new."

Bach's great compositions include his "Preludes and Fugues" for the organ, works so difficult and elaborate as perhaps to be above the average comprehension, but sources of delight and instruction to all musicians; the "Matthäus Passion," for two choruses and two orchestras, one of the masterpieces in music, which was not produced till a century after it was written; the "Oratorio of the Nativity of Jesus Christ;" and a very large number of masses, anthems, cantatas, chorals, hymns, etc. These works, from their largeness and dignity of form, as also from their depth of musical science, have been to all succeeding composers an art-armoury, whence they have derived and furbished their brightest weapons. In the study of Bach's works the student finds the deepest and highest reaches in the science of music; for his mind seems to have grasped all its resources, and to have embodied them with austere purity and precision of form. As Spenser is called the poet for poets, and Laplace the mathematician for mathematicians, so Bach is the musician for musicians. While Handel may be considered a purely independent and parallel growth, it is not too much to assert that without Sebastian Bach and his matchless studies for the piano, organ, and orchestra, we could not have had the varied musical development in sonata and symphony from such masters as Haydn, Mozart, and Beethoven. Three of Sebastian Bach's sons became distinguished musicians, and to Emanuel we owe the artistic development of the sonata, which in its turn became the foundation of the symphony.

HANDEL.

I.

To the modern Englishman Handel is almost a contemporary. Paintings and busts of this great minstrel are scattered everywhere throughout the land. He lies in Westminster Abbey among the great poets, warriors, and statesmen, a giant memory in his noble art. A few hours after death the sculptor Roubiliac took a cast of his face, which he wrought into imperishable marble; "moulded in colossal calm," he towers above his tomb, and accepts the homage of the world benignly like a god. Exeter Hall and the Foundling Hospital in London are also adorned with marble statues of him.

There are more than fifty known pictures of Handel, some of them by distinguished artists. In the best of these pictures Handel is seated in the gay costume of the period, with sword, shot-silk breeches, and coat embroidered with gold. The face is noble in its repose. Benevolence is seated about the finely-shaped mouth, and the face wears the mellow dignity of years, without weakness or austerity. There are few collectors of prints in England and America who have not a woodcut or a lithograph of him. His face and his music are alike familiar to the English-speaking world.

Handel came to England in the year 1710, at the age of twenty-five. Four years before he had met, at Naples, Scarlatti, Porpora, and Corelli. That year had been the turning-point in his life. With one stride he reached the front rank, and felt that no musician alive could teach him anything.

GEORGE FREDERICK HANDEL (or Händel, as the name is written in German) was born at Halle, Lower Saxony, in the year 1685. Like German literature, German music is a comparatively recent growth. What little feeling existed for the musical art employed itself in cultivating the alien flowers of Italian song. Even eighty years after this Mozart and Haydn were treated like lackeys and vagabonds, just as great actors were treated in England at the same period. Handel's father looked on music as an occupation having very little dignity.

Determined that his young son should become a doctor like himself, and leave the divine art to Italian fiddlers and French buffoons, he did not allow him to go to a public school even, for fear he should learn the gamut. But the boy Handel, passionately fond of sweet sounds, had, with the connivance of his nurse, hidden in the garret a poor spinet, and in stolen hours taught himself how to play. At last the senior Handel had a visit to make to another son in the service of the Duke of Saxe-Weissenfels, and the young George was taken along to the ducal palace. The boy strayed into the chapel, and was irresistibly drawn to the organ. His stolen performance was made known to his father and the duke, and the former was very much enraged at such a direct evidence of disobedience. The duke, however, being astonished at the performance of the youthful genius, interceded for him, and recommended that his taste should be encouraged and cultivated instead of repressed.

From this time forward fortune showered upon him a combination of conditions highly favourable to rapid development. Severe training, ardent friendship, the society of the first composers, and incessant practice were vouchsafed him. As the pupil of the great organist Zachau, he studied the whole existing mass of German and Italian music, and soon exacted from his master the admission that he had nothing more to teach him. Thence he went to Berlin to study the opera-school, where Ariosti and Bononcini were favourite composers. The first was friendly, but the latter, who with a first-rate head had a cankered heart, determined to take the conceit out of the Saxon boy. He challenged him to play at sight an elaborate piece. Handel played it with perfect precision, and thenceforward Bononcini, though he hated the youth as a rival, treated him as an equal.

On the death of his father Handel secured an engagement at the Hamburg opera-house, where he soon made his mark by the ability with which, on several occasions, he conducted rehearsals.

At the age of nineteen Handel received the offer of the Lübeck organ, on condition that he would marry the daughter of the retiring organist. He went down with his friend Mattheson, who it seems had been offered the same terms. They both returned, however, in single blessedness to Hamburg.

Though the Lübeck maiden had stirred no bad blood between them, musical rivalry did. A dispute in the theatre resulted in a duel. The only thing that saved Handel's life was a great brass button that shivered his antagonist's point, when they were parted to become firm friends again.

While at Hamburg Handel's first two operas were composed, "Almira" and "Nero." Both of these were founded on dark tales of crime and sorrow, and, in spite of some beautiful airs and clever instrumentation, were musical failures, as might be expected.

Handel had had enough of manufacturing operas in Germany, and so in July 1706 he went to Florence. Here he was cordially received; for Florence was second to no city in Italy in its passion for encouraging the arts. Its noble specimens of art creations in architecture, painting, and sculpture produced a powerful impression upon the young musician. In little more than a week's time he composed an opera, "Rodrigo," for which he obtained one hundred sequins. His next visit was to Venice, where he arrived at the height of the carnival. Whatever effect Venice, with its weird and mysterious beauty, with its marble palaces, façades, pillars, and domes, its magnificent shrines and frescoes, produced on Handel, he took Venice by storm. Handel's power as an organist and a harpsichord player was only second to his strength as a composer, even when, in the full zenith of his maturity, he composed the "Messiah" and "Judas Maccabæus."

"Il caro Sassone," the dear Saxon, found a formidable opponent as well as dear friend in the person of Scarlatti. One night at a masked ball, given by a nobleman, Handel was present in disguise. He sat at the harpsichord, and astonished the company with his playing; but no one could tell who it was that ravished the ears of the assembly. Presently another masquerader came into the room, walked up to the instrument, and called out: "It is either the devil or the Saxon!" This was Scarlatti, who afterwards had with Handel, in Florence and Rome, friendly contests of skill, in which it seemed difficult to decide which was victor. To satisfy the Venetian public, Handel composed the opera "Agrippina," which made a *furore* among all the connoisseurs of the city.

So, having seen the summer in Florence and the carnival in Venice, he must hurry on to be in time for the great Easter celebrations in Rome. Here he lived under the patronage of Cardinal Ottoboni, one of the wealthiest and most liberal of the Sacred College. The cardinal was a modern representative of the ancient patrician. Living himself in princely luxury, he endowed hospitals and surgeries for the public. He distributed alms, patronised men of science and art, and entertained the public with comedies, operas, oratorios, puppet-shows, and academic disputes. Under the auspices of this patron, Handel composed three operas and two oratorios. Even at this early period the young composer was parting company with the strict old musical traditions, and his works showed an extraordinary variety and strength of treatment.

From Rome he went to Naples, where he spent his second Italian summer, and composed the original Italian "Aci e Galatea," which in its English version, afterwards written for the Duke of Chandos, has continued a marked favourite with the musical world. Thence, after a lingering return through the sunny land where he had been so warmly welcomed, and which had taught him most effectually, in convincing him that his musical life had nothing in common with the traditions of Italian musical art, he returned to Germany, settling at the court of George of Brunswick, Elector of Hanover, and afterwards King of England. He received commission in the course of a few months from the elector to visit England, having been warmly invited thither by some English noblemen. On his return to Hanover, at the end of six months, he found the dull and pompous little court unspeakably tiresome after the bustle of London. So it is not to be marvelled at that he took the earliest opportunity of returning to the land which he afterwards adopted. At this period he was not yet twenty-five years old, but already famous as a performer on the organ and harpsichord, and as a composer of Italian operas.

When Queen Anne died and Handel's old patron became King of England, Handel was forbidden to appear before him, as he had not forgotten the musician's escapade; but his peace was at last made by a little ruse. Handel had a friend at court, Baron Kilmansegge, from whom he learned that the king was, on a certain day, going to take an excursion on the Thames. So he set to work to compose music for the occasion, which he arranged to have performed on a boat which followed the king's barge. As the king floated down the river he heard the new and delightful "Water-Music." He knew that only one man could have composed such music; so he sent for Handel, and sealed his pardon with a pension of two hundred pounds a-year.

II.

Let us take a glance at the society in which the composer moved in the heyday of his youth. His greatness was to be perfected in after-years by bitter rivalries, persecution, alternate oscillations of poverty and affluence, and a multitude of bitter experiences. But at this time Handel's life was a serene and delightful one. Rival factions had not been organised to crush him. Lord Burlington lived much at his mansion, which was then out of town, although the house is now in the heart of Piccadilly. The intimate friendship of this nobleman helped to bring the young musician into contact with many distinguished people.

It is odd to think of the people Handel met daily without knowing that their names and his would be in a century famous. The following picture sketches Handel and his friends in a sprightly fashion :—

"Yonder heavy, ragged-looking youth standing at the corner of Regent Street, with a slight and rather more refined-looking companion, is the obscure Samuel Johnson, quite unknown to fame. He is walking with Richard Savage. As Signor Handel, 'the composer of Italian music,' passes by, Savage becomes excited, and nudges his friend, who takes only a languid interest in the foreigner. Johnson did not care for music; of many noises he considered it the least disagreeable.

"Toward Charing Cross comes, in shovel-hat and cassock, the renowned ecclesiastic, Dean Swift. He has just nodded patronisingly to Bononcini in the Strand, and suddenly meets Handel, who cuts him dead. Nothing disconcerted, the dean moves on, muttering his famous epigram—

> 'Some say that Signor Bononcini,
> Compared to Handel, is a ninny;
> While others vow that to him Handel
> Is hardly fit to hold a candle.
> Strange that such difference should be
> 'Twixt tweedledum and tweedledee.'

"As Handel enters the 'Turk's Head' at the corner of Regent Street, a noble coach and four drives up. It is the Duke of Chandos, who is inquiring for Mr. Pope. Presently a deformed little man, in an iron-grey suit, and with a face as keen as a razor, hobbles out, makes a low bow to the burly Handel, who, helping him into the chariot, gets in after him, and they drive off together to Cannons, the duke's mansion at Edgeware. There they meet Mr. Addison, the poet Gay, and the witty Arbuthnot, who have been asked to luncheon. The last number of the *Spectator* is on the table, and a brisk discussion soon arises between

Pope and Addison concerning the merits of the Italian opera, in which Pope would have the better if he only knew a little more about music, and could keep his temper. Arbuthnot sides with Pope in favour of Mr. Handel's operas; the duke endeavours to keep the peace. Handel probably uses his favourite exclamation, 'Vat te tevil I care!' and consumes the *recherché* wines and rare viands with undiminished gusto.

"The Magnificent, or the Grand Duke, as he was called, had built himself a palace for £230,000. He had a private chapel, and appointed Handel organist in the room of the celebrated Dr. Pepusch, who retired with excellent grace before one manifestly his superior. On week-days the duke and duchess entertained all the wits and grandees in town, and on Sundays the Edgeware Road was thronged with the gay equipages of those who went to worship at the ducal chapel and hear Mr. Handel play on the organ.

"The Edgeware Road was a pleasant country drive, but parts of it were so solitary that highwaymen were much to be feared. The duke was himself attacked on one occasion; and those who could afford it never travelled so far out of town without armed retainers. Cannons was the pride of the neighbourhood, and the duke—of whom Pope wrote,

'Thus gracious Chandos is beloved at sight'—

was as popular as he was wealthy. But his name is made still more illustrious by the Chandos anthems. They were all written at Cannons between 1718 and 1720, and number in all eleven overtures, thirty-two solos, six duets, a trio, quartet, and forty-seven choruses. Some of the above are real masterpieces; but, with the exception of 'The waves of the sea rage horribly,' and 'Who is God but the Lord?' few of them are ever heard now. And yet these anthems were most significant in the variety of the choruses and in the range of the accompaniments; and it was then, no doubt, that Handel was feeling his way toward the great and immortal sphere of his oratorio music.

Indeed, his first oratorio, 'Esther,' was composed at Cannons, as also the English version of 'Acis and Galatea.'"

But Handel had other associates, and we must now visit Thomas Britton, the musical coal-heaver. "There goes the famous small-coal man, a lover of learning, a musician, and a companion of gentlemen." So the folks used to say as Thomas Britton, the coal-heaver of Clerkenwell Green, paced up and down the neighbouring streets with his sack of small coal on his back, destined for one of his customers. Britton was great among the great. He was courted by the most fashionable folk of his day. He was a cultivated coal-heaver, who, besides his musical taste and ability, possessed an extensive knowledge of chemistry and the occult sciences.

Britton did more than this. He gave concerts in Aylesbury Street, Clerkenwell, where this singular man had formed a dwelling-house, with a concert-room and a coal-store, out of what was originally a stable. On the ground-floor was the small-coal repository, and over that the concert-room—very long and narrow, badly lighted, and with a ceiling so low that a tall man could scarcely stand upright in it. The stairs to this room were far from pleasant to ascend, and the following facetious lines by Ward, the author of the "London Spy," confirm this:—

> " Upon Thursdays repair
> To my palace, and there
> Hobble up stair by stair,
> But I pray ye take care
> That you break not your shins by a stumble ;
>
> "And without e'er a souse
> Paid to me or my spouse,
> Sit as still as a mouse
> At the top of the house,
> And there you shall hear how we fumble."

Nevertheless, beautiful duchesses and the best society in town flocked to Britton's on Thursdays—not to order coals, but to sit out his concerts.

Let us follow the short, stout little man on a concert-day. The customers are all served, or as many as can be. The coal-shed is made tidy and swept up, and the coal-heaver awaits his company. There he stands at the door of his stable, dressed in his blue blouse, dustman's hat, and maroon kerchief tightly fastened round his neck. The concert-room is almost full, and, pipe in hand, Britton awaits a new visitor—the beautiful Duchess of B——. She is somewhat late (the coachman, possibly, is not quite at home in the neighbourhood).

Here comes a carriage, which stops at the coal-shop; and, laying down his pipe, the coal-heaver assists her grace to alight, and in the genteelest manner escorts her to the narrow staircase leading to the music-room. Forgetting Ward's advice, she trips laughingly and carelessly up the stairs to the room, from which proceed faint sounds of music, increasing to quite an *olla podrida* of sound as the apartment is reached—for the musicians are tuning up. The beautiful duchess is soon recognised, and as soon in deep gossip with her friends. But who is that gentlemanly man leaning over the chamber-organ? That is Sir Roger L'Estrange, an admirable performer on the violoncello, and a great lover of music. He is watching the subtile fingering of Mr. Handel, as his dimpled hands drift leisurely and marvellously over the keys of the instrument.

There, too, is Mr. Bannister with his fiddle—the first Englishman, by-the-by, who distinguished himself upon the violin; there is Mr. Woolaston, the painter, relating to Dr. Pepusch of how he had that morning thrown up his window upon hearing Britton crying "Small coal!" near his house in Warwick Lane, and, having beckoned him in, had made a sketch for a painting of him; there, too, is Mr. John Hughes, author of the "Siege of Damascus." In the background also are Mr. Philip Hart, Mr. Henry Symonds, Mr. Obadiah Shuttleworth, Mr. Abiell Whichello; while in the extreme corner of the room is Robe, a justice of the peace, letting out to Henry Needler of the Excise Office the last bit of scandal that has come into his court.

And now, just as the concert has commenced, in creeps "Soliman the Magnificent," also known as Mr. Charles Jennens, of Great Ormond Street, who wrote many of Handel's librettos, and arranged the words for the "Messiah."

"Soliman the Magnificent" is evidently resolved to do justice to his title on this occasion, with his carefully-powdered wig, frills, maroon-coloured coat, and buckled shoes; and as he makes his progress up the room, the company draw aside for him to reach his favourite seat near Handel. A trio of Corelli's is gone through; then Madame Cuzzoni sings Handel's last new air; Dr. Pepusch takes his turn at the harpsichord; another trio of Hasse, or a solo on the violin by Bannister; a selection on the organ from Mr. Handel's new oratorio; and then the day's programme is over. Dukes, duchesses, wits and philosophers, poets and musicians, make their way down the satirised stairs to go, some in carriages, some in chairs, some on foot, to their own palaces, houses, or lodgings.

III.

We do not now think of Handel in connection with the opera. To the modern mind he is so linked to the oratorio, of which he was the father and the consummate master, that his operas are curiosities but little known except to musical antiquaries. Yet some of the airs from the Handel operas are still cherished by singers as among the most beautiful songs known to the concert-stage.

In 1720 Handel was engaged by a party of noblemen, headed by his Grace of Chandos, to compose operas for the Royal Academy of Music at the Haymarket. An attempt had been made to put this institution on a firm foundation by a subscription of £50,000, and it was opened on May 2nd with a full company of singers engaged by Handel. In the course of eight years twelve operas were produced in rapid succession: "Floridante," December 9, 1721; "Ottone," January 12, 1723; "Flavio" and "Giulio Cesare," 1723;

"Tamerlano," 1724; "Rodelinda," 1725; "Scipione," 1726; "Alessandro," 1726; "Admeto," 1727; "Siroe," 1728; and "Tolommeo," 1728. They made as great a *furore* among the musical public of that day as would an opera from Gounod or Verdi in the present. The principal airs were sung throughout the land, and published as harpsichord pieces; for in these halcyon days of our composers the whole atmosphere of the land was full of the flavour and colour of Handel. Many of the melodies in these now forgotten operas have been worked up by modern composers, and so have passed into modern music unrecognised. It is a notorious fact that the celebrated song, "Where the Bee sucks," by Dr. Arne, is taken from a movement in "Rinaldo." Thus the new life of music is ever growing rich with the dead leaves of the past. The most celebrated of these operas was entitled "Otto." It was a work composed of one long string of exquisite gems, like Mozart's "Don Giovanni" and Gounod's "Faust." Dr. Pepusch, who had never quite forgiven Handel for superseding him as the best organist in England, remarked of one of the airs, "That great bear must have been inspired when he wrote that air." The celebrated Madame Cuzzoni made her *début* in it. On the second night the tickets rose to four guineas each, and Cuzzoni received two thousand pounds for the season.

The composer had already begun to be known for his irascible temper. It is refreshing to learn that operatic singers of the day, however whimsical and self-willed, were obliged to bend to the imperious genius of this man. In a spirit of ill-timed revolt Cuzzoni declined to sing an air. She had already given him trouble by her insolence and freaks, which at times were unbearable. Handel at last exploded. He flew at the wretched woman and shook her like a rat. "Ah! I always knew you were a fery tevil," he cried, "and I shall now let you know that I am Beelzebub, the prince of de tevils!" and, dragging her to the open window, was just on the point of pitching her into the street, when, in every sense of the word, she recanted.

So, when Carestini, the celebrated tenor, sent back an air, Handel was furious. Rushing into the trembling Italian's house, he said, in his four- or five-language style—"You tog! don't I know better as yourself vaat it pest for you to sing? If you vill not sing all de song vaat I give you, I vill not pay you ein stiver." Among the anecdotes told of Handel's passion is one growing out of the composer's peculiar sensitiveness to discords. The dissonance of the tuning-up period of an orchestra is disagreeable to the most patient. Handel, being peculiarly sensitive to this unfortunate necessity, always arranged that it should take place before the audience assembled, so as to prevent any sound of scraping or blowing. Unfortunately, on one occasion, some wag got access to the orchestra where the ready-tuned instruments were lying, and with diabolical dexterity put every string and crook out of tune. Handel enters. All the bows are raised together, and at the given beat all start off *con spirito*. The effect was startling in the extreme. The unhappy *maestro* rushes madly from his place, kicks to pieces the first double-bass he sees, and, seizing a kettle-drum, throws it violently at the leader of the band. The effort sends his wig flying, and, rushing bareheaded to the footlights, he stands a few moments amid the roars of the house, snorting with rage and choking with passion. Like Burleigh's nod, Handel's wig seemed to have been a sure guide to his temper. When things went well, it had a certain complacent vibration; but when he was out of humour, the wig indicated the fact in a very positive way. The Princess of Wales was wont to blame her ladies for talking instead of listening. "Hush, hush!" she would say. "Don't you see Handel's wig?"

For several years after the subscription of the nobility had been exhausted, our composer, having invested £10,000 of his own in the Haymarket, produced operas with remarkable affluence, some of them *pasticcio* works, composed of all sorts of airs, in which the singers could give their *bravura* songs. These were "Lotario," 1729; "Partenope," 1730; "Poro," 1731; "Ezio," 1732; "Sosarme," 1732; "Orlando,"

1733; "Ariadne," 1734; and also several minor works. Handel's operatic career was not so much the outcome of his choice as dictated to him by the necessity of time and circumstance. As time went on, his operas lost public interest. The audiences dwindled, and the overflowing houses of his earlier experience were replaced by empty benches. This, however, made little difference with Handel's royal patrons. The king and the Prince of Wales, with their respective households, made it an express point to show their deep interest in Handel's success. In illustration of this, an amusing anecdote is told of the Earl of Chesterfield. During the performance of "Rinaldo" this nobleman, then an equerry of the king, was met quietly retiring from the theatre in the middle of the first act. Surprise being expressed by a gentleman who met the earl, the latter said, "I don't wish to disturb his Majesty's privacy."

Handel paid his singers in those days what were regarded as enormous prices. Senisino and Carestini had each twelve hundred pounds, and Cuzzoni two thousand, for the season. Towards the end of what may be called the Handel season nearly all the singers and nobles forsook him, and supported Farinelli, the greatest singer living, at the rival house in Lincoln's Inn Fields.

IV.

From the year 1729 the career of Handel was to be a protracted battle, in which he was sometimes victorious, sometimes defeated, but always undaunted and animated with a lofty sense of his own superior power. Let us take a view of some of the rival musicians with whom he came in contact. Of all these Bononcini was the most formidable. He came to England in 1720 with Ariosti, also a meritorious composer. Factions soon began to form themselves around Handel and Bononcini, and a bitter struggle ensued between these old foes. The same drama repeated itself, with new actors, about thirty years afterwards, in

Paris. Gluck was then the German hero, supported by Marie Antoinette, and Piccini fought for the Italian opera under the colours of the king's mistress, Du Barry, while all the *littérateurs* and nobles ranged themselves on either side in bitter contest. The battle between Handel and Bononcini, as the exponents of German and Italian music, was also repeated in after-years between Mozart and Salieri, Weber and Rossini, and to-day is seen in the acrimonious disputes going on between Wagner and the Italian school. Bononcini's career in England came to an end very suddenly. It was discovered that a madrigal brought out by him was pirated from another Italian composer; whereupon Bononcini left England, humiliated to the dust, and finally died obscure and alone, the victim of a charlatan alchemist, who succeeded in obtaining all his savings.

Another powerful rival of Handel was Porpora, or, as Handel used to call him, "Old Borbora." Without Bononcini's fire or Handel's daring originality, he represented the dry contrapuntal school of Italian music. He was also a great singing master, famous throughout Europe, and upon this his reputation had hitherto principally rested. He came to London in 1733, under the patronage of the Italian faction, especially to serve as a thorn in the side of Handel. His first opera, "Ariadne," was a great success; but when he had the audacity to challenge the great German in the field of oratorio, his defeat was so overwhelming that he candidly admitted his rival's superiority. But he believed that no operas in the world were equal to his own, and he composed fifty of them during his life, extending to the days of Haydn, whom he had the honour of teaching, while the father of the symphony, on the other hand, cleaned Porpora's boots and powdered his wig for him.

Another Italian opponent was Hasse, a man of true genius, who in his old age instructed some of the most splendid singers in the history of the lyric stage. He also married one of the most gifted and most beautiful divas of Europe, Faustina Bordoni. The following anecdote does equal credit to Hasse's heart and penetration: In after-years, when he had left England, he was again sent for to take Handel's place as conductor of opera and oratorio. Hasse inquired, "What! is Handel dead?" On being told no, he indignantly refused, saying he was not worthy to tie Handel's shoe-latchets.

There are also Dr. Pepusch, the Anglicised Prussian, and Dr. Greene, both names well known in English music. Pepusch had had the leading place, before Handel's arrival, as organist and conductor, and made a distinct place for himself even after the sun of Handel had obscured all of his contemporaries. He wrote the music of the "Beggar's Opera," which was the great sensation of the times, and which still keeps possession of the stage. Pepusch was chiefly notable for his skill in arranging the popular songs of the day, and probably did more than any other composer to give the English ballad its artistic form.

The name of Dr. Greene is best known in connection with choral compositions. His relations with Handel and Bononcini are hardly creditable to him. He seems to have flattered each in turn. He upheld Bononcini in the great madrigal controversy, and appears to have wearied Handel by his repeated visits. The great Saxon easily saw through the flatteries of a man who was in reality an ambitious rival, and joked about him, not always in the best taste. When he was told that Greene was giving concerts at the "Devil Tavern," near Temple Bar, "Ah!" he exclaimed, "mein poor friend, Toctor Greene—so he is gone to de Tevil!"

From 1732 to 1740 Handel's life presents the suggestive and often-repeated experience in the lives of men of genius —a soul with a great creative mission, of which it is half unconscious, partly yielding to and partly struggling against the tendencies of the age, yet gradually crystallising into its true form, and getting consecrated to its true work. In these eight years Handel presented to the public ten operas and five oratorios. It was in 1731 that the great significant fact, though unrecognised by himself and others, occurred, which stamped the true bent of his genius. This was the production of his first oratorio in England. He was already playing his operas to empty houses, the subject of incessant scandal and abuse on the part of his enemies, but holding his way with steady cheerfulness and courage. Twelve years before this he had composed the oratorio of "Esther," but it was still in manuscript, uncared for and neglected. It was finally produced by a society called Philharmonic, under the direction of Bernard Gates, the royal-chapel master. Its fame spread wide, and we read these significant words in one of the old English newspapers—"'Esther,' an English oratorio, was performed six times, and very full."

Shortly after this Handel himself conducted "Esther" at the Haymarket by royal command. His success encouraged him to write "Deborah," another attempt in the same field, and it met a warm reception from the public, March 17, 1733.

For about fifteen years Handel had struggled heroically in the composition of Italian operas. With these he had at first succeeded; but his popularity waned more and more, and he became finally the continued target for satire, scorn, and malevolence. In obedience to the drift of opinion, all the great singers, who had supported him at the outset, joined the rival ranks or left England. In fact, it may be almost said that the English public were becoming dissatisfied with the whole system and method of Italian music. Colley Cibber, the actor and dramatist, explains why Italian opera could never satisfy the requirement of Handel, or be anything more than an artificial luxury in England: "The truth is, this kind of entertainment is entirely sensational." Still both Handel and his friends and his foes, all the exponents of musical opinion in England, persevered obstinately in warming this foreign exotic into a new lease of life.

The quarrel between the great Saxon composer and his opponents raged incessantly both in public and private. The newspaper and the drawing-room rang alike with venomous diatribes. Handel was called a swindler, a drunkard, and a blasphemer, to whom Scripture even was not sacred. The idea of setting Holy Writ to music scandalised the Pharisees, who revelled in the licentious operas and love-songs of the Italian school. All the small wits of the time showered on Handel epigram and satire unceasingly. The greatest of all the wits, however, Alexander Pope, was his firm friend and admirer; and in the "Dunciad," wherein the wittiest of poets impaled so many of the small fry of the age with his pungent and vindictive shaft, he also slew some of the most malevolent of Handel's foes.

Fielding, in *Tom Jones*, has an amusing hit at the taste of the period—"It was Mr. Western's custom every afternoon, as soon as he was drunk, to hear his daughter play on the harpsichord; for he was a great lover of music, and perhaps, had he lived in town, might have passed as a connoisseur, for he always excepted against the finest compositions of Mr. Handel."

So much had it become the fashion to criticise Handel's new effects in vocal and instrumental composition, that some years later Mr. Sheridan makes one of his characters fire a pistol simply to shock the audience, and makes him say in a stage whisper to the gallery, "This hint, gentlemen, I took from Handel."

The composer's Oxford experience was rather amusing and suggestive. We find it recorded that in July 1733, "one Handell, a foreigner, was desired to come to Oxford to perform in music." Again the same writer says— "Handell, with his lousy crew, a great number of foreign fiddlers, had a performance for his own benefit at the theatre." One of the dons writes of the performance as follows:—"This is an innovation; but everyone paid his five shillings to try how a little fiddling would sit upon him. And, notwithstanding the barbarous and inhuman combination of such a parcel of unconscionable scamps, he [Handel] disposed of the most of his tickets."

"Handel and his lousy crew," however, left Oxford with

the prestige of a magnificent victory. His third oratorio, "Athaliah," was received with vast applause by a great audience. Some of his university admirers, who appreciated academic honours more than the musician did, urged him to accept the degree of Doctor of Music, for which he would have to pay a small fee. The characteristic reply was a Parthian arrow: "Vat te tevil I trow my money away for dat vich the blockhead vish? I no vant!"

V.

In 1738 Handel was obliged to close the theatre and suspend payment. He had made and spent during his operatic career the sum of £10,000 sterling, besides dissipating the sum of £50,000 subscribed by his noble patrons. The rival house lasted but a few months longer, and the Duchess of Marlborough and her friends, who ruled the opposition clique and imported Bononcini, paid £12,000 for the pleasure of ruining Handel. His failure as an operatic composer is due in part to the same causes which constituted his success in oratorio and cantata. It is a little significant to notice that, alike by the progress of his own genius and by the force of conditions, he was forced out of the operatic field at the very time when he strove to tighten his grip on it.

His free introduction of choral and instrumental music, his creation of new forms and remodelling of old ones, his entire subordination of the words in the story to a pure musical purpose, offended the singers and retarded the action of the drama in the eyes of the audience; yet it was by virtue of these unpopular characteristics that the public mind was being moulded to understand and love the form of the oratorio.

From 1734 to 1738 Handel composed and produced a number of operatic works, the principal ones of which were "Alcina," 1735; "Arminio," 1737; and "Berenice," 1737. He also during these years wrote the magnificent music to Dryden's "Alexander's Feast," and the great funeral anthem on the occasion of Queen Caroline's death in the latter part of the year 1737.

We can hardly solve the tenacity of purpose with which Handel persevered in the composition of operatic music after it had ruined him; but it was still some time before he fully appreciated the true turn of his genius, which could not be trifled with or ignored. In his adversity he had some consolation. His creditors were patient, believing in his integrity. The royal family were his firm friends.

Southey tells us that Handel, having asked the youthful Prince of Wales, then a child, and afterward George the Third, if he loved music, answered, when the prince expressed his pleasure, "A good boy, a good boy! You shall protect my fame when I am dead." Afterwards, when the half-imbecile George was crazed with family and public misfortunes, he found his chief solace in the Waverley novels and Handel's music.

It is also an interesting fact that the poets and thinkers of the age were Handel's firm admirers. Such men as Gay, Arbuthnot, Hughes, Colley Cibber, Pope, Fielding, Hogarth, and Smollett, who recognised the deep, struggling tendencies of the times, measured Handel truly. They defended him in print, and never failed to attend his performances, and at his benefit concerts their enthusiastic support always insured him an overflowing house.

The popular instinct was also true to him. The aristocratic classes sneered at his oratorios and complained at his innovations. His music was found to be good bait for the popular gardens and the holiday-makers of the period. Jonathan Tyers was one of the most liberal managers of this class. He was proprietor of Vauxhall Gardens, and Handel (*incognito*) supplied him with nearly all his music. The composer did much the same sort of thing for Marylebone Gardens, furbishing up old and writing new strains with an ease that well became the urgency of the circumstances.

"My grandfather," says the Rev. J. Fountagne, "as I

have been told, was an enthusiast in music, and cultivated most of all the friendship of musical men, especially of Handel, who visited him often, and had a great predilection for his society. This leads me to relate an anecdote which I have on the best authority. While Marylebone Gardens were flourishing, the enchanting music of Handel, and probably of Arne, was often heard from the orchestra there. One evening, as my grandfather and Handel were walking together and alone, a new piece was struck up by the band. 'Come, Mr. Fountagne,' said Handel, 'let us sit down and listen to this piece; I want to know your opinion about it.' Down they sat, and after some time the old parson, turning to his companion, said, 'It is not worth listening to; it's very poor stuff.' 'You are right, Mr. Fountagne,' said Handel, 'it is very poor stuff; I thought so myself when I had finished it.' The old gentleman, being taken by surprise, was beginning to apologise; but Handel assured him there was no necessity, that the music was really bad, having been composed hastily, and his time for the production limited; and that the opinion given was as correct as it was honest."

VI.

The period of Handel's highest development had now arrived. For seven years his genius had been slowly but surely maturing, in obedience to the inner law of his being. He had struggled long in the bonds of operatic composition, but even here his innovations showed conclusively how he was reaching out toward the form with which his name was to be associated through all time. The year 1739 was one of prodigious activity. The oratorio of "Saul" was produced, of which the "Dead March" is still recognised as one of the great musical compositions of all time, being one of the few intensely solemn symphonies written in a major key. Several works now forgotten were composed, and the great "Israel in Egypt" was written in the incredibly short space of twenty-seven days. Of this work a distinguished writer on music says—"Handel was now fifty-five years old, and had entered, after many a long and weary contest, upon his last and greatest creative period. His genius culminates in the 'Israel.' Elsewhere he has produced longer recitatives and more pathetic arias; nowhere has he written finer tenor songs than 'The enemy said,' or finer duets than 'The Lord is a man of war;' and there is not in the history of music an example of choruses piled up like so many Ossas on Pelions in such majestic strength, and hurled in open defiance at a public whose ears were itching for Italian love-lays and English ballads. In these twenty-eight colossal choruses we perceive at once a reaction against and a triumph over the tastes of the age. The wonder is, not that the 'Israel' was unpopular, but that it should have been tolerated; but Handel, while he appears to have been for years driven by the public, had been, in reality, driving them. His earliest oratorio, 'Il Trionfo del Tempo' (composed in Italy), had but two choruses; into his operas more and more were introduced, with disastrous consequences; but when, at the zenith of his strength, he produced a work which consisted almost entirely of these unpopular peculiarities, the public treated him with respect, and actually sat out three performances in one season!" In addition to these two great oratorios, our composer produced the beautiful music to Dryden's "St. Cæcilia Ode," and Milton's "L'Allegro" and "Il Penseroso." Henceforth neither praise nor blame could turn Handel from his appointed course. He was not yet popular with the musical *dilettanti*, but we find no more catering to an absurd taste, no more writing of silly operatic froth.

Our composer had always been very fond of the Irish, and, at the invitation of the lord-lieutenant and prominent Dublin amateurs, he crossed the channel in 1741. He was received with the greatest enthusiasm, and his house became the resort of all the musical people in the city of Dublin. One after another his principal works were produced before admiring audiences in the new Music Hall in Fishamble Street. The crush to hear the "Allegro" and "Penseroso" at the opening performances was so great that the doors had to be closed. The papers declared there never had been seen such a scene before in Dublin.

Handel gave twelve performances at very short intervals, comprising all of his finest works. In these concerts the "Acis and Galatea" and "Alexander's Feast" were the most admired; but the enthusiasm culminated in the rendition of the "Messiah," produced for the first time on 13th April 1742. The performance was a beneficiary one in aid of poor and distressed prisoners for debt in the Marshalsea in Dublin. So, by a remarkable coincidence, the first performance of the "Messiah" literally meant deliverance to the captives. The principal singers were Mrs. Cibber (daughter-in-law of Colley Cibber, and afterwards one of the greatest actresses of her time), Mrs. Avoglio, and Mr. Dubourg. The town was wild with excitement. Critics, poets, fine ladies, and men of fashion tore rhetoric to tatters in their admiration. A clergyman so far forgot his Bible in his rapture as to exclaim to Mrs. Cibber, at the close of one of her airs, "Woman, for this be all thy sins forgiven thee." The penny-a-liners wrote that "words were wanting to express the exquisite delight," etc. And—supreme compliment of all, for Handel was a cynical bachelor—the fine ladies consented to leave their hoops at home for the second performance, that a couple of hundred or so extra listeners might be accommodated. This event was the grand triumph of Handel's life. Years of misconception, neglect, and rivalry were swept out of mind in the intoxicating delight of that night's success.

VII.

Handel returned to London, and composed a new oratorio, "Samson," for the following Lenten season. This, together with the "Messiah," heard for the first time in London, made the stock of twelve performances. The fashionable world ignored him altogether; the newspapers kept a contemptuous silence; comic singers were hired to parody his noblest airs at the great houses; and impudent Horace Walpole had the audacity to say that he "had hired all the goddesses from farces and singers of roast-beef, from between the acts of both theatres, with a man with one note in his voice, and a girl with never a one; and so they sang and made brave hallelujahs."

The new field into which Handel had entered inspired his genius to its greatest energy. His new works for the season of 1744 were the "Dettingen Te Deum," "Semele," and "Joseph and his Brethren;" for the next year (he had again rented the Haymarket Theatre), "Hercules," "Belshazzar," and a revival of "Deborah." All these works were produced in a style of then uncommon completeness; and the great expense he incurred, combined with the active hostility of the fashionable world, forced him to close his doors and suspend payment. From this time forward Handel gave concerts whenever he chose, and depended on the people, who so supported him by their gradually growing appreciation, that in two years he had paid off all his debts, and in ten years had accumulated a fortune of £10,000. The works produced during these latter years were "Judas Maccabæus," 1747; "Alexander," 1748; "Joshua," 1748; "Susannah," 1749; "Solomon," 1749; "Theodora," 1750; "Choice of Hercules," 1751; "Jephthah," 1752, closing with this a stupendous series of dramatic oratorios. While at work on the last, his eyes suffered an attack which finally resulted in blindness.

Like Milton in the case of "Paradise Lost," Handel preferred one of his least popular oratorios, "Theodora." It was a great favourite with him, and he used to say that the chorus, "He saw the lovely youth," was finer than anything in the "Messiah." The public were not of this opinion, and he was glad to give away tickets to any professors who applied for them. When the "Messiah" was again produced, two of these gentlemen who had neglected "Theodora" applied for admission. "Oh! your sarvant, meine Herren!" exclaimed the indignant composer. "You are tamnable dainty! You would not go to 'Theodora'—dere was room enough to dance dere when dat was perform." When Handel heard that an enthusiast had offered to make himself responsible for all the boxes the next time the despised oratorio should be given—"He is a fool," said he; "the Jews will not come to it as to 'Judas Maccabæus,' because it is a Christian story; and the ladies will not come, because it is a virtuous one."

Handel's triumph was now about to culminate in a serene and acknowledged pre-eminence. The people had recognised his greatness, and the reaction at last conquered all classes. Publishers vied with each other in producing his works, and their performance was greeted with great audiences and enthusiastic applause. His last ten years were a peaceful and beautiful ending of a stormy career.

VIII.

Thought lingers pleasantly over this sunset period. Handel throughout life was so wedded to his art, that he cared nothing for the delights of woman's love. His recreations were simple—rowing, walking, visiting his friends, and playing on the organ. He would sometimes try to play the people out of St. Paul's Cathedral, and hold them indefinitely. He would resort at night to his favourite tavern, the Queen's Head, where he would smoke and drink beer with his chosen friends. Here he would indulge in roaring conviviality and fun, and delight his friends with sparkling satire and pungent humour, of which he was a great master, helped by his amusing compound of English, Italian, and German. Often he would visit the picture galleries, of which he was passionately fond. His clumsy but noble figure could be seen almost any morning rolling through Charing Cross; and everyone who met old Father Handel treated him with the deepest reverence.

The following graphic narrative, taken from the *Somerset House Gazette*, offers a vivid portraiture. Schoelcher, in his *Life of Handel*, says that "its author had a relative, Zachary Hardcastle, a retired merchant, who was intimately acquainted with all the most distinguished men of his time, artists, poets, musicians, and physicians." This old gentleman, who lived at Paper Buildings, was accustomed to take his morning walk in the garden of Somerset House, where he happened to meet with another old man, Colley Cibber, and proposed to him to go and hear a competition which was to take place at midday for the post of organist to the Temple, and he invited him to breakfast, telling him at the same time that Dr. Pepusch and Dr. Arne were to be with him at nine o'clock. They go in; Pepusch arrives punctually at the stroke of nine; presently there is a knock, the door is opened, and Handel unexpectedly presents himself. Then follows the scene :—

"Handel: 'Vat! mein dear friend Hardgasdle—vat! you are merry py dimes! Vat! and Misder Golley Cibbers, too! aye, and Togder Peepbush as vell! Vell, dat is gomigal. Vell, mein friendts, andt how vags the vorldt wid you, mein tdears? Bray, bray, do let me sit town a momend.'

"Pepusch took the great man's hat, Colley Cibber took his stick, and my great-uncle wheeled round his reading-chair, which was somewhat about the dimensions of that in which our kings and queens are crowned; and then the great man sat him down.

"'Vell, I thank you, gentlemen; now I am at mein ease vonce more. Upon mein vord, dat is a picture of a ham. It is very pold of me to gome to preak my fastd wid you uninvided; and I have brought along wid me a nodable abbetite; for the wader of old Fader Dems is it not a fine pracer of the stomach?'

"'You do me great honour, Mr. Handel,' said my great-uncle. 'I take this early visit as a great kindness.'

"'A delightful morning for the water,' said Colley Cibber.

"'Pray, did you come with oars or scullers, Mr. Handel?' said Pepusch.

"'Now, how gan you demand of me dat zilly question, you who are a musician and a man of science, Togder Peepbush? Vat gan it concern you whether I have one votdermans or two votdermans—whether I bull out mine burce for to pay von shilling or two? Diavolo! I gannot go here, or I gannot go dere, but some one shall send it to some newsbaber, as how Misder Chorge Vrederick Handel did go somedimes last week in a votderman's wherry, to preak his fastd wid Misder Zac. Hardgasdle; but it shall be all the fault wid himeself, if it shall be but in print, whether I was rowed by one votdermans or by two votdermans. So, Togder Peepbush, you will blease to excuse me from dat.'

"Poor Dr. Pepusch was for a moment disconcerted, but it was soon forgotten in the first dish of coffee.

"'Well, gentlemen,' said my great-uncle Zachary, looking at his tompion, 'it is ten minutes past nine. Shall we wait more for Dr. Arne?'

"'Let us give him another five minutes' chance, Master Hardcastle,' said Colley Cibber; 'he is too great a genius to keep time.'

"'Let us put it to the vote,' said Dr. Pepusch, smiling. 'Who holds up hands?'

"'I will segond your motion wid all mine heardt,' said Handel. 'I will hold up mine feeble hands for mine oldt friendt Custos (Arne's name was Augustine), for I know not who I wouldt waidt for, over andt above mine oldt rival, Master Dom (meaning Pepusch). Only by your bermission, I vill dake a snag of your ham, andt a slice of French roll, or a modicum of chicken; for to dell you the honest fagd, I am all pote famished, for I laid me down on mine billow in bed the lastd nightd widout mine supper, at the instance of mine physician, for which I am not altogeddere inglined to extend mine fastd no longer.' Then, laughing: 'Berhaps, Mister Golley Cibbers, you may like to pote this to the vote? But I shall not segond the motion, nor shall I holdt up mine hand, as I will, by bermission, embloy it some dime in a better office. So, if you please, do me the kindness for to gut me a small slice of ham.'

"At this instant a hasty footstep was heard on the stairs, accompanied by the humming of an air, all as gay as the morning, which was beautiful and bright. It was the month of May.

"'Bresto! be quick,' said Handel; he knew it was Arne; 'fifteen minutes of dime is butty well for an *ad libitum.*'

"'Mr. Arne,' said my great-uncle's man.

"A chair was placed, and the social party commenced their *déjeuner.*

"'Well, and how do you find yourself, my dear sir?' inquired Arne, with friendly warmth.

"'Why, by the mercy of Heaven, and the waders of Aix-la-Chapelle, andt the addentions of mine togders andt physicians, and oggulists, of lade years, under Providence, I am surbrizingly pedder—thank you kindly, Misder Custos. Andt you have also been doing well of lade, as I am bleased to hear. You see, sir,' pointing to his plate, 'you see, sir, dat I am in the way for to regruit mine flesh wid the good viands of Misder Zachary Hardgasdle.'

"'So, sir, I presume you are come to witness the trial of skill at the old round church? I understand the amateurs expect a pretty sharp contest,' said Arne.

"'Gondest,' echoed Handel, laying down his knife and fork. 'Yes, no doubt; your amadeurs have a bassion for gondest. Not vot it vos in our remembrance. Hey, mine friendt? Ha, ha, ha!'

"'No, sir, I am happy to say those days of envy and bickering, and party feeling, are gone and past. To be sure we had enough of such disgraceful warfare: it lasted too long.'

"'Why, yes; it tid last too long, it bereft me of mine poor limbs: it tid bereave of that vot is the most blessed gift of Him vot made us, andt not wee ourselves. And for vot? Vy, for noding in the vorldt pode the bleasure and bastime of them who, having no widt, nor no want, set at loggerheads such men as live by their widts, to worry and destroy one andt anodere as wild beasts in the Golloseum in the dimes of the Romans.'

"Poor Dr. Pepusch during this conversation, as my great-uncle observed, was sitting on thorns; he was in the confederacy professionally only.

"'I hope, sir,' observed the doctor, 'you do not include me among those who did injustice to your talents?'

"'Nod at all, nod at all; God forbid! I am a great admirer of the airs of the 'Peggar's Obera,' andt every professional gendtleman must do his best for to live.'

"This mild return, couched under an apparent compliment, was well received; but Handel, who had a talent for sarcastic drolling, added—

"'Pute why blay the Peggar yourself, Togder, andt adapt oldt pallad humsdrum, ven, as a man of science, you could gombose original airs of your own? Here is mine friendt, Custos Arne, who has made a road for himself, for to drive along his own genius to the demple of fame.' Then, turning to our illustrious Arne, he continued, 'Min friendt Custos, you and I must meed togeder somedimes before it is long, and hold a *tête-à-tête* of old days vat is gone; ha, ha! Oh! it is gomigal now dat id is all gone by. Custos, to nod you remember as it was almost only of yesterday dat she-devil Guzzoni, andt dat other brecious taughter of iniquity, Pelzebub's spoiled child, the bretty-faced Faustina? Oh! the mad rage vot I have to answer for, vot with one and the oder of these fine latdies' airs andt graces. Again, to you nod remember dat ubstardt buppy Senesino, and the goxgomb Farinelli? Next, again, mine somedimes nodtable rival Bononcini, and old Borbora? Ha, ha, ha! all at war wid me, andt all at war wid themselves. Such a gonfusion of rivalshibs, andt double-facedness, andt hybocrisy, and malice, vot would make a gomigal subject for a boem in rhymes, or a biece for the stage, as I hopes to be saved.'"

IX.

We now turn from the man to his music. In his daily life with the world we get a spectacle of a quick, passionate temper, incased in a great burly frame, and raging into whirlwinds of excitement at small provocation; a gourmand devoted to the pleasure of the table, sometimes indeed gratifying his appetite in no seemly fashion, resembling his friend Dr. Samuel Johnson in many notable ways. Handel as a man was of the earth, earthly, in the extreme, and marked by many whimsical and disagreeable faults. But in his art we recognise a genius so colossal, massive, and self-poised as to raise admiration to its superlative of awe. When Handel had disencumbered himself of tradition, convention, the trappings of time and circumstances, he attained a place in musical creation, solitary and unique. His genius found expression in forms large and austere, disdaining the luxuriant and trivial. He embodied the spirit of Protestantism in music ; and a recognition of this fact is probably the key of the admiration felt for him by the Anglo-Saxon races.

Handel possessed an inexhaustible fund of melody of the noblest order; an almost unequalled command of musical expression ; perfect power over all the resources of his science ; the faculty of wielding huge masses of tone with perfect ease and felicity ; and he was without rival in the sublimity of ideas. The problem which he so successfully solved in the oratorio was that of giving such dramatic force to the music, in which he clothed the sacred texts, as to be able to dispense with all scenic and stage effects. One of the finest operatic composers of the time, the rival of Bach as an instrumental composer, and performer on the harpsichord or organ, the unanimous verdict of the musical world is that no one has ever equalled him in completeness, range of effect, elevation and variety of conception, and sublimity in the treatment of sacred music. We can readily appreciate Handel's own words when describing his own sensations in writing the "Messiah"—"I did think I did see all heaven before me, and the great God himself."

The great man died on Good Friday night, 1759, aged seventy-five years. He had often wished "he might breathe his last on Good Friday, in hope," he said, "of meeting his good God, his sweet Lord and Saviour, on the day of his resurrection." The old blind musician had his wish.

GLUCK.

I.

GLUCK is a noble and striking figure in musical history, alike in the services he rendered to his art and the dignity and strength of his personal character. As the predecessor of Wagner and Meyerbeer, who among the composers of this century have given opera its largest and noblest expression, he anticipated their important reforms, and in his musical creations we see all that is best in what is called the new school.

The man, the Ritter CHRISTOPH WILIBALD VON GLUCK, is almost as interesting to us as the musician. He moved in the society of princes with a calm and haughty dignity, their conscious peer, and never prostituted his art to gain personal advancement or to curry favour with the great ones of the earth. He possessed a majesty of nature which was the combined effect of personal pride, a certain lofty self-reliance, and a deep conviction that he was the apostle of an important musical mission.

Gluck's whole life was illumined by an indomitable sense of his own strength, and lifted by it into an atmosphere high above that of his rivals, whom the world has now almost forgotten, except as they were immortalised by being his enemies. Like Milton and Bacon, who put on record their knowledge that they had written for all time, Gluck had a magnificent consciousness of himself. "I have written," he says, "the music of my 'Armida' in such a manner as to prevent its soon growing old." This is a sublime vanity inseparable from the great aggressive geniuses of the world, the wind of the speed which measures their force of impact.

Duplessis's portrait of Gluck almost takes the man out of paint to put him in flesh and blood. He looks down with wide-open eyes, swelling nostrils, firm mouth, and massive chin. The noble brow, dome-like and expanded, relieves the massiveness of his face; and the whole countenance and figure express the repose of a powerful and passionate nature schooled into balance and symmetry: altogether the presentment of a great man, who felt that he could move the world and had found the *pou sto*. Of a large and robust type of physical beauty, Nature seems to have endowed him on every hand with splendid gifts. Such a man as this could say with calm simplicity to Marie Antoinette, who inquired one night about his new opera of "Armida," then nearly finished—"*Madame, il est bientôt fini, et vraiment ce sera superbe.*"

One night Handel listened to a new opera from a young and unknown composer, the "Caduta de' Giganti," one of Gluck's very earliest works, written when he was yet corrupted with all the vices of the Italian method. "Mein Gott! he is an idiot," said Handel; "he knows no more of counterpoint then mein cook." Handel did not see with prophetic eyes. He never met Gluck afterwards, and we do not know his later opinion of the composer of "Orpheus and Eurydice" and "Iphigenia in Tauris." But Gluck had ever the profoundest admiration for the author of the "Messiah." There was something in these two strikingly similar, as their music was alike characterised by massive simplicity and strength, not rough-hewn, but shaped into austere beauty.

Before we relate the great episode of our composer's life, let us take a backward glance at his youth. He was the son of a forester in the service of Prince Lobkowitz, born at Weidenwang in the Upper Palatinate, 2nd July 1714. Gluck was devoted to music from early childhood, but received, in connection with the musical art, an excellent education at the Jesuit College of Kommotau. Here he learned singing, the organ, the violin and harpsichord, and had a mind to get his living by devoting his musical talents to the Church. The Prague public recognised in him a musician of fair talent, but he found but little encouragement to stay at the Bohemian capital. So he decided to finish his musical education at Vienna, where more distinguished masters could be had. Prince Lobkowitz, who remembered his gamekeeper's son, introduced the young man to the Italian Prince Melzi, who induced him to accompany him to Milan. As the pupil of the Italian organist and composer, Sammartini, he made rapid progress in operatic composition. He was successful in pleasing Italian audiences, and in four years produced eight operas, for which the world has forgiven him in forgetting them. Then Gluck must go to London to see what impression he could make on English critics; for London then, as now, was one of the great musical centres, where every successful composer or singer must get his brevet.

Gluck's failure to please in London was, perhaps, an important epoch in his career. With a mind singularly sensitive to new impressions, and already struggling with fresh ideas in the laws of operatic composition, Handel's great music must have had a powerful effect in stimulating his unconscious progress. His last production in England, "Pyramus and Thisbe," was a *pasticcio* opera, in which he embodied the best bits out of his previous works. The experiment was a glaring failure, as it ought to have been; for it illustrated the Italian method, which was designed for mere vocal display, carried to its logical absurdity.

II.

In 1748 Gluck settled in Vienna, where almost immediately his opera of "Semiramide" was produced. Here he conceived a passion for Marianne, the daughter of Joseph Pergin, a rich banker; but on account of the father's distaste for a musical son-in-law, the marriage did not occur till 1750. "Telemacco" and "Clemenza di Tito" were composed about this time, and performed in Vienna, Rome, and Naples. In 1755 our composer received the order of the Golden Spur from the Roman pontiff in recognition of the merits of two operas performed at Rome, called "Il Trionfo di Camillo" and "Antigono." Seven years were now actively employed in producing operas for Vienna and Italian cities, which, without possessing great value, show the change which had begun to take place in this composer's theories of dramatic music. In Paris he had been struck with the operas of Rameau, in which the declamatory form was strongly marked. His early Italian training had fixed in his mind the importance of pure melody. From Germany he obtained his appreciation of harmony, and had made a deep study of the uses of the orchestra. So we see this great reformer struggling on with many faltering steps towards that result which he afterwards summed up in the following concise description—" My purpose was to restrict music to its true office, that of ministering to the expression of poetry, without interrupting the action."

In Calzabigi Gluck had met an author who fully appreciated his ideas, and had the talent of writing a libretto in accordance with them. This coadjutor wrote all the librettos that belonged to Gluck's greatest period. He had produced his "Orpheus and Eurydice" and "Alceste" in Vienna with a fair amount of success; but his tastes drew him strongly to the French stage, where the art of acting and declamation was cultivated then, as it is now, to a height unknown in other parts of Europe. So we find him gladly accepting an offer from the managers of the French Opera to migrate to the great city, in which were fermenting with much noisy fervour those new ideas in art, literature, politics, and society, which were turning the eyes of all Europe to the French capital.

The world's history has hardly a more picturesque and striking spectacle, a period more fraught with the working of powerful forces, than that exhibited by French society in the latter part of Louis XV.'s reign. We see a court rotten to the core with indulgence in every form of sensuality and vice, yet glittering with the veneer of a social polish which made it the admiration of the world. A dissolute king was ruled by a succession of mistresses, and all the courtiers vied in emulating the vice and extravagance of their master. Yet in this foul compost-heap art and literature flourished with a tropical luxuriance. Voltaire was at the height of his splendid career, the most brilliant wit and philosopher of his age. The lightnings of his mockery attacked with an incessant play the social, political, and religious shams of the period. People of all classes, under the influence of his unsparing satire, were learning to see with clear eyes what an utterly artificial and polluted age they lived in, and the cement which bound society in a compact whole was fast melting under this powerful solvent.

Rousseau, with his romantic philosophy and eloquence, had planted his new ideas deep in the hearts of his contemporaries, weary with the artifice and the corruption of a time which had exhausted itself and had nothing to promise under the old social *régime*. The ideals uplifted in the *Nouvelle Héloïse* and the *Confessions* awakened men's minds with a great rebound to the charms of Nature, simplicity, and a social order untrammelled by rules or conventions. The eloquence with which these theories were propounded carried the French people by storm, and Rousseau was a demigod at whose shrine worshipped alike duchess and peasant. The Encyclopedists stimulated the ferment by their literary enthusiasm, and the heartiness with which they co-operated with the whole current of revolutionary thought.

The very atmosphere was reeking with the prophecy of imminent change. Versailles itself did not escape the contagion. Courtiers and aristocrats, in worshipping the beautiful ideals set up by the new school, which were as far removed as possible from their own effete civilisation, did not realise that they were playing with the fire which was to burn out the whole social edifice of France with such a terrible conflagration; for, back and beneath all this, there was a people groaning under long centuries of accumulated wrong, in whose imbruted hearts the theories applauded by their oppressors with a sort of *doctrinaire* delight were working with a fatal fever.

III.

In this strange condition of affairs Gluck found his new sphere of labour—Gluck, himself overflowing with the revolutionary spirit, full of the enthusiasm of reform. At first he carried everything before him. Protected by royalty, he produced, on the basis of an admirable libretto by Du Rollet, one of the great wits of the time, "Iphigenia in Aulis." It was enthusiastically received. The critics, delighted to establish the reputation of one especially favoured by the Dauphiness Marie Antoinette, exhausted superlatives on the new opera. The Abbé Arnaud, one of the leading *dilettanti*, exclaimed—"With such music one might found a new religion!" To be sure, the connoisseurs could not understand the complexities of the music; but, following the rule of all connoisseurs before or since, they considered it all the more learned and profound. So led, the general public clapped their hands, and agreed to consider Gluck as a great composer. He was called the Hercules of music; the opera-house was crammed night after night; his footsteps were dogged in the streets by admiring enthusiasts; the wits and poets occupied themselves with composing sonnets in his praise; brilliant courtiers and fine ladies showered valuable gifts on the new musical oracle; he was hailed as the exponent of Rousseauism in music. We read that it was considered to be a priceless privilege to be admitted to the rehearsal of a new opera, to see Gluck conduct in nightcap and dressing-gown.

Fresh adaptations of "Orpheus and Eurydice" and of "Alceste" were produced. The first, brought out in 1784, was received with an enthusiasm which could be contented only with forty-nine consecutive performances. The second act of this work has been called one of the most astonishing productions of the human mind. The public began to show signs of fickleness, however, on the production of the "Alceste." On the first night a murmur arose among the spectators—"The piece has fallen." Abbé Arnaud, Gluck's devoted defender, arose in his box and replied, "Yes!

fallen from heaven." While Mademoiselle Levasseur was singing one of the great airs, a voice was heard to say, "Ah! you tear out my ears;" to which the caustic rejoinder was, "How fortunate, if it is to give you others!"

Gluck himself was badly bitten, in spite of his hatred of shams and shallowness, with the pretences of the time, which professed to dote on nature and simplicity. In a letter to his old pupil, Marie Antoinette, wherein he disclaims any pretension of teaching the French a new school of music, he says—"I see with satisfaction that the language of Nature is the universal language."

So, here on the crumbling crust of a volcano, where the volatile French court danced and fiddled and sang, unreckoning of what was soon to come, our composer and his admirers patted each other on the back with infinite complacency.

But after this high tide of prosperity there was to come a reverse. A powerful faction, that for a time had been crushed by Gluck's triumph, after a while raised their heads and organised an attack. There were second-rate composers whose scores had been laid on the shelf in the rage for the new favourite; musicians who were shocked and enraged at the difficulties of his instrumentation; wits who, having praised Gluck for a while, thought they could now find a readier field for their quills in satire; and a large section of the public who changed for no earthly reason but that they got tired of doing one thing.

Therefore, the Italian Piccini was imported to be pitted against the reigning deity. The French court was broken up into hostile ranks. Marie Antoinette was Gluck's patron, but Madame Du Barry, the king's mistress, declared for Piccini. Abbé Arnaud fought for Gluck; but the witty Marmontel was the advocate of his rival. The keen-witted Du Rollet was Gluckist; but La Harpe, the eloquent, was Piccinist. So this battle-royal in art commenced and raged with virulence. The green-room was made unmusical with contentions carried out in polite Billingsgate. Gluck tore up his unfinished score in rage when he learned that his rival was to compose an opera on the same libretto. La Harpe said—"The famous Gluck may puff his own compositions, but he can't prevent them from boring us to death." Thus the wags of Paris laughed and wrangled over the musical rivals. Berton, the new director, fancied he could soften the dispute and make the two composers friends; so at a dinner-party, when they were all in their cups, he proposed that they should compose an opera jointly. This was demurred to; but it was finally arranged that they should compose an opera on the same subject.

"Iphigenia in Tauris," Gluck's second "Iphigenia," produced in 1779, was such a masterpiece that his rival shut his own score in his portfolio, and kept it two years. All Paris was enraptured with this great work, and Gluck's detractors were silenced in the wave of enthusiasm which swept the public. Abbé Arnaud's opinion was the echo of the general mind—"There was but one beautiful part, and that was the whole of it." This opera may be regarded as the most perfect example of Gluck's school in making the music the full reflex of the dramatic action. While Orestes sings in the opera, "My heart is calm," the orchestra continues to paint the agitation of his thoughts. During the rehearsal the musician failed to understand the exigency and ceased playing. The composer cried out, in a rage, "Don't you see he is lying? Go on, go on; he has just killed his mother."

On one occasion, when he was praising Rameau's chorus of "Castor and Pollux," an admirer of his flattered him with the remark, "But what a difference between this chorus and that of your 'Iphigenia!'" "Yet it is very well done," said Gluck; "one is only a religious ceremony, the other is a real funeral." He was wont to say that in composing he always tried to forget he was a musician.

Gluck, however, a few months subsequent to this, was so much humiliated at the non-success of "Echo and Narcissus," that he left Paris in bitter irritation, in spite of Marie Antoinette's pleadings that he should remain at the French capital.

The composer was now advanced in years, and had become impatient and fretful. He left Paris for Vienna in 1780, having amassed considerable property. There, as an old, broken-down man, he listened to the young Mozart's new symphonies and operas, and applauded them with great zeal: for Gluck, though fiery and haughty in the extreme, was singularly generous in recognising the merits of others.

This was exhibited in Paris in his treatment of Méhul, the Belgian composer, then a youth of sixteen, who had just arrived in the gay city. It was on the eve of the first representation of "Iphigenia in Tauris," when the operatic battle was agitating the public. With all the ardour of a novice and a devotee, the young musical student immediately threw himself into the affray, and by the aid of a friend he succeeded in gaining admittance to the theatre for the final rehearsal of Gluck's opera. This so enchanted him that he resolved to be present at the public performance. But, unluckily for the resolve, he had no money, and no prospect of obtaining any; so, with a determination and a love for art which deserve to be remembered, he decided to hide himself in one of the boxes and there to wait for the time of representation.

"At the end of the rehearsal," writes George Hogarth in his *Memoirs of the Drama*, "he was discovered in his place of concealment by the servants of the theatre, who proceeded to turn him out very roughly. Gluck, who had not left the house, heard the noise, came to the spot, and found the young man, whose spirit was roused, resisting the indignity with which he was treated. Méhul, finding in whose presence he was, was ready to sink with confusion; but, in answer to Gluck's questions, he told him that he was a young musical student from the country, whose anxiety to be present at the performance of the opera had led him into the commission of an impropriety. Gluck, as may be supposed, was delighted with a piece of enthusiasm so flattering to himself, and not only gave his young admirer a ticket of admission, but desired his acquaintance." From this artistic *contretemps*, then, arose a friendship alike creditable to the goodness and generosity of Gluck, as it was to the sincerity and high order of Méhul's musical talent.

Gluck's death, in 1787, was caused by over-indulgence in wine at a dinner which he gave to some of his friends. The love of stimulants had grown upon him in his old age, and had become almost a passion. An enforced abstinence of some months was succeeded by a debauch, in which he drank an immense quantity of brandy. The effects brought on a fit of apoplexy, of which he died, aged seventy-three.

Gluck's place in musical history is peculiar and well marked. He entered the field of operatic composition when it was hampered with a great variety of dry forms, and utterly without soul and poetic spirit. The object of composers seemed to be to show mere contrapuntal learning, or to furnish singers opportunity to display vocal agility. The opera, as a large and symmetrical expression of human emotions, suggested in the collisions of a dramatic story, was utterly an unknown quantity in art. Gluck's attention was early called to this radical inconsistency; and, though he did not learn for many years to develop his musical ideas according to a theory, and never carried that theory to the logical results insisted on by his great after-type, Wagner, he accomplished much in the way of sweeping reform. He elaborated the recitative or declamatory element in opera with great care, and insisted that his singers should make this the object of their most careful efforts. The arias, duos, quartets, etc., as well as the choruses and orchestral parts, were made consistent with the dramatic motive and situations. In a word, Gluck aimed with a single-hearted purpose to make music the expression of poetry and sentiment.

The principles of Gluck's school of operatic writing may be briefly summarised as follows:—That dramatic music can only reach its highest power and beauty when joined to a simple and poetic text, expressing passions true to Nature; that music can be made the language of all the varied emotions of the heart; that the music of an opera must exactly follow the rhythm and melody of the words; that the orchestra must be only used to strengthen and intensify the feeling embodied in the vocal parts, as demanded by the text or dramatic situation. We get some further light on these principles from Gluck's letter of dedication to the Grand-Duke of Tuscany on the publication of "Alceste." He writes :—"I am of opinion that music must be to poetry what liveliness of colour and a happy mixture of light and shade are for a faultless and well-arranged drawing, which serve to add life to the figures without injuring the outlines; . . . that the overture should prepare the auditors for the character of the action which is to be presented, and hint at the progress of the same; that the instruments must be employed according to the degree of interest and passion; that the composer should avoid too marked a disparity in the dialogue between the air and recitative, in order not to break the sense of a period, or interrupt the energy of the action. . . . Finally, I have even felt compelled to sacrifice rules to the improvement of the effect."

We find in this composer's music, therefore, a largeness and dignity of treatment which have never been surpassed. His command of melody is quite remarkable, but his use of it is under severe artistic restraint; for it is always characterised by breadth, simplicity, and directness. He aimed at and attained the symmetrical balance of an old Greek play.

HAYDN.

I.

"Papa Haydn!" Thus did Mozart ever speak of his foster-father in music, and the title, transmitted to posterity, admirably expressed the sweet, placid, gentle nature, whose possessor was personally beloved no less than he was admired. His life flowed, broad and unruffled. like some great river, unvexed for the most part by the rivalries, jealousies, and sufferings, oftentimes self-inflicted, which have harassed the careers of other great musicians. He remained to the last the favourite of the imperial court of Vienna, and princes followed his remains to their last resting-place.

JOSEPH HAYDN was the eldest of the twenty children of Matthias Haydn, a wheelwright at Rohrau, Lower Austria, where he was born in 1732. At the age of twelve years he was engaged to sing in Vienna. He became a chorister in St. Stephen's Church, but offended the choir-master by the revolt on the part of himself and parents from submitting to the usual means then taken to perpetuate a fine soprano in boys. So Haydn, who had surreptitiously picked up a good deal of musical knowledge apart from the art of singing, was at the age of sixteen turned out on the world. A compassionate barber, however, took him in, and Haydn dressed and powdered wigs downstairs, while he worked away at a little worm-eaten harpsichord at night in his room. Unfortunate boy! he managed to get himself engaged to the barber's daughter, Anne Keller, who was for a good while the Xantippe of his gentle life, and he paid dearly for his father-in-law's early hospitality.

The young musician soon began to be known, as he played the violin in one church, the organ in another, and got some pupils. His first rise was his acquaintance with Metastasio, the poet-laureate of the court. Through him Haydn got introduced to the mistress of the Venetian ambassador, a great musical enthusiast, and in her circle he met Porpora, the best music-master in the world, but a crusty, snarling old man. Porpora held at Vienna the position of musical dictator and censor, and he exercised the tyrannical privileges of his post mercilessly. Haydn was a small, dark-complexioned, insignificant-looking youth, and Porpora, of course, snubbed him most contemptuously. But Haydn wanted instruction, and no one in the world could give it so well as the savage old *maestro*. So he performed all sorts of menial services for him, cleaned his shoes, powdered his wig, and ran all his errands. The result was that Porpora softened and consented to give his young admirer lessons—no great hardship, for young Haydn proved a most apt and gifted pupil. And it was not long either before the young musician's compositions attracted public attention and found a sale. The very curious relations between Haydn and Porpora are brilliantly sketched in George Sand's *Consuelo*.

At night Haydn, accompanied by his friends, was wont to wander about Vienna by moonlight, and serenade his patrons with trios and quartets of his own composition. He happened one night to stop under the window of Bernardone Kurz, a director of a theatre and the leading clown of Vienna. Down rushed Kurz very excitedly. "Who are you?" he shrieked. "Joseph Haydn." "Whose music is it?" "Mine." "The deuce it is! And at your age, too!" "Why, I must begin with something." "Come along upstairs."

The enthusiastic director collared his prize, and was soon deep in explaining a wonderful libretto, entitled "The Devil on Two Sticks." To write music for this was no easy matter; for it was to represent all sorts of absurd things, among others a tempest. The tempest made Haydn despair, and he sat at the piano, banging away in a reckless fashion, while the director stood behind him, raving in a disconnected way as to his meaning. At last the distracted pianist brought his fists simultaneously down upon the key-board, and made a rapid sweep of all the notes.

"Bravo! bravo! that is the tempest!" cried Kurz.

The buffoon also laid himself on a chair, and had it carried about the room, during which he threw out his limbs in imitation of the act of swimming. Haydn supplied an accompaniment so suitable that Kurz soon landed on *terra firma*, and congratulated the composer, assuring him that he was the man to compose the opera. By this stroke of good luck our young musician received one hundred and thirty florins.

II.

At the age of twenty-eight Haydn composed his first symphony. Soon after this he attracted the attention of the old Prince Esterhazy, all the members of whose family have become known in the history of music as generous Mæcenases of the art.

"What! you don't mean to say that little blackamoor" (alluding to Haydn's brown complexion and small stature) "composed that spmphony?"

"Surely, prince," replied the director Friedburg, beckoning to Joseph Haydn, who advanced towards the orchestra.

"Little Moor," says the old gentleman, "you shall enter my service. I am Prince Esterhazy. What's your name?"

"Haydn."

"Ah! I've heard of you. Get along and dress yourself like a *Kapellmeister*. Clap on a new coat, and mind your wig is curled. You're too short. You shall have red heels; but they shall be high, that your stature may correspond with your merit."

So he went to live at Eisenstadt in the Esterhazy household, and received a salary of four hundred florins, which was afterwards raised to one thousand by Prince Nicholas Esterhazy. Hadyn continued the intimate friend and associate of Prince Nicholas for thirty years, and death only dissolved the bond between them. In the Esterhazy household the life of Haydn was a very quiet one, a life of incessant and happy industry; for he poured out an incredible number of works, among them not a few of his most famous ones. So he spent a happy life in hard labour, alternated with delightful recreations at the Esterhazy country-seat, mountain rambles, hunting and fishing, open-air concerts, musical evenings, etc.

A French traveller who visited Esterhazy about 1782 says —"The château stands quite solitary, and the prince sees nobody but his officials and servants, and strangers who come hither from curiosity. He has a puppet-theatre, which is certainly unique in character. Here the grandest operas are produced. One knows not whether to be amazed or to laugh at seeing 'Alceste,' 'Alcides,' etc., put on the stage with all due solemnity and played by puppets. His orchestra is one of the best I ever heard, and the great Haydn is his court and theatre composer. He employs a poet for his singular theatre, whose humour and skill in suiting the grandest subjects for the stage, and in parodying the gravest effects, are often exceedingly happy. He often engages a troupe of wandering players for months at a time, and he himself and his retinue form the entire audience. They are allowed to come on the stage uncombed, drunk, their parts not half learned, and half dressed. The prince is not for the serious and tragic, and he enjoys it when the players, like Sancho Panza, give loose reins to their humour."

Yet Haydn was not perfectly contented. He would have been had it not been for his terrible wife, the hair-dresser's daughter, who had a dismal, mischievous, sullen nature, a venomous tongue, and a savage temper. She kept Haydn in hot water continually, till at last he broke loose from this plague by separating from her. Scandal says that Haydn, who had a very affectionate and sympathetic nature, found ample consolation for marital infelicity in the charms and society of the lovely Boselli, a great singer. He had her picture painted, and humoured all her whims and caprices, to the sore depletion of his pocket.

In after-years again he was mixed up in a little affair with the great Mrs. Billington, whose beautiful person was no less marked than her fine voice. Sir Joshua Reynolds was painting her portrait for him, and had represented her as St. Cecilia listening to celestial music. Haydn paid her a charming compliment at one of the sittings.

"What do you think of the charming Billington's picture?" said Sir Joshua.

"Yes," said Haydn, "it is indeed a beautiful picture. It is just like her, but there's a strange mistake."

"What is that?"

"Why, you have painted her listening to the angels, when you ought to have painted the angels listening to her."

At one time, during Haydn's connection with Prince Esterhazy, the latter, from motives of economy, determined to dismiss his celebrated orchestra, which he supported at great expense. Haydn was the leader, and his patron's purpose caused him sore pain, as indeed it did all the players, among whom were many distinguished instrumentalists. Still, there was nothing to be done but for all concerned to make themselves as cheerful as possible under the circumstances; so, with that fund of wit and humour which seems to have been concealed under the immaculate coat and formal wig of the strait-laced Haydn, he set about composing a work for the last performance of the royal band, a work which has ever since borne the appropriate title of the "Farewell Symphony."

On the night appointed for the last performance a brilliant company, including the prince, had assembled. The music of the new symphony began gaily enough—it was even merry. As it went on, however, it became soft and dreamy. The strains were sad and "long drawn out." At length a sorrowful wailing began. One instrument after another left off, and each musician, as his task ended, blew out his lamp and departed with his music rolled up under his arm.

Haydn was the last to finish, save one, and this was the prince's favourite violinist, who said all that he had to say in a brilliant violin cadenza, when, behold! he made off.

The prince was astonished. "What is the meaning of all this?" cried he.

"It is our sorrowful farewell," answered Haydn.

This was too much. The prince was overcome, and, with a good laugh, said: "Well, I think I must reconsider my decision. At anyrate we will not say 'good-bye' now."

III.

During the thirty years of Haydn's quiet life with the Esterhazys he had been gradually acquiring an immense reputation in France, England and Spain, of which he himself was unconscious. His great symphonies had stamped him world-wide as a composer of remarkable creative genius. Haydn's modesty prevented him from recognising his own celebrity. Therefore, we can fancy his astonishment when, shortly after the death of Prince Nicholas Esterhazy, a stranger called on him and said, "I am Salomon, from London, and must strike a bargain with you for that city immediately."

Haydn was dazed with the suddenness of the proposition, but the old ties were broken up, and his grief needed recreation and change. Still, he had many beloved friends, whose society it was hard to leave. Chief among these was Mozart. "Oh, papa," said Mozart, "you have had no training for the wide world, and you speak so few languages." "Oh, my language is understood all over the world," said Papa Haydn, with a smile. When he departed for England, December 15, 1790, Mozart could with difficulty tear himself away, and said, with pathetic tears, "We shall doubtless now take our last farewell."

Haydn and Mozart were perfectly in accord, and each thought and did well towards the other. Mozart, we know, was born when Haydn had just reached manhood, so that when Mozart became old enough to study composition the earlier works of Haydn's chamber music had been written; and these undoubtedly formed the studies of the boy Mozart, and greatly influenced his style; so that Haydn was the model, and, in a sense, the instructor of Mozart. Strange is it then to find, in after-years, the master borrowing (perhaps with interest!) from the pupil. Such, however, was the fact, as every amateur knows. At this we can hardly wonder, for Haydn possessed unbounded admiration not only for Mozart, but also for his music, which the following shows. Being asked by a friend at Prague to send him an opera, he replied :—

"With all my heart, if you desire to have it for yourself alone, but if you wish to perform it in public, I must be excused; for, being written specially for my company at the Esterhazy Palace, it would not produce the proper effect elsewhere. I would do a new score for your theatre, but what a hazardous step it would be to stand in comparison with Mozart! Oh, Mozart! If I could instil into the soul of every lover of music the admiration I have for his matchless works, all countries would seek to be possessed of so great a treasure. Let Prague keep him, ah! and well reward him, for without that the history of geniuses is bad; alas! we see so many noble minds crushed beneath adversity. Mozart is incomparable, and I am annoyed that he is unable to obtain any court appointment. Forgive me if I get excited when speaking of him, I am so fond of him."

Mozart's admiration for Haydn's music, too, was very marked. He and Herr Kozeluch were one day listening to a composition of Haydn's which contained some bold modulations. Kozeluch thought them strange, and asked Mozart whether he would have written them. "I think not," smartly replied Mozart, "and for this reason: because they would not have occurred either to you or me!"

On another occasion we find Mozart taking to task a Viennese professor of some celebrity, who used to experience great delight in turning to Haydn's compositions to find therein any evidence of the master's want of sound theoretical training—a quest in which the pedant occasionally succeeded. One day he came to Mozart with a great crime to unfold. Mozart as usual endeavoured to turn the conversation, but the learned professor still went chattering on, till at last Mozart shut his mouth with the following pill—"Sir, if you and I were both melted down together, we should not furnish materials for one Haydn."

It was one of the most beautiful friendships in the history of art, full of tender offices, and utterly free from the least taint of envy or selfishness.

IV.

Haydn landed in England after a voyage which delighted him in spite of his terror of the sea—a feeling which seems to be usual among people of very high musical sensibilities.

In his diary we find recorded—"By four o'clock we had come twenty miles. The large vessel stood out to sea five hours longer, till the tide carried it into the harbour. I remained on deck the whole passage, in order to gaze my fill at that huge monster—the ocean."

The novelty of Haydn's concerts—of which he was to give twenty at fifty pounds a-piece—consisted of their being his own symphonies, conducted by himself in person. Haydn's name, during his serene, uneventful years with the Esterhazys, had become world-famous. His reception was most brilliant. Dinner parties, receptions, invitations without end, attested the enthusiasm of the sober English; and his appearance at concerts and public meetings was the signal for stormy applause. How, in the press of all this pleasure in which he was plunged, he continued to compose the great number of works produced at this time, is a marvel. He must have been little less than a Briareus. It was in England that he wrote the celebrated Salomon symphonies—the "twelve grand," as they are called. They may well be regarded as the crowning-point of Haydn's efforts in that form of writing. He took infinite pains with them, as, indeed, is well proved by an examination of the scores. More elaborate, more beautiful, and scored for a fuller orchestra than any others of the one hundred and twenty or thereabouts which he composed, the Salomon set also bears marks of the devout and pious spirit in which Haydn ever laboured.

It is interesting to see how, in many of the great works which have won the world's admiration, the religion of the author has gone hand-in-hand with his energy and his genius; and we find Haydn not ashamed to indorse his score with his prayer and praise, or to offer the fruits of his talents to the Giver of all. Thus, the symphony in D (No. 6) bears on the first page of the score the inscription, "*In nomine Domini: di me Giuseppe Haydn, maia* 1791, *in London;*" and on the last page, "*Fine, Laus Deo,* 238."

That genius may sometimes be trusted to judge of its

own work may be gathered from Haydn's own estimate of these great symphonies.

"Sir," said the well-satisfied Salomon, after a successful performance of one of them, "I am strongly of opinion that you will never surpass these symphonies."

"No!" replied Haydn; "I never mean to try."

The public, as we have said, was enthusiastic; but such a full banquet of severe orchestral music was a severe trial to many, and not a few heads would keep time to the music by steady nods during the slow movements. Haydn, therefore, composed what is known as the "Surprise" symphony. The slow movement is of the most lulling and soothing character, and about the time the audience should be falling into its first snooze, the instruments having all died away into the softest *pianissimo*, the full orchestra breaks out with a frightful BANG. It is a question whether the most vigorous performance of this symphony would startle an audience nowadays, accustomed to the strident effects of Wagner and Liszt. A wag in a recent London journal tells us, indeed, that at the most critical part in the work a gentleman opened one eye sleepily and said, "Come in."

Simple-hearted Haydn was delighted at the attention lavished on him in London. He tells us how he enjoyed his various entertainments and feastings by such dignitaries as William Pitt, the Lord Chancellor, and the Duke of Lids (Leeds). The gentlemen drank freely the whole night, and the songs, the crazy uproar, and smashing of glasses were very great. He went down to stay with the Prince of Wales (George IV.), who played on the violoncello, and charmed the composer by his kindness. "He is the handsomest man on God's earth. He has an extraordinary love of music, and a great deal of feeling, but very little money."

To stem the tide of Haydn's popularity, the Italian faction had recourse to Giardini; and they even imported a pet pupil of Haydn, Pleyel, to conduct the rival concerts. Our composer kept his temper, and wrote, "He [Pleyel] behaves himself with great modesty." Later we read, "Pleyel's presumption is a public laughing-stock;" but he adds, "I go to all his concerts and applaud him."

Far different were the amenities that passed between Haydn and Giardini. "I won't know the German hound," says the latter. Haydn wrote, "I attended his concert at Ranelagh, and he played the fiddle like a hog."

Among the pleasant surprises Haydn had in England was his visit to Herschel, the great astronomer, in whom he recognised one of his old oboe-players. The big telescope amazed him, and so did the patient star-gazer, who often sat out-of-doors in the most intense cold for five or six hours at a time.

Our composer returned to Vienna in May 1795, with the little fortune of 12,000 florins in his pocket.

v.

In his charming little cottage near Vienna Haydn was the centre of a brilliant society. Princes and nobles were proud to do honour to him; and painters, poets, scholars, and musicians made a delightful coterie, which was not even disturbed by the political convulsions of the time. The baleful star of Napoleon shot its disturbing influences throughout Europe, and the roar of his cannon shook the established order of things with the echoes of what was to come. Haydn was passionately attached to his country and his emperor, and regarded anxiously the rumblings and quakings of the period; but he did not intermit his labour, or allow his consecration to his divine art to be in the least shaken. Like Archimedes of old, he toiled serenely at his appointed work, while the political order of things was crumbling before the genius and energy of the Corsican adventurer.

In 1798 he completed his great oratorio of "The Creation," on which he had spent three years of toil, and which embodied his brightest genius. Haydn was usually a very rapid composer, but he seems to have laboured at the "Creation" with a sort of reverential humility, which never permitted him to think his work worthy or complete. It soon went the round of Germany, and passed to England and France, everywhere awakening enthusiasm by its great symmetry and beauty. Without the sublimity of Handel's "Messiah," it is marked by a richness of melody, a serene elevation, a matchless variety in treatment, which make it the most characteristic of Haydn's works. Napoleon, the first consul, was hastening to the opera-house to hear this, 24th January 1801, when he was stopped by an attempt at assassination.

Two years after "The Creation" appeared "The Seasons," founded on Thomson's poem, also a great work, and one of his last; for the grand old man was beginning to think of rest, and he only composed two or three quartets after this. He was now seventy years old, and went but little from his own home. His chief pleasure was to sit in his shady garden, and see his friends, who loved to solace the musical patriarch with cheerful talk and music. Haydn often fell into deep melancholy, and he tells us that God revived him; for no more sweet, devout nature ever lived. His art was ever a religion. A touching incident of his old age occurred at a grand performance of "The Creation" in 1808. Hadyn was present, but he was so old and feeble that he had to be wheeled in a chair into the theatre, where a princess of the house of Esterhazy took her seat by his side. This was the last time that Haydn appeared in public, and a very impressive sight it must have been to see the aged father of music listening to "The Creation" of his younger days, but too old to take any active share in the performance. The presence of the old man roused intense enthusiasm among the audience, which could no longer be suppressed as the chorus and orchestra burst in full power upon the superb passage, "And there was light."

Amid the tumult of the enraptured audience the old composer was seen striving to raise himself. Once on his feet, he mustered up all his strength, and, in reply to the applause of the audience, he cried out as loud as he was able—"No, no! not from me, but," pointing to heaven, "from thence—from heaven above—comes all!" saying which, he fell back in his chair, faint and exhausted, and had to be carried out of the room.

One year after this Vienna was bombarded by the French, and a shot fell in Haydn's garden. He requested to be led to his piano, and played the "Hymn to the Emperor" three times over with passionate eloquence and pathos. This was his last performance. He died five days afterwards, aged seventy-seven, and lies buried in the cemetery of Gumpfenzdorf, in his own beloved Vienna.

VI.

The serene, genial face of Haydn, as seen in his portraits, measures accurately the character of his music. In both we see healthfulness, good-humour, vivacity, devotional feeling, and warm affections; a mind contented, but yet attaching high importance to only one thing in life, the composing of music. Haydn pursued this with a calm, insatiable industry, without haste, without rest. His works number eight hundred, comprising cantatas, symphonies, oratorios, masses, concertos, trios, sonatas, quartets, minuets, etc., and also twenty-two operas, eight German and fourteen Italian.

As a creative mind in music, Haydn was the father of the quartet and symphony. Adopting the sonata form as scientifically illustrated by Emanuel Bach, he introduced it into compositions for the orchestra and the chamber. He developed these into a completeness and full-orbed symmetry, which have never been improved. Mozart is richer, Beethoven more sublime, Schubert more luxuriant, Mendelssohn more orchestral and passionate; but Haydn has never been surpassed in his keen perception of the capacities of instruments, his subtile distribution of parts, his variety in treating his themes, and his charmingly legitimate effects. He fills a large space in musical history, not merely from the number, originality, and beauty of his compositions, but as one who represents an era in art-development.

In Haydn genius and industry were happily united. With a marvellously rich flow of musical ideas, he clearly knew what he meant to do, and never neglected the just elaboration of each one. He would labour on a theme till it had shaped itself into perfect beauty.

Haydn is illustrious in the history of art as a complete artistic life, which worked out all of its contents as did the great Goethe. In the words of a charming writer: "His life was a rounded whole. There was no broken light about it; it orbed slowly, with a mild, unclouded lustre, into a perfect star. Time was gentle with him, and Death was kind, for both waited upon his genius until all was won. Mozart was taken away at an age when new and dazzling effects had not ceased to flash through his brain: at the very moment when his harmonies began to have a prophetic ring of the nineteenth century, it was decreed that he should not see its dawn. Beethoven himself had but just entered upon an unknown 'sea whose margin seemed to fade forever and forever as he moved;' but good old Haydn had come into port over a calm sea and after a prosperous voyage. The laurel wreath was this time woven about silver locks; the gathered-in harvest was ripe and golden."

MOZART.

I.

THE life of WOLFGANG AMADEUS MOZART, one of the immortal names in music, contradicts the rule that extraordinary youthful talent is apt to be followed by a sluggish and commonplace maturity. His father entered the room one day with a friend, and found the child bending over a music score. The little Mozart, not yet five years old, told his father he was writing a concerto for the piano. The latter examined it, and tears of joy and astonishment rolled down his face on perceiving its accuracy.

"It is good, but too difficult for general use," said the friend.

"Oh," said Wolfgang, "it must be practised till it is learned. This is the way it goes." So saying, he played it with perfect correctness.

About the same time he offered to take the violin at a performance of some chamber music. His father refused, saying, "How can you? You have never learned the violin."

"One needs not study for that," said this musical prodigy; and taking the instrument, he played second violin with ease and accuracy. Such precocity seems almost incredible, and only in the history of music does it find any parallel.

Born in Salzburg, 27th January 1756, he was carefully trained by his father, who resigned his place as court musician to devote himself more exclusively to his family. From the earliest age he showed an extraordinary passion for music and mathematics, scrawling notes and diagrams in every place accessible to his insatiate pencil.

Taken to Vienna, the six-year-old virtuoso astonished the court by his brilliant talents. The future Queen of France, Marie Antoinette, was particularly delighted with him, and the little Mozart naïvely said he would like to marry her, for she was so good to him. His father devoted several years to an artistic tour, with him and his little less talented sister, through the German cities, and it was also extended to Paris and London. Everywhere the greatest enthusiasm was evinced in this charming bud of promise. The father writes home—"We have swords, laces, mantillas, snuff-boxes, gold cases, sufficient to furnish a shop; but as for money, it is a scarce article, and I am positively poor."

At Paris they were warmly received at the court, and the boy is said to have expressed his surprise when Mme. Pompadour refused to kiss him, saying, "Who is she, that she will not kiss me? Have I not been kissed by the queen?" In London his improvisations and piano sonatas excited the greatest admiration. Here he also published his third work. These journeys were an uninterrupted chain of triumphs for the child-virtuoso on the piano, organ, violin, and in singing. He was made honorary member of the Academies of Bologna and Verona, decorated with orders, and received at the age of thirteen an order to write the opera of "Mithridates," which was successfully produced at Milan in 1770. Several other fine minor compositions were also written to order at this time for his Italian admirers. At Rome Mozart attended the Sistine Chapel and wrote the score of Allegri's great mass, forbidden by the Pope to be copied, from the memory of a single performance.

The record of Mozart's youthful triumphs might be extended at great length; but aside from the proof they furnish of his extraordinary precocity, they have lent little vital significance in the great problem of his career, except so far as they stimulated the marvellous boy to lay a deep foundation for his greater future, which, short as it was, was fruitful in undying results.

II.

Mozart's life in Paris, where he lived with his mother in 1778 and 1779, was a disappointment, for he despised the French nation. His deep, simple, German nature revolted from Parisian frivolity, in which he found only sensuality and coarseness, disguised under a thin veneering of social grace. He abhorred French music in these bitter terms— "The French are and always will be downright donkeys. They cannot sing, they scream." It was just at this time that Gluck and Piccini were having their great art-duel. We get a glimpse of the pious tendency of the young composer in his characterisation of Voltaire.—"The ungodly arch-villain, Voltaire, has just died like a dog." Again he writes—" Friends who have no religion cannot long be my friends. . . . I have such a sense of religion that I shall never do anything that I would not do before the whole world."

With Mozart's return to Germany in 1779, being then twenty-three years of age, comes the dawn of his classical period as a composer. The greater number of his masses had already been written, and now he settled himself in serious earnest to the cultivation of a true German operatic school. This found its dawn in the production of "Idomeneo," his first really great work for the lyric stage.

The young composer had hard struggles with poverty in these days. His letters to his father are full of revelations of his friction with the little worries of life. Lack of money pinched him close, yet his cheerful spirit was ever buoyant. "I have only one small room; it is quite crammed with a piano, a table, a bed, and a chest of drawers," he writes.

Yet he would marry; for he was willing to face poverty in the companionship of a loving woman who dared to face it with him. At Mannheim he had met a beautiful young singer, Aloysia Weber, and he went to Munich to offer her marriage. She, however, saw nothing attractive in the thin, pale young man, with his long nose, great eyes, and little head; for he was anything but prepossessing. A younger sister, Constance, however, secretly loved Mozart, and he soon transferred his repelled affections to this charming woman, whom he married in 1782 at the house of Baroness Waldstetten. His *naïve* reasons for marrying show Mozart's ingenuous nature. He had no one to take care of his linen, he would not live dissolutely like other young men, and he loved Constance Weber. His answer to his father, who objected on account of his poverty, is worth quoting :—

" Constance is a well-conducted, good girl, of respectable parentage, and I am in a position to earn at least *daily bread* for her. We love each other, and are resolved to marry. All that you have written or may possibly write on the subject can be nothing but well-meant advice, which, however good and sensible, can no longer apply to a man who has gone so far with a girl."

Poor as Mozart was, he possessed such integrity and independence that he refused a most liberal offer from the King of Prussia to become his chapel-master, for some unexplained reason which involved his sense of right and wrong. The first year of his marriage he wrote "Il Seraglio," and made the acquaintance of the aged Gluck, who took a deep interest in him and warmly praised his genius. Haydn, too, recognised his brilliant powers. "I tell you, on the word of an honest man," said the author of the "Creation" to Leopold Mozart, the father, who asked his opinion, "that I consider your son the greatest composer I have ever heard. He writes with taste, and possesses a thorough knowledge of composition."

Poverty and increasing expense pricked Mozart into intense, restless energy. His life had no lull in its creative industry. His splendid genius, insatiable and tireless, broke down his body, like a sword wearing out its scabbard. He poured out symphonies, operas, and sonatas with such prodigality as to astonish us, even when recollecting how fecund the musical mind has often been. Alike as artist and composer, he never ceased his labours. Day after day and night after night he hardly snatched an hour's rest. We can almost fancy he foreboded how short his brilliant life was to be, and was impelled to crowd into its brief compass its largest measure of results.

Yet he was always pursued by the spectre of want. Oftentimes his sick wife could not obtain needed medicines. He made more money than most musicians, yet was always impoverished. But it was his glory that he was never impoverished by sensual indulgence, extravagance, and riotous living, but by his lavish generosity to those who in many instances needed help less than himself. Like many other men of genius and sensibility, he could not say "no" to even the pretence of distress and suffering.

III.

The culminating point of Mozart's artistic development was in 1786. The "Marriage of Figaro" was the first of a series of masterpieces which cannot be surpassed alike for musical greatness and their hold on the lyric stage. The next year "Don Giovanni" saw the light, and was produced at Prague. The overture of this opera was composed and scored in less than six hours. The inhabitants of Prague greeted the work with the wildest enthusiasm, for they seemed to understand Mozart better than the Viennese.

During this period he made frequent concert tours to recruit his fortunes, but with little financial success. Presents of watches, snuff-boxes, and rings were common, but the returns were so small that Mozart was frequently obliged to pawn his gifts to purchase a dinner and lodging. What a comment on the period which adored genius, but allowed it to starve! His audiences could be enthusiastic enough to carry him to his hotel on their shoulders, but probably never thought that the wherewithal of a hearty supper was a more seasonable homage. So our musician struggled on through the closing years of his life with the wolf constantly at his door, and an invalid wife whom he passionately loved, yet must needs see suffer from the want of common necessaries. In these modern days, when distinguished artists make princely fortunes by the exercise of their musical gifts, it is not easy to believe that Mozart, recognised as the greatest pianoforte player and composer of his time by all of musical Germany, could suffer such dire extremes of want as to be obliged more than once to beg for a dinner.

In 1791 he composed the score of the "Magic Flute" at the request of Schikaneder, a Viennese manager, who had written the text from a fairy tale, the fantastic elements of which are peculiarly German in their humour. Mozart put great earnestness into the work, and made it the first German opera of commanding merit, which embodied the essential intellectual sentiment and kindly warmth of popular German life. The manager paid the composer but a trifle for a work whose transcendent success enabled him to build a new opera-house, and laid the foundation of a large fortune. We are told, too, that at the time of Mozart's death in extreme want, when his sick wife, half-maddened with grief, could not buy a coffin for the dead composer, this hard-hearted wretch, who owed his all to the genius of the great departed, rushed about through Vienna bewailing the loss to music with sentimental tears, but did not give the heart-broken widow one kreutzer to pay the expense of a decent burial.

In 1791 Mozart's health was breaking down with great rapidity, though he himself would never recognise his own swiftly advancing fate. He experienced, however, a deep melancholy which nothing could remove. For the first time his habitual cheerfulness deserted him. His wife had been enabled through the kindness of her friends to visit the healing waters of Baden, and was absent.

An incident now occurred which impressed Mozart with an ominous chill. One night there came a stranger, singularly dressed in grey, with an order for a requiem to be composed without fail within a month. The visitor, without revealing his name, departed in mysterious gloom, as he came. Again the stranger called, and solemnly reminded Mozart of his promise. The composer easily persuaded himself that this was a visitor from the other world, and that the requiem would be his own; for he was exhausted with labour and sickness, and easily became the prey of superstitious fancies. When his wife returned, she found him with a fatal pallor on his face, silent and melancholy, labouring with intense absorption on the funereal mass. He would sit brooding over the score till he swooned away in his chair, and only come to consciousness to bend his waning energies again to their ghastly work. The mysterious visitor, whom Mozart believed to be the precursor of his death, we now know to have been Count Walseck, who had recently lost his wife, and wished a musical memorial.

His final sickness attacked the composer while labouring at the requiem. The musical world was ringing with the fame of his last opera. To the dying man was brought the offer of the rich appointment of organist of St. Stephen's Cathedral. Most flattering propositions were made him by eager managers, who had become thoroughly awake to his genius when it was too late. The great Mozart was dying in the very prime of his youth and his powers, when success was in his grasp and the world opening wide its arms to welcome his glorious gifts with substantial recognition; but all too late, for he was doomed to die in his spring-tide, though "a spring mellow with all the fruits of autumn."

The unfinished requiem lay on the bed, and his last efforts were to imitate some peculiar instrumental effects, as he breathed out his life in the arms of his wife and his friend, Süssmaier.

The epilogue to this life-drama is one of the saddest in the history of art: a pauper funeral for one of the world's greatest geniuses. "It was late one winter afternoon," says an old record, "before the coffin was deposited on the side aisles on the south side of St. Stephen's. Van Swieten, Salieri, Süssmaier, and two unknown musicians were the only persons present besides the officiating priest and the pall-bearers. It was a terribly inclement day; rain and sleet came down fast; and an eye-witness describes how the little band of mourners stood shivering in the blast, with their umbrellas up, round the hearse, as it left the door of the church. It was then far on in the dark, cold December afternoon, and the evening was fast closing in before the solitary hearse had passed the Stubenthor, and reached the distant graveyard of St. Marx, in which, among the 'third class,' the great composer of the 'G minor Symphony' and the 'Requiem' found his resting-place. By this time the weather had proved too much for all the mourners; they had dropped off one by one, and Mozart's body was accompanied only by the driver of the carriage. There had been already two pauper funerals that day—one of them a midwife—and Mozart was to be the third in the grave and the uppermost.

"When the hearse drew up in the slush and sleet at the gate of the graveyard, it was welcomed by a strange pair— Franz Harruschka, the assistant grave-digger, and his mother, Katharina, known as 'Frau Katha,' who filled the quaint office of official mendicant to the place.

"The old woman was the first to speak: 'Any coaches or mourners coming?'

"A shrug from the driver of the hearse was the only response.

"'Whom have you got there, then?' continued she.

"'A bandmaster,' replied the other.

"'A musician? they're a poor lot; then I've no more money to look for to-day. It is to be hoped we shall have better luck in the morning.'

"To which the driver said, with a laugh, 'I'm devilish thirsty, too—not a kreutzer of drink-money have I had.'

"After this curious colloquy the coffin was dismounted and shoved into the top of the grave already occupied by the two paupers of the morning; and such was Mozart's last appearance on earth."

To-day no stone marks the spot where were deposited the last remains of one of the brightest of musical spirits; indeed, the very grave is unknown, for it was the grave of a pauper.

IV.

Mozart's charming letters reveal to us such a gentle, sparkling, affectionate nature, as to inspire as much love for the man as admiration for his genius. Sunny humour and tenderness bubble in almost every sentence. A clever writer says that "opening these is like opening a painted tomb. . . . The colours are all fresh, the figures are all distinct."

No better illustration of the man Mozart can be had than in a few extracts from his correspondence. He writes to his sister from Rome while yet a mere lad :—

"I am, thank God! except my miserable pen, well, and send you and mamma a thousand kisses. I wish you were in Rome; I am sure it would please you. Papa says I am a little fool, but that is nothing new. Here we have but one bed; it is easy to understand that I can't rest comfortably with papa. I shall be glad when we get into new quarters. I have just finished drawing the Holy Peter with his keys, the Holy Paul with his sword, and the Holy Luke with my sister. I have had the honour of kissing St. Peter's foot; and because I am so small as to be unable to reach it, they had to lift me up. I am the same old "WOLFGANG."

Mozart was very fond of this sister Nannerl, and he used to write to her in a playful mosaic of French, German, and Italian. Just after his wedding he writes:—

"My darling is now a hundred times more joyful at the idea of going to Salzburg, and I am willing to stake—ay, my very life, that you will rejoice still more in my happiness when you know her; if, indeed, in your estimation, as in mine, a high-principled, honest, virtuous, and pleasing wife ought to make a man happy."

Late in his short life he writes the following characteristic note to a friend, whose life does not appear to have been one of the most regular:—

"Now tell me, my dear friend, how you are. I hope you are all as well as we are. You cannot fail to be happy, for you possess everything that you can wish for at your age and in your position, especially as you now seem to have entirely given up your former mode of life. Do you not every day become more convinced of the truth of the little lectures I used to inflict on you? Are not the pleasures of a transient, capricious passion widely different from the happiness produced by rational and true love? I feel sure that you often in your heart thank me for my admonitions. I shall feel quite proud if you do. But, jesting apart, you do really owe me some little gratitude if you are become worthy of Fräulein N——, for I certainly played no insignificant part in your improvement or reform.

"My great-grandfather used to say to his wife, my great-grandmother, who in turn told it to her daughter, my grandmother, who again repeated it to her daughter, my mother, who repeated it to her daughter, my own sister, that it was a very great art to talk eloquently and well, but an equally great one to know the right moment to stop. I therefore shall follow the advice of my sister, thanks to our mother, grandmother, and great-grandmother, and thus end, not only my moral ebullition, but my letter."

His playful tenderness lavished itself on his wife in a thousand quaint ways. He would, for example, rise long before her to take his horseback exercise, and always kiss her sleeping face and leave a little note like the following resting on her forehead—"Good-morning, dear little wife! I hope you have had a good sleep and pleasant dreams. I shall be back in two hours. Behave yourself like a good little girl, and don't run away from your husband."

Speaking of an infant child, our composer would say merrily, "That boy will be a true Mozart, for he always cries in the very key in which I am playing."

Mozart's musical greatness, shown in the symmetry of his art as well as in the richness of his inspirations, has been unanimously acknowledged by his brother composers. Meyerbeer could not restrain his tears when speaking of him. Weber, Mendelssohn, Rossini, and Wagner always praise him in terms of enthusiastic admiration. Haydn called him the greatest of composers. In fertility of invention, beauty of form, and exactness of method, he has never been surpassed, and has but one or two rivals. The composer of three of the greatest operas in musical history, besides many of much more than ordinary excellence ; of symphonies that rival Haydn's for symmetry and melodic affluence ; of a great number of quartets, quintets, etc. ;

and of pianoforte sonatas which rank high among the best; of many masses that are standard in the service of the Catholic Church; of a great variety of beautiful songs—there is hardly any form of music which he did not richly adorn with the treasures of his genius. We may well say, in the words of one of the most competent critics:—

"Mozart was a king and a slave—king in his own beautiful realm of music; slave of the circumstances and the conditions of this world. Once over the boundaries of his own kingdom, and he was supreme; but the powers of the earth acknowledged not his sovereignty."

BEETHOVEN.

I.

The name and memory of this composer awaken, in the heart of the lover of music, sentiments of the deepest reverence and admiration. His life was so marked with affliction and so isolated as to make him, in his environment of conditions as a composer, an unique figure.

The principal fact which made the exterior life of Beethoven so bare of the ordinary pleasures that brighten and sweeten existence, his total deafness, greatly enriched his spiritual life. Music finally became to him a purely intellectual conception, for he was without any sensual enjoyment of its effects. To this Samson of music, for whom the ear was like the eye to other men, Milton's lines may indeed well apply:—

> "Oh! dark, dark, dark, amid the blaze of noon!
> Irrecoverably dark—total eclipse,
> Without all hope of day!
> Oh first created Beam, and thou, great Word,
> 'Let there be light,' and light was over all,
> Why am I thus bereaved thy prime decree?
> The sun to me is dark."

To his severe affliction we owe alike many of the defects of his character and the splendours of his genius. All his powers, concentrated into a spiritual focus, wrought such things as lift him into a solitary greatness. The world has agreed to measure this man as it measures Homer, Dante, and Shakespeare. We do not compare him with others.

Beethoven had the reputation among his contemporaries of being harsh, bitter, suspicious, and unamiable. There is much to justify this in the circumstances of his life; yet our readers will discover much to show, on the other hand, how deep, strong, and tender was the heart which was so wrung and tortured, and wounded to the quick by—

" The slings and arrows of outrageous fortune."

Weber gives a picture of Beethoven—"The square Cyclopean figure attired in a shabby coat with torn sleeves." Everybody will remember his noble, austere face, as seen in the numerous prints: the square, massive head, with the forest of rough hair; the strong features, so furrowed with the marks of passion and sadness; the eyes, with their look of introspection and insight; the whole expression of the countenance as of an ancient prophet. Such was the impression made by Beethoven on all who saw him, except in his moods of fierce wrath, which towards the last were not uncommon, though short-lived. A sorely tried, sublimely gifted man, he met his fate stubbornly, and worked out his great mission with all his might and main, through long years of weariness and trouble. Posterity has rewarded him by enthroning him on the highest peaks of musical fame.

II.

Ludwig van Beethoven was born at Bonn in 1770. It is a singular fact that at an early age he showed the deepest distaste for music, unlike the other great composers, who evinced their bent from their earliest years. His father was obliged to whip him severely before he would consent to sit down at the harpsichord; and it was not till he was past ten that his genuine interest in music showed itself. His first compositions displayed his genius. Mozart heard him play them, and said, "Mind, you will hear that boy talked of." Haydn, too, met Beethoven for the first and only time when the former was on his way to England, and recognised his remarkable powers. He gave him a few lessons in composition, and was after that anxious to claim the young Titan as a pupil.

"Yes," growled Beethoven, who for some queer reason never liked Haydn, "I had some lessons of him, indeed, but I was not his disciple. I never learned anything from him."

Beethoven made a profound impression even as a youth on all who knew him. Aside from the palpable marks of his power, there was an indomitable *hauteur*, a mysterious, self-wrapped air as of one constantly communing with the invisible, an unconscious assertion of mastery about him, which strongly impressed the imagination.

At the very outset of his career, when life promised all fair and bright things to him, two comrades linked themselves to him, and ever after that refused to give him up — grim poverty and still grimmer disease. About the same time that he lost a fixed salary through the death of his friend, the Elector of Cologne, he began to grow deaf. Early in 1800, walking one day in the woods with his devoted friend and pupil, Ferdinand Ries, he disclosed the sad secret to him that the whole joyous world of sound was being gradually closed up to him; the charm of the human voice, the notes of the woodland birds, the sweet babblings of Nature, jargon to others, but intelligible to genius, the full-born splendours of *heard* music—all, all were fast receding from his grasp.

Beethoven was extraordinarily sensitive to the influences of Nature. Before his disease became serious he writes— "I wander about here with music-paper among the hills, and dales, and valleys, and scribble a good deal. No man on earth can love the country as I do." But one of

Nature's most delightful modes of speech to man was soon to be utterly lost to him. At last he became so deaf that the most stunning crash of thunder or the *fortissimo* of the full orchestra were to him as if they were not. His bitter, heart-rending cry of agony, when he became convinced that the misfortune was irremediable, is full of eloquent despair—" As autumn leaves wither and fall, so are my hopes blighted. Almost as I came, I depart. Even the lofty courage, which so often animated me in the lovely days of summer, is gone forever. O Providence! vouchsafe me one day of pure felicity! How long have I been estranged from the glad echo of true joy! When, O my God! when shall I feel it again in the temple of Nature and man? Never!"

And the small-souled, mole-eyed gossips and critics called him hard, churlish, and cynical—him, for whom the richest thing in Nature's splendid dower had been obliterated, except a soul, which never in its deepest sufferings lost its noble faith in God and man, or allowed its indomitable courage to be one whit weakened. That there were periods of utterly rayless despair and gloom we may guess; but not for long did Beethoven's great nature cower before its evil genius.

III.

Within three years, from 1805 to 1808, Beethoven composed some of his greatest works—the oratorio of " The Mount of Olives," the opera of " Fidelio," and the two noble symphonies, " Pastorale " and " Eroica," besides a large number of concertos, sonatas, songs, and other occasional pieces. However gloomy the externals of his life, his creative activities knew no cessation.

The " Sinfonia Eroica," the " Choral " only expected, is the longest of the immortal nine, and is one of the greatest examples of musical portraiture extant. All the great composers from Handel to Wagner have attempted what is called descriptive music with more or less success, but never have musical genius and skill achieved a result so admirable in its relation to its purpose and by such strictly legitimate means as in this work.

"The 'Eroica,'" says a great writer, "is an attempt to draw a musical portrait of an historical character—a great statesman, a great general, a noble individual; to represent in music—Beethoven's own language—what M. Thiers has given in words, and Paul Delaroche in painting." Of Beethoven's success another writer has said—"It wants no title to tell its meaning, for throughout the symphony the hero is visibly portrayed."

It is anything but difficult to realise why Beethoven should have admired the first Napoleon. Both the soldier and musician were made of that sturdy stuff which would and did defy the world; and it is not strange that Beethoven should have desired in some way—and he knew of no better course than through his art—to honour one so characteristically akin to himself, and who at that time was the most prominent man in Europe. Beethoven began the work in 1802, and in 1804 it was completed, and bore the following title:—

> Sinfonia grande
> "Napoleon Bonaparte"
> 1804 in August
> del Sigr
> Louis van Beethoven
> Sinfonia 3.
> Op. 55.

This was copied and the original score despatched to the ambassador for presentation, while Beethoven retained the copy. Before the composition was laid before Napoleon, however, the great general had accepted the title of Emperor. No sooner did Beethoven hear of this from his pupil Ries than he started up in a rage, and exclaimed—"After all, then, he's nothing but an ordinary mortal! He will trample the rights of men under his feet!" saying which, he rushed to his table, seized the copy of the score, and tore the title-page completely off. From this time Beethoven hated Napoleon, and never again spoke of him in connection with the symphony until he heard of his death in St. Helena, when he observed, " I have already composed music for this calamity," evidently referring to the " Funeral March " in this symphony.

The opera of " Fidelio," which he composed about the same time, may be considered, in the severe sense of a great and symmetrical musical work, the finest lyric drama ever written, with the possible exception of Gluck's " Orpheus and Eurydice " and " Iphigenia in Tauris." It is rarely performed, because its broad, massive, and noble effects are beyond the capacity of most singers, and belong to the domain of pure music, demanding but little alliance with the artistic clap-trap of startling scenery and histrionic extravagance. Yet our composer's conscience shows its completeness in his obedience to the law of opera ; for the music he has written to express the situations cannot be surpassed for beauty, pathos, and passion. Beethoven, like Mendelssohn, revolted from the idea of lyric drama as an art-inconsistency, but he wrote " Fidelio " to show his possibilities in a direction with which he had but little sympathy. He composed four overtures for this opera at different periods, on account of the critical caprices of the Viennese public—a concession to public taste which his stern independence rarely made.

IV.

Beethoven's relations with women were peculiar and characteristic, as were all the phases of a nature singularly self-poised and robust. Like all men of powerful imagination and keen (though perhaps not delicate) sensibility, he was strongly attracted towards the softer sex. But a certain austerity of morals, and that purity of feeling which is the inseparable shadow of one's devotion to lofty aims, always kept him within the bounds of Platonic affection. Yet there is enough in Beethoven's letters, as scanty as their indications are in this direction, to show what ardour and glow of feeling he possessed.

About the time that he was suffering keenly with the knowledge of his fast-growing infirmity, he was bound by a strong tie of affection to Countess Giulietta Guicciardi, his "immortal beloved," "his angel," "his all," "his life," as he called her in a variety of passionate utterances. It was to her that he dedicated his song "Adelaida," which, as an expression of lofty passion, is world-famous. Beethoven was very much dissatisfied with the work even in the glow of composition. Before the notes were dry on the music paper, the composer's old friend Barth was announced. "Here," said Beethoven, putting a roll of score paper in Barth's hands, "look at that. I have just finished it, and don't like it. There is hardly fire enough in the stove to burn it, but I will try." Barth glanced through the composition, then sang it, and soon grew into such enthusiasm as to draw from Beethoven the expression, "No? then we will not burn it, old fellow." Whether it was the reaction of disgust, which so often comes to genius after the tension of work, or whether his ideal of its lovely theme was so high as to make all effort seem inadequate, the world came very near losing what it could not afford to have missed.

The charming countess, however, preferred rank, wealth, and unruffled ease to being linked even with a great genius, if, indeed, the affair ever looked in the direction of marriage. She married another, and Beethoven does not seem to have been seriously disturbed. It may be that, like Goethe, he valued the love of woman not for itself or its direct results, but as an art-stimulus which should enrich and fructify his own intellectual life.

We get glimpses of successors to the fair countess. The beautiful Marie Pachler was for some time the object of his adoration. The affair is a somewhat mysterious one, and the lady seems to have suffered from the fire through which her powerful companion passed unscathed. Again, quaintest and oddest of all, is the fancy kindled by that "mysterious sprite of genius," as one of her contemporaries calls her, Bettina Brentano, the gifted child-woman, who fascinated all who came within her reach, from Goethe and

Beethoven down to princes and nobles. Goethe's correspondence with this strange being has embalmed her life in classic literature.

Our composer's intercourse with women—for he was always alive to the charms of female society—was for the most part homely and practical in the extreme, after his deafness destroyed the zest of the more romantic phases of the divine passion. He accepted adoration, as did Dean Swift, as a right. He permitted his female admirers to knit him stockings and comforters, and make him dainty puddings and other delicacies, which he devoured with huge gusto. He condescended, in return, to go to sleep on their sofas, after picking his teeth with the candle-snuffers (so says scandal), while they thrummed away at his sonatas, the artistic slaughter of which Beethoven was mercifully unable to hear.

v.

The friendship of the Archduke Rudolph relieved Beethoven of the immediate pressure of poverty; for in 1809 he settled a small life-pension upon him. The next ten years were passed by him in comparative ease and comfort, and in this time he gave to the world five of his immortal symphonies, and a large number of his finest sonatas and masses. His general health improved very much; and in his love for his nephew Karl, whom Beethoven had adopted, the lonely man found an outlet for his strong affections, which was medicine for his soul, though the object was worthless and ungrateful.

We get curious and amusing insights into the daily tenor of Beethoven's life during this period—things sometimes almost grotesque, were they not so sad. The composer lived a solitary life, and was very much at the mercy of his servants on account of his self-absorption and deafness. He was much worried by these prosaic cares. One story of a slatternly servant is as follows:—The master was working at the mass in D, the great work which he commenced in

1819 for the celebration of the appointment of the Archduke Rudolph as Archbishop of Olmütz, and which should have been completed by the following year. Beethoven, however, became so engrossed with his work, and increased its proportions so much, that it was not finished until some two years after the event which it was intended to celebrate. While Beethoven was engaged upon this score, he one day woke up to the fact that some of his pages were missing. "Where on earth could they be?" he asked himself, and the servant too; but the problem remained unsolved. Beethoven, beside himself, spent hours and hours in searching, and so did the servant, but it was all in vain. At last they gave up the task as a useless one, and Beethoven, mad with despair, and pouring the very opposite to blessings upon the head of her who, he believed, was the author of the mischief, sat down with the conclusion that he must rewrite the missing part. He had no sooner commenced a new Kyrie—for this was the movement which was not to be found—than some loose sheets of score paper were discovered in the kitchen! Upon examination they proved to be the identical pages that Beethoven so much desired, and which the woman, in her anxiety to be "tidy" and to "keep things straight," had appropriated at some time or other for wrapping up, not only old boots and clothes, but also some superannuated pots and pans that were greasy and black!

Thus he was continually fretted by the carelessness or the rascality of the servants in whom he was obliged to trust. He writes in his diary—"Nancy is too uneducated for a housekeeper—indeed, quite a beast." "My precious servants were occupied from seven o'clock till ten trying to kindle a fire." "The cook's off again." "I shied half-a-dozen books at her head." They made his dinner so nasty he couldn't eat it. "No soup to-day, no beef, no eggs. Got something from the inn at last."

His temper and peculiarities, too, made it difficult for him to live in peace with landlords and fellow-lodgers. As his deafness increased, he struck and thumped harder at the keys of his piano, the sound of which he could scarcely hear. Nor was this all. The music that filled his brain gave him no rest. He became an inspired madman. For hours he would pace the room "howling and roaring" (as his pupil Ries puts it); or he would stand beating time with hand and foot to the music which was so vividly present to his mind. This soon put him into a feverish excitement, when, to cool himself, he would take his water-jug, and, thoughtless of everything, pour its contents over his hands, after which he could sit down to his piano. With all this it can easily be imagined that Beethoven was frequently remonstrated with. The landlord complained of a damaged ceiling, and the fellow-lodgers declared that either they or the madman must leave the house, for they could get no rest where he was. So Beethoven never for long had a resting-place. Impatient at being interfered with, he immediately packed up and went off to some other vacant lodging. From this cause he was at one time paying the rent of four lodgings at once. At times he would get tired of this changing from one place to another —from the suburbs to the town—and then he would fall back upon the hospitable home of a patron, once again taking possession of an apartment which he had vacated, probably without the least explanation or cause. One admirer of his genius, who always reserved him a chamber in his establishment, used to say to his servants—" Leave it empty ; Beethoven is sure to come back again."

The instant that Beethoven entered the house he began to write and cipher on the walls, the blinds, the table, everything, in the most abstracted manner. He frequently composed on slips of paper, which he afterwards misplaced, so that he had great difficulty in finding them. At one time, indeed, he forgot his own name and the date of his birth.

It is said that he once went into a Viennese restaurant, and, instead of giving an order, began to write a score on the back of the bill-of-fare, absorbed and unconscious of time and place. At last he asked how much he owed. " You owe nothing, sir," said the waiter. " What ! do you think I have not dined?" "Most assuredly." "Very well, then, give me something." "What do you wish?" "Anything."

These infirmities do not belittle the man of genius, but set off his greatness as with a foil. They illustrate the thought of Goethe: "It is all the same whether one is great or small, he has to pay the reckoning of humanity."

VI.

Yet beneath these eccentricities what wealth of tenderness, sympathy, and kindliness existed! His affection for his graceless nephew Karl is a touching picture. With the rest of his family he had never been on very cordial terms. His feeling of contempt for snobbery and pretence is very happily illustrated in his relations with his brother Johann. The latter had acquired property, and he sent Ludwig his card, inscribed "Johann von Beethoven, land-owner." The caustic reply was a card, on which was written, "Ludwig von Beethoven, brain-owner." But on Karl all the warmest feelings of a nature which had been starving to love and be loved poured themselves out. He gave the scapegrace every luxury and indulgence, and, self-absorbed as he was in an ideal sphere, felt the deepest interest in all the most trivial things that concerned him. Much to the uncle's sorrow, Karl cared nothing for music; but, worst of all, he was an idle, selfish, heartless fellow, who sneered at his benefactor, and valued him only for what he could get from him. At last Beethoven became fully aware of the lying ingratitude of his nephew, and he exclaims—"I know now you have no pleasure in coming to see me, which is only natural, for my atmosphere is too pure for you. God has never yet forsaken me, and no doubt some one will be found to close my eyes." Yet the generous old man forgave him, for he says in the codicil of his will, "I appoint my nephew Karl my sole heir."

Frequently, glimpses of the true vein showed themselves in such little episodes as that which occurred when

Moscheles, accompanied by his brother, visited the great musician for the first time.

"Arrived at the door of the house," writes Moscheles, "I had some misgivings, knowing Beethoven's strong aversion to strangers. I therefore told my brother to wait below. After greeting Beethoven, I said, 'Will you permit me to introduce my brother to you?'

"'Where is he?' he suddenly replied.

"'Below.'

"'What, downstairs?' and Beethoven immediately rushed off, seized hold of my brother, saying, 'Am I such a savage that you are afraid to come near me?'

"After this he showed great kindness to us."

While referring to the relations of Moscheles and Beethoven, the following anecdote related by Mme. Moscheles will be found suggestive. The pianist had been arranging some numbers of "Fidelio," which he took to the composer. He, *à la* Haydn, had inscribed the score with the words, "By God's help." Beethoven did not fail to perceive this, and he wrote underneath this phylactory the characteristic advice—"O man, help thyself."

The genial and sympathetic nature of Beethoven is illustrated in this quaint incident:—

It was in the summer of 1811 that Ludwig Löwe, the actor, first met Beethoven in the dining-room of the Blue Star at Töplitz. Löwe was paying his addresses to the landlord's daughter; and conversation being impossible at the hour he dined there, the charming creature one day whispered to him, "Come at a later hour, when the customers are gone and only Beethoven is here. He cannot hear, and will therefore not be in the way." This answered for a time; but the stern parents, observing the acquaintanceship, ordered the actor to leave the house and not to return. "How great was our despair!" relates Löwe. "We both desired to correspond, but through whom? Would the solitary man at the opposite table assist us? Despite his serious reserve and seeming churlishness, I believe he is not unfriendly. I have often caught a kind smile across his bold, defiant face." Löwe determined to try. Knowing Beethoven's custom, he contrived to meet the master when he was walking in the gardens. Beethoven instantly recognised him, and asked the reason why he no longer dined at the Blue Star. A full confession was made, and then Löwe timidly asked if he would take charge of a letter to give to the girl.

"Why not?" pleasantly observed the rough-looking musician. "You mean what is right." So pocketing the note, he was making his way onward when Löwe again interfered.

"I beg your pardon, Herr von Beethoven, that is not all."

"So, so," said the master.

"You must also bring back the answer," Löwe went on to say.

"Meet me here at this time to-morrow," said Beethoven.

Löwe did so, and there found Beethoven awaiting him, with the coveted reply from his lady-love. In this manner Beethoven carried the letters backward and forward for some five or six weeks—in short, as long as he remained in the town.

His friendship with Ferdinand Ries commenced in a way which testified how grateful he was for kindness. When his mother lay ill at Bonn, he hurried home from Vienna just in time to witness her death. After the funeral he suffered greatly from poverty, and was relieved by Ries, the violinist. Years afterwards young Ries waited on Beethoven with a letter of introduction from his father. The composer received him with cordial warmth, and said, "Tell your father I have not forgotten the death of my mother." Ever afterwards he was a helpful and devoted friend to young Ries, and was of inestimable value in forwarding his musical career.

Beethoven in his poverty never forgot to be generous. At a concert given in aid of wounded soldiers, where he conducted, he indignantly refused payment with the words, "Say Beethoven never accepts anything where humanity is concerned." To an Ursuline convent he gave an entirely new symphony to be performed at their benefit concert. Friend or enemy never applied to him for help that he did not freely give, even to the pinching of his own comfort.

VII.

Rossini could write best when he was under the influence of Italian wine and sparkling champagne. Paesiello liked the warm bed in which to jot down his musical notions, and we are told that "it was between the sheets that he planned the 'Barber of Seville,' the 'Molinara,' and so many other *chefs-d'œuvre* of ease and gracefulness." Mozart could chat and play at billiards or bowls at the same time that he composed the most beautiful music. Sacchini found it impossible to write anything of any beauty unless a pretty woman was by his side, and he was surrounded by his cats, whose graceful antics stimulated and affected him in a marked fashion. "Gluck," Bombet says, "in order to warm his imagination and to transport himself to Aulis or Sparta, was accustomed to place himself in the middle of a beautiful meadow. In this situation, with his piano before him, and a bottle of champagne on each side, he wrote in the open air his two 'Iphigenias,' his 'Orpheus,' and some other works." The agencies which stimulated Beethoven's grandest thoughts are eminently characteristic of the man. He loved to let the winds and storms beat on his bare head, and see the dazzling play of the lightning. Or, failing the sublimer moods of Nature, it was his delight to walk in the woods and fields, and take in at every pore the influences which she so lavishly bestows on her favourites. His true life was his ideal life in art. To him it was a mission and an inspiration, the end and object of all things; for these had value only as they fed the divine craving within.

"Nothing can be more sublime," he writes, "than to draw nearer to the Godhead than other men, and to diffuse here on earth these Godlike rays among mortals." Again: "What is all this compared to the grandest of all Masters of Harmony—above, above?"

> " All experience seemed an arch, wherethrough
> Gleamed that untravelled world, whose margin fades
> Forever and forever as we move."

The last four years of our composer's life were passed amid great distress from poverty and feebleness. He could compose but little; and, though his friends solaced his latter days with attention and kindness, his sturdy independence would not accept more. It is a touching fact that Beethoven voluntarily suffered want and privation in his last years, that he might leave the more to his selfish and ungrateful nephew. He died in 1827, in his fifty-seventh year, and is buried in the Wahring Cemetery near Vienna. Let these extracts from a testamentary paper addressed to his brothers in 1802, in expectation of death, speak more eloquently of the hidden life of a heroic soul than any other words could:—

"O ye, who consider or declare me to be hostile, obstinate, or misanthropic, what injustice ye do me! Ye know not the secret causes of that which to you wears such an appearance. My heart and my mind were from childhood prone to the tender feelings of affection. Nay, I was always disposed even to perform great actions. But, only consider that, for the last six years, I have been attacked by an incurable complaint, aggravated by the unskilful treatment of medical men, disappointed from year to year in the hope of relief, and at last obliged to submit to the endurance of an evil the cure of which may last perhaps for years, if it is practicable at all. Born with a lively, ardent disposition, susceptible to the diversions of society, I was forced at an early age to renounce them, and to pass my life in seclusion. If I strove at any time to set myself above all this, oh how cruelly was I driven back by the doubly painful experience of my defective hearing! and yet it was not possible for me to say to people, 'Speak louder—bawl—for I am deaf!' Ah! how could I proclaim the defect of a sense that I once possessed in the highest perfection—in a perfection in which few of my colleagues possess or ever did possess it? Indeed, I cannot! Forgive me, then, if ye see me draw back when I would gladly mingle among you. Doubly mortifying is my misfortune to me, as it must tend to cause me to be misconceived. From recreation in the society of my fellow-creatures, from the pleasures of conversation, from the effusions of friendship, I am cut off. Almost alone in the world, I dare not venture into society more than absolute necessity requires. I am obliged to live as an exile. If I go into company, a painful anxiety comes over me, since I am apprehensive of being exposed to the danger of betraying my situation. Such has been my state, too, during this half year that I have spent in the country. Enjoined by my intelligent physician to spare my hearing as much as possible, I have been almost encouraged by him in my present natural disposition, though, hurried away by my fondness for society, I sometimes suffered myself to be enticed into it. But what a humiliation when any one standing beside me could hear at a distance a flute that I could not hear, or any one heard the shepherd singing, and I could not distinguish a sound! Such circumstances brought me to the brink of despair, and had well-nigh made me put an end to my life—nothing but my art held my hand. Ah! it seemed to me impossible to quit the world before I had produced all that I felt myself called to accomplish. And so I endured this wretched life—so truly wretched, that a somewhat speedy change is capable of transporting me from the best into the worst condition. Patience—so I am told—I must choose for my guide. Steadfast, I hope, will be my resolution to persevere, till it shall please the inexorable Fates to cut the thread.

"Perhaps there may be an amendment—perhaps not; I am prepared for the worst—I, who so early as my twenty-eighth year was forced to become a philosopher—it is not easy—for the artist more difficult than for any other. O God! thou lookest down upon my misery; thou knowest that it is accompanied with love of my fellow-creatures, and a disposition to do good! O men! when ye shall read this, think that ye have wronged me; and let the child of affliction take comfort on finding one like himself, who, in spite of all the impediments of Nature, yet did all that lay in his power to obtain admittance into the rank of worthy artists and men. . . . I go to meet Death with joy. If he comes before I have had occasion to develop all my professional abilities, he will come too soon for me, in spite of my hard fate, and I should wish that he had delayed his arrival. But even then I am content, for he will release me from a state of endless suffering. Come when thou wilt, I shall meet thee with firmness. Farewell, and do not quite forget me after I am dead; I have deserved that you should think of me, for in my lifetime I have often thought of you to make you happy. May you ever be so!"

VIII.

The music of Beethoven has left a profound impress on art. In speaking of his genius it is difficult to keep expression within the limits of good taste. For who has so passed into the very inner *penetralia* of his great art, and revealed to the world such heights and depths of beauty and power in sound?

Beethoven composed nine symphonies, which, by one voice, are ranked as the greatest ever written, reaching in the last, known as the "Choral," the full perfection of his power and experience. Other musicians have composed symphonic works remarkable for varied excellences, but in Beethoven this form of writing seems to have attained its highest possibilities, and to have been illustrated by the greatest variety of effects, from the sublime to such as are simply beautiful and melodious. His hand swept the whole range of expression with unfaltering mastery. Some passages may seem obscure, some too elaborately wrought, some startling and abrupt, but on all is stamped the die of his great genius.

Beethoven's compositions for the piano, the sonatas, are no less notable for range and power of expression, their adaptation to meet all the varied moods of passion and sentiment. Other pianoforte composers have given us more warm and vivid colour, richer sensual effects of tone, more wild and bizarre combination, perhaps even greater sweetness in melody; but we look in vain elsewhere for the spiritual passion and poetry, the aspiration and longing, the lofty humanity, which make the Beethoven sonatas the *suspiria de profundis* of the composer's inner life. In addition to his symphonies and sonatas, he wrote the great opera of "Fidelio," and in the field of oratorio asserted his equality with Handel and Haydn by composing "The Mount of Olives." A great variety of chamber music, masses, and songs bear the same imprint of power. He may be called the most original and conscientious of all the composers. Handel, Haydn, Mozart, Schubert, and Mendelssohn were inveterate thieves, and pilfered the choicest gems from old and forgotten writers without scruple. Beethoven seems to have been so fecund in great conceptions, so lifted on the wings of his tireless genius, so austere in artistic morality, that he stands for the most part above the reproach deservedly borne by his brother composers.

Beethoven's principal title to fame is in his superlative place as a symphonic composer. In the symphony music finds its highest intellectual dignity; in Beethoven the symphony has found its loftiest master.

SCHUBERT AND SCHUMANN.

I.

HEINRICH HEINE, in his preface to a translation of *Don Quixote*, discusses the creative powers of different peoples. To the Spaniard Cervantes is awarded the first place in novel-writing, and to our own Shakespeare, of course, the transcendent rank in drama.

"And the Germans," he goes on to say, "what palm is due to them? Well, we are the best writers of songs in the world. No people possesses such beautiful *Lieder* as the Germans. Just at present the nations have too much political business on hand; but, after that has once been settled, we Germans, English, Spaniards, Frenchmen, and Italians will all go to the green forest and sing, and the nightingale shall be umpire. I feel sure that in this contest the song of Wolfgang Goethe will gain the prize."

There are few, if any, who will be disposed to dispute the verdict of the German poet, himself no mean rival, in depth and variety of lyric inspiration, even of the great Goethe. But a greater poet than either one of this great pair bears the suggestive and impersonal name of "The People." It is to the countless wealth of the German race in folk-songs, an affluence which can be traced back to the very dawn of civilisation among them, that the possibility of such lyric poets as Goethe, Heine, Rückert, and Uhland is due. From the days of the "Nibelungenlied," that great epic which, like the Homeric poems, can hardly be credited to any one author, every hamlet has rung with beautiful national songs, which sprung straight from the fervid heart of the people. These songs are balmy with the breath of the forest, the meadow, and river, and have that simple and bewitching freshness of motive and rhythm which unconsciously sets itself to music.

The German *Volkslied*, as the exponent of the popular heart, has a wide range, from mere comment on historical events, and quaint, droll satire, such as may be found in Hans Sachs, to the grand protest against spiritual bondage which makes the burden of Luther's hymn, "Ein' feste Burg." But nowhere is the beauty of the German song so marked as in those *Lieder* treating of love, deeds of arms, and the old mystic legends so dear to the German heart. Tieck writes of the "Minnesinger period"—"Believers sang of faith, lovers of love; knights described knightly actions and battles, and loving, believing knights were their chief audiences. The spring, beauty, gaiety, were objects that could never tire; great duels and deeds of arms carried away every hearer, the more surely the stronger they were painted; and as the pillars and dome of the church encircled the flock, so did Religion, as the highest, encircle poetry and reality, and every heart in equal love humbled itself before her."

A similar spirit has always inspired the popular German song, a simple and beautiful reverence for the unknown, the worship of heroism, a vital sympathy with the various manifestations of Nature. Without the fire of the French *chansons*, the sonorous grace of the Tuscan *stornelli*, these artless ditties, with their exclusive reliance on true feeling, possess an indescribable charm.

The German *Lied* always preserved its characteristic beauty. Goethe, and the great school of lyric poets clustered around him, simply perfected the artistic form, without departing from the simplicity and soulfulness of the stock from which it came. Had it not been for the rich soil of popular song, we should not have had the peerless lyrics of modern Germany. Had it not been for the poetic inspiration of such word-makers as Goethe and Heine, we should not have had such music-makers in the sphere of song as Schubert and Franz.

The songs of these masters appeal to the interest and admiration of the world, then, not merely in virtue of musical beauty, but in that they are the most vital outgrowths of Teutonic nationality and feeling.

The immemorial melodies to which the popular songs of Germany were set display great simplicity of rhythm, even monotony, with frequent recurrence of the minor keys, so well adapted to express the melancholy tone of many of the poems. The strictly strophic treatment is used, or, in other words, the repetition of the melody of the first stanza in all the succeeding ones. The chasm between this and the varied form of the artistic modern song is deep and wide, yet it was overleaped in a single swift bound by the remarkable genius of Franz Schubert, who, though his compositions were many and matchless of their kind, died all too young; for, as the inscription on his tombstone pathetically has it, he was "rich in what he gave, richer in what he promised."

II.

The great masters of the last century tried their hands in the domain of song with only comparative success, partly because they did not fully realise the nature of this form of art, partly because they could not limit the sweep of the creative power within such narrow limits. Schubert was a revelation to his countrymen in his musical treatment of subjective passion, in his instinctive command over condensed, epigrammatic expression. This rich and gifted life, however quiet in its exterior facts, was great in its creative and spiritual manifestation. Born at Vienna of humble parents, January 31, 1797, the early life of Franz Schubert was commonplace in the extreme, the most interesting feature being the extraordinary development of his genius. At the age of fourteen he had made himself a master of counterpoint and harmony, and composed a large mass of chamber-music and works for the piano. His poverty was such that he was oftentimes unable to obtain the music-paper with which to fasten the immortal thoughts that thronged through his brain. It was two years later that his special creative function found exercise in the production of the two great songs, the "Erl-King" and the "Serenade," the former of which proved the source of most of the fame and money emolument he enjoyed during life. It is hardly needful to speak of the power and beauty of this composition, the weird sweetness of its melodies, the dramatic contrasts, the wealth of colour and shading in its varying phrases, the subtilty of the accompaniment, which elaborates the spirit of the song itself. The piece was composed in less than an hour. One of Schubert's intimates tells us that he left him reading Goethe's great poem for the first time. He instantly conceived and arranged the melody, and when the friend returned after a short absence Schubert was rapidly noting the music from his head on paper. When the song was finished he rushed to the Stadtconvict school, his only *alma mater*, and sang it to the scholars. The music-master, Rucziszka, was overwhelmed with rapture and astonishment, and embraced the young composer in a transport of joy. When this immortal music was first sung to Goethe, the great poet said, " Had music, instead of words, been my instrument of thought, it is so I would have framed the legend."

The "Serenade" is another example of the swiftness of Schubert's artistic imagination. He and a lot of jolly boon-companions sat one Sunday afternoon in an obscure Viennese tavern, known as the Biersack. The surroundings were anything but conducive to poetic fancies—dirty tables, floor, and ceiling, the clatter of mugs and dishes, the loud dissonance of the beery German roisterers, the squalling of children, and all the sights and noises characteristic of the beer-cellar. One of our composer's companions had a volume of poems, which Schubert looked at in a lazy way, laughing and drinking the while. Singling out some verses, he said, " I have a pretty melody in my head for these lines, if I could only get a piece of ruled paper." Some staves were drawn on the back of a bill-of-fare, and here, amid all the confusion and riot, the divine melody of the "Serenade" was born, a tone-poem which embodies the most delicate dream of passion and tenderness that the heart of man ever conceived.

Both these compositions were eccentric and at odds with the old canons of song, fancied with a grace, warmth, and variety of colour hitherto characteristic only of the more pretentious forms of music, which had already been brought to a great degree of perfection. They inaugurate the genesis of the new school of musical lyrics, the golden wedding of the union of poetry with music.

For a long time the young composer was unsuccessful in his attempts to break through the barren and irritating drudgery of a schoolmaster's life. At last a wealthy young dilettante, Franz von Schober, who had become an admirer of Schubert's songs, persuaded his mother to offer him a fixed home in her house. The latter gratefully accepted the overture of friendship, and thence became a daily guest at Schober's house. He made at this time a number of strong friendships with obscure poets, whose names only live through the music of the composer set to verses furnished by them; for Schubert, in his affluence of creative power, merely needed the slightest excuse for his genius to flow forth. But, while he wrote nothing that was not beautiful, his masterpieces are based only on themes furnished by the lyrics of such poets as Goethe, Heine, and Rückert. It is related, in connection with his friendship with Mayrhofer, one of his rhyming associates of these days, that he would set the verses to music much faster than the other could compose them.

The songs of the obscure Schubert were gradually finding their way to favour among the exclusive circles of Viennese aristocracy. A celebrated singer of the opera, Vogl, though then far advanced in years, was much sought after for the drawing-room concerts so popular in Vienna, on account of the beauty of his art. Vogl was a warm admirer of Schubert's genius, and devoted himself assiduously to the task of interpreting it—a friendly office of no little value. Had it not been for this, our composer would have sunk to his early grave probably without even the small share of reputation and monetary return actually vouchsafed to him. The strange, dreamy unconsciousness of Schubert is very well illustrated in a story told by Vogl after his friend's death. One day Schubert left a new song at the singer's apartments, which, being too high, was transposed. Vogl, a fortnight afterwards, sang it in the lower key to his friend, who remarked: "Really, that *Lied* is not bad; who composed it?"

III.

Our great composer, from the peculiar constitution of his gifts, the passionate subjectiveness of his nature, might be supposed to have been peculiarly sensitive to the fascinations of love, for it is in this feeling that lyric inspiration has found its most fruitful root. But not so. Warmly susceptible to the charms of friendship, Schubert for the most part enacted the *rôle* of the woman-hater, which was not all affected; for the Hamlet-like mood is only in part a simulated madness with souls of this type. In early youth he would sneer at the amours of his comrades. It is true he fell a victim to the charms of Theresa Gröbe, a beautiful soprano, who afterwards became the spouse of a master-baker. But the only genuine love-sickness of Schubert was of a far different type, and left indelible traces on his nature, as its very direction made it of necessity unfortunate. This was his attachment to Countess Caroline Esterhazy.

The Count Esterhazy, one of those great feudal princes still extant among the Austrian nobility, took a traditional pride in encouraging genius, and found in Franz Schubert a noble object for his generous patronage. He was almost a boy (only nineteen), except in the prodigious development of his genius, when he entered the Esterhazy family as teacher of music, though always treated as a dear and familiar friend. During the summer months, Schubert went with the Esterhazys to their country seat at Zelész, in Hungary. Here, amid beautiful scenery, and the sweetness of a social life perfect of its kind, our poet's life flew on rapid wings, the one bright, green spot of unalloyed happiness, for the dream was delicious while it lasted. Here, too, his musical life gathered a fresh inspiration, since he became acquainted with the treasures of the national Hungarian music, with its weird, wild rhythms and striking melodies. He borrowed the motives of many of his most characteristic songs from these reminiscences of hut and hall, for the Esterhazys were royal in their hospitality, and exercised a wide patriarchal sway.

The beautiful Countess Caroline, an enthusiastic girl of great beauty, became the object of a romantic passion. A young, inexperienced maiden, full of *naïve* sweetness, the finest flower of the haughty Austrian caste, she stood at an infinite distance from Schubert, while she treated him with childlike confidence and fondness, laughing at his eccentricities, and worshipping his genius. He bowed before this idol, and poured out all the incense of his heart. Schubert's exterior was anything but that of the ideal lover. Rude, unshapely features, thick nose, coarse, protruding mouth, and a shambling, awkward figure, were redeemed only by eyes of uncommon splendour and depth, aflame with the unmistakable light of the soul.

The inexperienced maiden hardly understood the devotion of the artist, which found expression in a thousand ways peculiar to himself. Only once he was on the verge of a full revelation. She asked him why he had dedicated nothing to her. With abrupt, passionate intensity of tone Schubert answered, "What's the use of that? Everything belongs to you!" This brink of confession seems to have frightened him, for it is said that after this he threw much more reserve about his intercourse with the family, till it was broken off. Hints in his letters, and the deep despondency which increased after this, indicate, however, that the humbly-born genius never forgot his beautiful dream.

He continued to pour out in careless profusion songs, symphonies, quartets, and operas, many of which knew no existence but in the score till after his death, hardly knowing of himself whether the productions had value or not. He created because it was the essential law of his being, and never paused to contemplate or admire the beauties of his own work. Schubert's body had been mouldering for several years, when his wonderful symphony in C major, one of the *chefs-d'œuvre* of orchestral composition, was brought to the attention of the world by the critical admiration of Robert Schumann, who won the admiration of lovers of music, not less by his prompt vindication of neglected genius than by his own creative powers.

In the contest between Weber and Rossini which agitated Vienna, Schubert, though deeply imbued with the seriousness of art, and by nature closely allied in sympathies with the composer of "Der Freischütz," took no part. He was too easy-going to become a volunteer partisan, too shy and obscure to make his alliance a thing to be sought after. Besides, Weber had treated him with great brusqueness, and damned an opera for him, a slight which even good-natured Franz Schubert could not easily forgive.

The fifteen operas of Schubert, unknown now except to musicians, contain a wealth of beautiful melody which could easily be spread over a score of ordinary works. The purely lyric impulse so dominated him that dramatic arrangement was lost sight of, and the noblest melodies were likely to be lavished on the most unworthy situations. Even under the operatic form he remained essentially the song-writer. So in the symphony his affluence of melodic inspiration seems actually to embarrass him, to the detriment of that breadth and symmetry of treatment so vital to this form of art. It is in the musical lyric that our composer stands matchless.

During his life as an independent musician at Vienna, Schubert lived fighting a stern battle with want and despondency, while the publishers were commencing to make fortunes by the sale of his exquisite *Lieder*. At that time a large source of income for the Viennese composers was the public performance of their works in concerts under their own direction. From recourse to this, Schubert's bashfulness and lack of skill as a *virtuoso* on any instrument helped to bar him, though he accompanied his own songs with exquisite effect. Once only his friends organised a concert for him, and the success was very brilliant. But he was prevented from repeating the good fortune by that fatal illness which soon set in. So he lived out the last glimmers of his life, poverty-stricken, despondent, with few even of the amenities of friendship to soothe his declining days. Yet those who know the beautiful results of that life, and have even a faint glow of sympathy with the life of a man of genius, will exclaim with one of the most eloquent critics of Schubert—

"But shall we, therefore, pity a man who all the while revelled in the treasures of his creative ore, and from the very depths of whose despair sprang the sweetest flowers of song? Who would not battle with the iciest blast of the north if out of storm and snow he could bring back to his chamber the germs of the 'Winterreise?' Who would grudge the moisture of his eyes if he could render it immortal in the strains of Schubert's 'Lob der Thräne?'"

Schubert died in the flower of his youth, November 19, 1828; but he left behind him nearly a thousand compositions, six hundred of which were songs. Of his operas only the "Enchanted Harp" and "Rosamond" were put on the stage during his lifetime. "Fierabras," considered to be his finest dramatic work, has never been produced. His church music, consisting of six masses, many effertories, and the great "Hallelujah" of Klopstock, is still performed in Germany. Several of his symphonies are ranked among the greatest works of this nature. His pianoforte compositions are brilliant, and strongly in the style of Beethoven, who was always the great object of Schubert's devoted admiration, his artistic idol and model. It was his dying request that he should be buried by the side of Beethoven, of whom the art-world had been deprived the year before.

Compared with Schubert, other composers seem to have written in prose. His imagination burned with a passionate love of Nature. The lakes, the woods, the mountain heights, inspired him with eloquent reveries that burst into song; but he always saw Nature through the medium of human passion and sympathy, which transfigured it. He was the faithful interpreter of spiritual suffering, and the joy which is born thereof.

The genius of Schubert seems to have been directly formed for the expression of subjective emotion in music. That his life should have been simultaneous with the perfect literary unfolding of the old *Volkslied* in the superb lyrics of Goethe, Heine, and their school, is quite remarkable. Poetry and song clasped hands on the same lofty summits of genius. Liszt has given to our composer the title of *le musicien le plus poétique,* which very well expresses his place in art.

In the song as created by Schubert and transmitted to his successors, there are three forms, the first of which is that of the simple *Lied*, with one unchanged melody. A good example of this is the setting of Goethe's "Haideröslein," which is full of quaint grace and simplicity. A second and more elaborate method is what the Germans call "through-composed," in which all the different feelings are successively embodied in the changes of the melody, the sense of unity being preserved by the treatment of the accompaniment, or the recurrence of the principal motive at the close of the song. Two admirable models of this are found in the "Lindenbaum" and "Serenade."

The third and finest art-method, as applied by Schubert to lyric music, is the "declamatory." In this form we detect the consummate flower of the musical lyric. The vocal part is lifted into a species of passionate chant, full of dramatic fire and colour, while the accompaniment, which is extremely elaborate, furnishes a most picturesque setting. The genius of the composer displays itself here fully as much as in the vocal treatment. When the lyric feeling rises to its climax it expresses itself in the crowning melody, this high tide of the music and poetry being always in unison. As masterpieces of this form may be cited "Die Stadt" and "Der Erlkönig," which stand far beyond any other works of the same nature in the literature of music.

IV.

ROBERT SCHUMANN, the loving critic, admirer, and disciple of Schubert in the province of song, was in most respects a man of far different type. The son of a man of wealth and position, his mind and tastes were cultivated from early youth with the utmost care. Schumann is known in Germany no less as a philosophical thinker and critic than as a composer. As the editor of the *Neue Zeitschrift für Musik*, he exercised a powerful influence over contemporary thought in art-matters, and established himself both as a keen and incisive thinker and as a master of literary style. Schumann was at first intended for the law, but his unconquerable taste for music asserted itself in spite of family opposition. His acquaintance with the celebrated teacher, Wieck, whose gifted daughter, Clara, afterwards became his wife, finally established his career; for it was through Wieck's advice that the Schumann family yielded their opposition to the young man's bent.

Once settled in his new career, Schumann gave himself up to work with the most indefatigable ardour. The early part of the present century was a halcyon time for the *virtuosi*, and the fame and wealth that poured themselves on such players as Paganini and Liszt made such a pursuit tempting in the extreme. Fortunately, the young musician was saved from such a career. In his zeal of practice and desire to attain a perfectly independent action for each finger on the piano, Schumann devised some machinery, the result of which was to weaken the sinews of his third finger by undue distension. By this he lost the effective use of the whole right hand, and of course his career as a *virtuoso* practically closed.

Music gained in its higher walks what it lost in a lower. Schumann devoted himself to composition and æsthetic criticism, after he had passed through a thorough course of preparatory studies. Both as a writer and a composer Schumann fought against Philistinism in music. Ardent, progressive, and imaginative, he soon became the leader of the romantic school, and inaugurated the crusade which had its parallel in France in that carried on by Victor Hugo in the domain of poetry. His early pianoforte compositions bear the strong impress of this fiery, revolutionary spirit. His great symphonic works belong to a later period, when his whole nature had mellowed and ripened without losing its imaginative sweep and brilliancy. Schumann's compositions for the piano and orchestra are those by which his name is most widely honoured, but nowhere do we find a more characteristic exercise of his genius than in his songs, to which this article will call more special attention.

Such works as the "Etudes Symphoniques" and the "Kreisleriana" express much of the spirit of unrest and longing aspiration, the struggle to get away from prison-bars and limits, which seem to have sounded the key-note of Schumann's deepest nature. But these feelings could only find their fullest outlet in the musical form expressly suited to subjective emotion. Accordingly, the "Sturm and Drang" epoch of his life, when all his thoughts and conceptions were most unsettled and visionary, was most fruitful in lyric song. In Heinrich Heine he found a fitting poetical co-worker, in whose moods he seemed to see a perfect reflection of his own—Heine, in whom the bitterest irony was wedded to the deepest pathos, "the spoiled favourite of the Graces," "the knight with the laughing tear in his scutcheon"—Heine, whose songs are charged with the brightest light and deepest gloom of the human heart.

Schumann's songs never impress us as being deliberate attempts at creative effort, consciously selected forms through which to express thoughts struggling for speech. They are rather involuntary experiments to relieve oneself of some woeful burden, medicine for the soul. Schumann is never distinctively the lyric composer; his imagination had too broad and majestic a wing. But in those moods, peculiar to genius, where the soul is flung back on itself with a sense of impotence, our composer instinctively burst into song. He did not in the least advance or change its artistic form, as fixed by Schubert. This, indeed, would have been irreconcilable with his use of the song as a simple medium of personal feeling, an outlet and safeguard.

The peculiar place of Schumann as a song-writer is indicated by his being called the musical exponent of Heine, who seems to be the other half of his soul. The composer enters into each shade and detail of the poet's meaning with an intensity and fidelity which one can never cease admiring. It is this phase which gives the Schumann songs their great artistic value. In their clean-cut, abrupt, epigrammatic force there is something different from the work of any other musical lyrist. So much has this impressed the students of the composer that more than one able critic has ventured to prophesy that Schumann's greatest claim to immortality would yet be found in such works as the settings of "Ich grolle nicht" and the "Dichterliebe" series— a perverted estimate, perhaps, but with a large substratum of truth. The duration of Schumann's song-time was short, the greater part of his *Lieder* having been written in 1840. After this he gave himself up to oratorio, symphony, and chamber-music.

Note by the Editor.—The above account of Robert Schumann does not give an adequate impression of the composer; the following remarks are therefore appended, based in most part upon J. A. Fuller Maitland's "Schumann" in *The Great Musicians* Series. In 1832 the poet Grillparzer, in a critical article published in the *Wiener Musikallische Zeitung*, recognises that Schumann "belongs to no school, but creates of himself without making parade of outlandish ideas, . . . he has made himself a new ideal world in which he moves about as he wills, with a certain original *bizarrerie*." Moscheles, a friend of Schumann, wrote in his diary—"For mind (Geist) give me Schumann. The Romanticism in his works is a thing so completely new, his genius so great, that to weigh correctly the peculiar qualities and weakness of this new school I must go deeper and deeper into the study of his works." In the *Gazette Musicale* for November 12, 1837, Franz Liszt wrote a thoroughly sympathetic criticism of the composer's works, as a whole, and says—"The more closely we examine Schumann's ideas, the more power and life do we discover in them; and the more we study them, the more we are amazed at the wealth and fertility which had before escaped us." And Hector Berlioz, the great French Romanticist, looked upon him "as one of the most remarkable composers and critics in Germany." As a musical critic Schumann ranks very high. In 1834 he, with several friends, started a critical paper, *Neue Zeitschrift für Music*, in order "no longer to look on idly, but to try and make things better, so that the poetry of art may once more be duly honoured." The paper was very successful, and had a considerable influence in the musical world—more especially as it supplied a distinct want, for at the time of its appearance "musical criticism in Germany was of the most futile kind, silly, superficial admiration of mediocrity—Schumann used to call it 'Honey-daubing' —or the contemptuous depreciation of what was new or unknown; these were the order of the day in such of the journals as deigned to notice music at all." Schumann possessed all the qualities which are required in a musical critic, and it is said of him that in that capacity he has never been excelled. His aims were high and pure—to quote his own words, "to send light into the depth of the human heart—that is the artist's calling,"—and the chief object of his critical labour was "the elevation of German taste and intellect by German art, whether by pointing to the great models of old time, or by encouraging younger talents." His connection with the paper lasted ten years as a constant contributor, though he continued to write for it from time to time. The last article published by him in it was one written in favour of Johannes Brahms, who had been sent to him with a letter of introduction by Joseph Joachim, the violinist, "recommending to his notice a young composer of whose powers the writer had formed the highest opinion." "At once Schumann recognised the surpassing capabilities of the young man, and wrote to Joachim these words, and nothing more—'Das ist der, der kommen musste' ('This is he was wanted to come')." The article was entitled "New Paths," and is one of his most remarkable writings. "In it Schumann seems to sing his 'Nunc Dimittis,' hailing the advent of this young and ardent spirit, who was to carry on the great line of composers, and to prove himself no unworthy member of their glorious company." The concluding sentence of the article, which contained the composer's last printed words, is not a little remarkable, for it gives fullest expression to that principle which had always governed his own criticism. "In every age there is a secret band of kindred spirits. Ye who are of this fellowship, see that ye weld the circle firmly, so that the truth of art may shine ever more and more clearly, shedding joy and blessing far and near."

As a man Schumann was kind-hearted, generous, devoid of jealousy, and always ready and willing to recognise merit, great or small, in those with whom he came in contact. It was always easier for him to praise than to blame; so much so that in conducting an orchestra in rehearsal, it became impossible for him to find fault with the performers when necessity arose, and, if they did not find out their mistakes themselves, he allowed them to remain uncorrected! Although a faithful friend, he was eminently unsociable; he was very reserved and silent, and this peculiarity became more marked towards the latter part of his life, when his terrible malady was spreading its shadow over him. An amusing account of his silence is given in E. Hanslick's *Musikalischen Stationen*—"Wagner expressed himself thus to the author in 1846—'Schumann is a highly gifted musician, but an *impossible* man. When I came from Paris I went to see Schumann; I related to him my Parisian experiences, spoke of the state of music in France, then of that in Germany, spoke of literature and politics; but he remained as good as dumb for nearly an hour. One cannot go on talking quite alone. An impossible man!'" Schumann's account, apparently of the same interview, is as follows:—"I have seldom met him; but he is a man of education and spirit; he talks, however, unceasingly, and that one cannot endure for very long together."

Schumann has been described "as a man of moderately tall stature, well-built, and of a dignified and pleasant aspect. The outlines of his face, with its intellectual brow, and with its lower part inclining slightly to heaviness, are sufficiently familiar to us all; but we cannot see the dreamy, half-shut eyes kindle into animation at a word from some friend with whom he felt himself in sympathy." A description of him by his friend, Sterndale Bennett, is amusing, on the words of which S. Bennett wrote a little canon—

> "Herr Schumann ist ein guter mann,
> Er raucht Tabak als Niemand kann;
> Ein mann veilleicht von dreissig Jahr,
> Mit kurze nas' und kurze Haar."

> ("Herr Schumann is a first-rate man,
> He smokes as ne'er another can;
> A man of thirty, I suppose,
> Short is his hair, and short his nose.")

Schumann's latter days were very sorrowful, for he was afflicted with a great mental distress, caused, we are told by one of his biographers, by ossification of the brain. He was haunted by delusions—amongst others, by the constant hearing of a single musical note. "On one occasion he was under the impression that Schubert and Mendelssohn had visited him, and had given him a musical theme, which he wrote down, and upon which he set himself to write variations." He suffered from attacks of acute melancholy, and at length, during one of them, threw himself into the Rhine, but was, fortunately, rescued. At length it became necessary to confine him in a private asylum, where he was visited by his friends when his condition permitted it. He died on July 29, 1856, in presence of his wife, through whose exertions, in great part, we, in England, have become acquainted with his pianoforte works.

CHOPIN.

I.

NEVER has Paris, the Mecca of European art, genius, and culture, presented a more brilliant social spectacle than it did in 1832. Hitherward came pilgrims from all countries, poets, painters, and musicians, anxious to breathe the inspiring air of the French capital, where society laid its warmest homage at the feet of the artist. Here came, too, in dazzling crowds, the rich nobles and the beautiful women of Europe to find the pleasure, the freedom, the joyous unrestraint, with which Paris offers its banquet of sensuous and intellectual delights to the hungry epicure. Then as now the queen of the art-world, Paris absorbed and assimilated to herself the most brilliant influences in civilisation.

In all of brilliant Paris there was no more charming and gifted circle than that which gathered around the young Polish pianist and composer, Chopin, then a recent arrival in the gay city. His peculiarly original genius, his weird and poetic style of playing, which transported his hearers into a mystic fairy-land of sunlight and shadow, his strangely delicate beauty, the alternating reticence and enthusiasm of his manners, made him the idol of the clever men and women, who courted the society of the shy and sensitive musician; for to them he was a fresh revelation. Dr. Franz Liszt gives the world some charming pictures of this art-coterie, which was wont often to assemble at Chopin's rooms in the Chaussée d'Antin.

His room, taken by surprise, is all in darkness except the luminous ring thrown off by the candles on the piano, and the flashes flickering from the fire-place. The guests gather around informally as the piano sighs, moans, murmurs, or dreams under the fingers of the player. Heinrich Heine, the most poetic of humorists, leans on the instrument, and asks, as he listens to the music and watches the firelight, "if the roses always glowed with a flame so triumphant? if the trees at moonlight sang always so harmoniously?" Meyerbeer, one of the musical giants, sits near at hand lost in reverie; for he forgets his own great harmonies, forged with hammer of Cyclops, listening to the dreamy passion and poetry woven into such quaint fabrics of sound. Adolphe Nourrit, passionate and ascetic, with the spirit of some mediæval monastic painter, an enthusiastic servant of art in its purest, severest form, a combination of poet and anchorite, is also there; for he loves the gentle musician, who seems to be a visitor from the world of spirits. Eugène Delacroix, one of the greatest of modern painters, his keen eyes half closed in meditation, absorbs the vague mystery of colour which imagination translates from the harmony, and attains new insight and inspiration through the bright links of suggestion by which one art lends itself to another. The two great Polish poets, Niemcewicz and Mickiewicz (the latter the Dante of the Slavic race), exiles from their unhappy land, feed their sombre sorrow, and find in the wild, Oriental rhythms of the player only melancholy memories of the past. Perhaps Victor Hugo, Balzac, Lamartine, or the aged Chateaubriand, also drop in by-and-by, to recognise, in the music, echoes of the daring romanticism which they opposed to the classic and formal pedantry of the time.

Buried in a fauteuil, with her arms resting upon a table, sits Mdme. George Sand (that name so tragically mixed with Chopin's life), "curiously attentive, gracefully subdued." With the second sight of genius, which pierces through the mask, she saw the sweetness, the passion, the delicate emotional sensibility of Chopin; and her insatiate nature must unravel and assimilate this new study in human enjoyment and suffering. She had then just finished "Lelia," that strange and powerful creation, in which she embodied all her hatred of the forms and tyrannies of society, her craving for an impossible social ideal, her tempestuous hopes and desires, in such startling types. Exhausted by the struggle, she panted for the rest and luxury of a companionship in which both brain and heart could find sympathy. She met Chopin, and she recognised in the poetry of his temperament and the fire of his genius what she desired. Her personality, electric, energetic, and imperious, exercised the power of a magnet on the frail organisation of Chopin, and he loved once and forever, with a passion that consumed him; for in Mdme. Sand he found the blessing and curse of his life. This many-sided woman, at this point of her development, found in the fragile Chopin one phase of her nature which had never been expressed, and he was sacrificed to the demands of an insatiable originality, which tried all things in turn, to be contented with nothing but an ideal which could never be attained.

About the time of Chopin's arrival in Paris the political effervescence of the recent revolution had passed into art and letters. It was the oft-repeated battle of Romanticism against Classicism. There could be no truce between those who believed that everything must be fashioned after old models, that Procrustes must settle the height and depth, the length and breadth of art-forms, and those who, inspired with the new wine of liberty and free creative thought, held that the rule of form should always be the mere expression of the vital, flexible thought. The one side argued that supreme perfection already reached left the artist hope only in imitation; the other, that the immaterial beautiful could have no fixed absolute form. Victor Hugo among the poets, Delacroix among the painters, and Berlioz among the musicians, led the ranks of the romantic school.

Chopin found himself strongly enlisted in this contest on the side of the new school. His free, unconventional nature found in its teachings a musical atmosphere true to the artistic and political proclivities of his native Poland; for Chopin breathed the spirit and tendencies of his people in every fibre of his soul, both as man and artist. Our musician, however, in freeing himself from all servile formulas, sternly repudiated the charlatanism which would replace old abuses with new ones.

Chopin, in his views of his art, did not admit the least compromise with those who failed earnestly to represent progress, nor, on the other hand, with those who sought to make their art a mere profitable trade. With him, as with all the great musicians, his art was a religion—something so sacred that it must be approached with unsullied heart and hand. This reverential feeling was shown in the following touching fact:—It was a Polish custom to choose the garments in which one would be buried. Chopin, though among the first of contemporary artists, gave fewer concerts than any other; but, notwithstanding this, he left directions to be borne to the grave in the clothes he had worn on such occasions.

II

FREDERICK FRANCIS CHOPIN was born near Warsaw, in 1810, of French extraction. He learned music at the age of nine from Ziwny, a pupil of Sebastian Bach, but does not seem to have impressed anyone with his remarkable talent except Madame Catalani, the great singer, who gave him a watch. Through the kindness of Prince Radziwill, an enthusiastic patron of art, he was sent to Warsaw College, where his genius began to unfold itself. He afterwards became a pupil of the Warsaw Conservatory, and acquired there a splendid mastery over the science of music. His labour was prodigious in spite of his frail health; and his knowledge of contrapuntal forms was such as to exact the highest encomiums from his instructors.

Through his brother pupils he was introduced to the highest Polish society, for his fellows bore some of the proudest names in Poland. Chopin seems to have absorbed the peculiarly romantic spirit of his race, the wild, imaginative melancholy, which, almost gloomy in the Polish peasant, when united to grace and culture in the Polish noble, offered an indescribable social charm. Balzac sketches the Polish woman in these picturesque antitheses:—"Angel through love, demon through fantasy; child through faith, sage through experience; man through the brain, woman through the heart; giant through hope, mother through sorrow; and poet through dreams." The Polish gentleman was chivalrous, daring, and passionate; the heir of the most gifted and brilliant of the Slavic races, with a proud heritage of memory which gave his bearing an indescribable dignity, though the son of a fallen nation. Ardently devoted to pleasure, the Poles embodied in their national dances wild and inspiring rhythms, a glowing poetry of sentiment as well as motion, which mingled with their Bacchanal fire a chaste and lofty meaning that became at times funereal. Polish society at this epoch pulsated with an originality, an imagination, and a romance, which transfigured even the common things of life.

It was amid such an atmosphere that Chopin's early musical career was spent, and his genius received its lasting impress. One afternoon in after years he was playing to one of the most distinguished women in Paris, and she said that his music suggested to her those gardens in Turkey where bright parterres of flowers and shady bowers were strewed with gravestones and burial mounds. This underlying depth of melancholy Chopin's music expresses most eloquently, and it may be called the perfect artistic outcome of his people; for in his sweetest tissues of sound the imagination can detect agitation, rancour, revolt, and menace, sometimes despair. Chateaubriand dreamed of an Eve innocent, yet fallen; ignorant of all, yet knowing all; mistress, yet virgin. He found this in a Polish girl of seventeen, whom he paints as a "mixture of Odalisque and Valkyr." The romantic and fanciful passion of the Poles, bold, yet unworldly, is shown in the habit of drinking the health of a sweetheart from her own shoe.

Chopin, intensely spiritual by temperament and fragile in health, born an enthusiast, was coloured through and through with the rich dyes of Oriental passion; but with these were mingled the fantastic and ideal elements which,

"Wrapped in sense, yet dreamed of heavenlier joys."

And so he went to Paris, the city of his fate, ripe for the

tragedy of his life. After the revolution of 1830, he started to go to London, and, as he said, "passed through Paris." Yet Paris he did not leave till he left it with Mdme. Sand to live a brief dream of joy in the beautiful Isle of Majorca.

III.

Liszt describes Chopin in these words—"His blue eyes were more spiritual than dreamy; his bland smile never writhed into bitterness. The transparent delicacy of his complexion pleased the eye; his fair hair was soft and silky; his nose slightly aquiline; his bearing so distinguished, and his manners stamped with such high breeding, that involuntarily he was always treated *en prince*. His gestures were many and graceful; the tones of his voiced veiled, often stifled. His stature was low, his limbs were slight." Again, Mdme. Sand paints him even more characteristically in her novel, *Lucrezia Floriani*—"Gentle, sensitive, and very lovely, he united the charm of adolescence with the suavity of a more mature age; through the want of muscular development he retained a peculiar beauty, an exceptional physiognomy, which, if we may venture so to speak, belonged to neither age nor sex. . . . It was more like the ideal creations with which the poetry of the Middle Ages adorned the Christian temples. The delicacy of his constitution rendered him interesting in the eyes of women. The full yet graceful cultivation of his mind, the sweet and captivating originality of his conversation, gained for him the attention of the most enlightened men; while those less highly cultivated liked him for the exquisite courtesy of his manners."

All this reminds us of Shelley's dream of Hermaphroditus, or perhaps of Shelley himself, for Chopin was the Shelley of music.

His life in Paris was quiet and retired. The most brilliant and beautiful women desired to be his pupils, but Chopin refused except where he recognised in the petitioners exceptional earnestness and musical talent. He gave but few concerts, for his genius could not cope with great masses of people.

He said to Liszt, "I am not suited for concert-giving. The public intimidate me, their breath stifles me. You are destined for it; for when you do not gain your public, you have the force to assault, to overwhelm, to compel them." It was his delight to play to a few chosen friends, and to evoke for them such dreams from the ivory gate, which Virgil fabled to be the portal of Elysium, as to make his music

> "The silver key of the fountain of tears,
> Where the spirit drinks till the brain is wild;
> Softest grave of a thousand fears,
> Where their mother, Care, like a weary child,
> Is laid asleep in a bed of flowers."

He avoided general society, finding in the great artists and those sympathetic with art his congenial companions. His life was given up to producing those unique compositions which make him, *par excellence*, the king of the pianoforte. He was recognised by Liszt, Kalkbrenner, Pleyel, Field, and Meyerbeer, as being the most wonderful of players; yet he seemed to disdain such a reputation as a cheap notoriety, ceasing to appear in public after the first few concerts, which produced much excitement and would have intoxicated most performers. He sought largely the society of the Polish exiles, men and women of the highest rank who had thronged to Paris.

His sister Louise, whom he dearly loved, frequently came to Paris from Warsaw to see him; and he kept up a regular correspondence with his own family. Yet he abhorred writing so much that he would go to any shifts to avoid answering a note. Some of his beautiful countrywomen, however, possess precious memorials in the shape of letters written in Polish, which he loved much more than French. His thoughtfulness was continually sending pleasant little gifts and souvenirs to his Warsaw friends. This tenderness and consideration displayed itself too in his love of children. He would spend whole evenings in playing blind-man's-buff or telling them charming fairy stories from the folk-lore in which Poland is singularly rich.

Always gentle, he yet knew how to rebuke arrogance, and had sharp repartees for those who tried to force him into musical display. On one occasion, when he had just left the dining-room, an indiscreet host, who had had the simplicity to promise his guests some piece executed by him as a rare dessert, pointed him to an open piano. Chopin quietly refused, but on being pressed said, with a languid and sneering drawl:—"Ah, sir, I have just dined; your hospitality, I see, demands payment."

IV.

Mdme. Sand, in her *Lettres d'un Voyageur*, depicts the painful lethargy which seizes the artist when, having incorporated the emotion which inspired him in his work, his imagination still remains under the dominance of the insatiate idea, without being able to find a new incarnation. She was suffering in this way when the character of Chopin excited her curiosity and suggested a healthful and happy relief. Chopin dreaded to meet this modern Sibyl. The superstitious awe he felt was a premonition whose meaning was hidden from him. They met, and Chopin lost his fear in one of those passions which feed on the whole being with a ceaseless hunger.

In the fall of 1837 Chopin yielded to a severe attack of the disease which was hereditary in his frame. In company with Mdme. Sand, who had become his constant companion, he went to the isle of Majorca, to find rest and medicine in the balmy breezes of the Mediterranean. All the happiness of Chopin's life was gathered in the focus of this experience. He had a most loving and devoted nurse, who yielded to all his whims, soothed his fretfulness, and watched over him as a mother does over a child. The grounds of the villa where they lived were as perfect as Nature and art could make them, and exquisite scenes greeted the eye at every turn. Here they spent long golden days.

The feelings of Chopin for his gifted companion are best painted by herself in the pages of *Lucrezia Floriani*, where she is the "Floriani," Liszt "Count Salvator Albani," and Chopin "Prince Karol"—"It seemed as if this fragile being was absorbed and consumed by the strength of his affection. . . . But he loved for the sake of loving. . . . His love was his life, and, delicious or bitter, he had not the power of withdrawing himself a single moment from its domination." Slowly she nursed him back into temporary health, and in the sunlight of her love his mind assumed a gaiety and cheerfulness it had never known before.

It had been the passionate hope of Chopin to marry Mdme. Sand, but wedlock was alien alike to her philosophy and preference. After a protracted intimacy, she wearied of his persistent entreaties, or perhaps her self-development had exhausted what it sought in the poet-musician. An absolute separation came, and his mistress buried the episode in her life with the epitaph—"Two natures, one rich in its exuberance, the other in its exclusiveness, could never really mingle, and a whole world separated them." Chopin said—"All the cords that bind me to life are broken." His sad summary of all was that his life had been an episode which began and ended in Paris. What a contrast to the being of a few years before, of whom it is written—"He was no longer on the earth; he was in an empyrean of golden clouds and perfumes; his imagination, so full of exquisite beauty, seemed engaged in a monologue with God himself!"*

Both Liszt and Mdme. Dudevant have painted Chopin somewhat as a sickly sentimentalist, living in an atmosphere of moonshine and unreality. Yet this was not precisely true. In spite of his delicacy of frame and romantic imagination, Chopin was never ill till within the last ten years of his life, when the seeds of hereditary consumption developed themselves. As a young man he was lively and joyous, always ready for frolic, and with a great fund of humour, especially in caricature. Students of human character know how consistent these traits are with a deep undercurrent of melancholy, which colours the whole life when the immediate impulse of joy subsides.

* *Lucrezia Floriani.*

From the date of 1840 Chopin's health declined; but through the seven years during which his connection with Mdme. Sand continued, he persevered actively in his work of composition. The final rupture with the woman he so madly loved seems to have been his death-blow. He spoke of Mdme. Sand without bitterness, but his soul pined in the bitter-sweet of memory. He recovered partially, and spent a short season of concert-giving in London, where he was fêted and caressed by the best society as he had been in Paris. Again he was sharply assailed by his fatal malady, and he returned to Paris to die. Let us describe one of his last earthly experiences, on Sunday, the 15th of October 1849.

Chopin had lain insensible from one of his swooning attacks for some time. His sister Louise was by his side, and the Countess Delphine Potocka, his beautiful countrywoman and a most devoted friend, watched him with streaming eyes. The dying musician became conscious, and faintly ordered a piano to be rolled in from the adjoining room. He turned to the countess, and whispered, feebly, "Sing." She had a lovely voice, and, gathering herself for the effort, she sang that famous canticle to the Virgin which, tradition says, saved Stradella's life from assassins. "How beautiful it is!" he exclaimed. "My God! how very beautiful!" Again she sang to him, and the dying musician passed into a trance, from which he never fully aroused till he expired, two days afterwards, in the arms of his pupil, M. Gutman.

Chopin's obsequies took place at the Madeleine Church, and Lablache sang on this occasion the same passage, the "Tuba Mirum" of Mozart's Requiem Mass, which he had sung at the funeral of Beethoven in 1827; while the other solos were given by Mdme. Viardot Garcia and Mdme. Castellan. He lies in Père Lachaise, beside Cherubini and Bellini.

v.

The compositions of Chopin were exclusively for the piano; and alike as composer and virtuoso he is the founder of a new school, or perhaps may be said to share that honour with Robert Schumann—the school which to-day is represented in its advanced form by Liszt and Von Bülow. Schumann called him "the boldest and proudest poetic spirit of the times." In addition to this remarkable poetic power, he was a splendidly-trained musician, a great adept in style, and one of the most original masters of rhythm and harmony that the records of music show. All his works, though wanting in breadth and robustness of tone, are characterised by the utmost finish and refinement. Full of delicate and unexpected beauties, elaborated with the finest touch, his effects are so quaint and fresh as to fill the mind of the listener with pleasurable sensations, perhaps not to be derived from grander works.

Chopin was essentially the musical exponent of his nation; for he breathed in all the forms of his art the sensibilities, the fires, the aspirations, and the melancholy of the Polish race. This is not only evident in his polonaises, his waltzes and mazurkas, in which the wild Oriental rhythms of the original dances are treated with the creative skill of genius; but also in the *études*, the preludes, noctures, scherzos, ballads, etc., with which he so enriched musical literature. His genius could never confine itself within classic bonds, but, fantastic and impulsive, swayed and bent itself with easy grace to inspirations that were always novel and startling, though his boldness was chastened by deep study and fine art-sense.

All of the suggestions of the quaint and beautiful Polish dance-music were worked by Chopin into a variety of forms, and were greatly enriched by his skill in handling. He dreamed out his early reminiscences in music, and these national memories became embalmed in the history of art. The polonaises are marked by the fire and ardour of his soldier race, and the mazurkas are full of the coquetry and tenderness of his countrywomen; while the ballads are a free and powerful rendering of Polish folk-music, beloved alike in the herdsman's hut and the palace of the noble. In deriving his inspiration direct from the national heart,

Chopin did what Schumann, Schubert, and Weber did in Germany, what Rossini did in Italy, and shares with them a freshness of melodic power to be derived from no other source. Rather tender and elegiac than vigorous, the deep sadness underlying the most sparkling forms of his work is most notable. One can at times almost recognise the requiem of a nation in the passionate melancholy on whose dark background his fancy weaves such beautiful figures and colours.

Franz Liszt, in characterising Chopin as a composer, furnishes an admirable study—"We meet with beauties of a high order, expressions entirely new, and a harmonic tissue as original as erudite. In his compositions boldness is always justified; richness, often exuberance, never interferes with clearness; singularity never degenerates into the uncouth and fantastic; the sculpturing is never disordered; the luxury of ornament never overloads the chaste eloquence of the principal lines. His best works abound in combinations which may be said to be an epoch in the handling of musical style. Daring, brilliant, and attractive, they disguise their profundity under so much grace, their science under so many charms, that it is with difficulty we free ourselves sufficiently from their magical enthralment, to judge coldly of their theoretical value."

As a romance composer Chopin struck out his own path, and has no rival. Full of originality, his works display the utmost dignity and refinement. He revolted from the bizarre and eccentric, though the peculiar influences which governed his development might well have betrayed one less finely organised.

As a musical poet, embodying the feelings and tendencies of a people, Chopin advances his chief claim to his place in art. He did not task himself to be a national musician; for he is utterly without pretence and affectation, and sings spontaneously, without design or choice, from the fullness of a rich nature. He collected "in luminous sheaves the impressions felt everywhere through his country—vaguely felt, it is true, yet in fragments pervading all hearts."

Chopin was repelled by the lusty and almost coarse humour sometimes displayed by Schubert, for he was painfully fastidious. He could not fully understand nor appreciate Beethoven, whose works are full of lion-marrow, robust and masculine alike in conception and treatment. He did not admire Shakespeare, because his great delineations are too vivid and realistic. Our musician was essentially a dreamer and idealist. His range was limited, but within it he reached perfection of finish and originality never surpassed. But, with all his limitations, the art-judgment of the world places him high among those

> "... whom Art's service pure
> Hallows and claims, whose hearts are made her throne,
> Whose lips her oracle, ordained secure
> To lead a priestly life and feed the ray
> Of her eternal shrine; to them alone
> Her glorious countenance unveiled is shown."

WEBER.

I.

THE genius which inspired the three great works, "Der Freischütz," "Euryanthe," and "Oberon," has stamped itself as one of the most original and characteristic in German music. Full of bold and surprising strokes of imagination, these operas are marked by the true atmosphere of national life and feeling, and we feel in them the fresh, rich colour of the popular traditions and song-music which make the German *Lieder* such an inexhaustible treasure-trove. As Weber was maturing into that fullness of power which gave to the world his greater works, Germany had been wrought into a passionate patriotism by the Napoleonic wars. The call to arms resounded from one end of the Fatherland to the other. Every hamlet thrilled with fervour, and all the resources of national tradition were evoked to heighten the love of country into a puissance which should save the land. Germany had been humiliated by a series of crushing defeats, and national pride was stung to vindicate the grand old memories. France, in answer to a similar demand for some art-expression of its patriotism, had produced its Rouget de Lisle; Germany produced the poet Körner and the musician Weber.

It is not easy to appreciate the true quality and significance of Weber's art-life without considering the peculiar state of Germany at the time; for if ever creative imagination was forged and fashioned by its environments into a logical expression of public needs and impulses, it was in the case of the father of German romantic opera. This inspiration permeated the whole soil of national thought, and its embodiment in art and letters has hardly any parallel except in that brilliant morning of English thought which we know as the Elizabethan era. To understand Weber the composer, then, we must think of him not only as the musician, but as the patriot and revivalist of ancient tendencies in art, drawn directly from the warm heart of the people.

KARL MARIA VON WEBER was born at Eutin, in Holstein, December 18, 1786. His father had been a soldier, but, owing to extravagance and folly, had left the career of arms, and, being an educated musician, had become by turns attached to an orchestra, director of a theatre, Kapellmeister, and wandering player—never remaining long in one position, for he was essentially vagrant and desultory in character. Whatever Karl Maria had to suffer from his father's folly and eccentricity, he was indebted to him for an excellent training in the art of which he was to become so brilliant an ornament. He had excellent masters in singing and the piano, as also in drawing and engraving. So he grew up a melancholy, imaginative recluse, absorbed in his studies, and living in a dreamland of his own, which he peopled with ideal creations. His passionate love of

Nature, tinged with old German superstition, planted in his imagination those fruitful germs which bore such rich results in after years.

In 1797 Weber studied the piano and composition under Hanschkel, a thoroughly scientific musician, and found in his severe drill a happy counter-balancing influence to the more desultory studies which had preceded. Major Weber's restless tendencies did not permit his family to remain long in one place. In 1798 they moved to Salzburg, where young Weber was placed at the musical institute of which Michael Haydn, brother of the great Joseph, was director. Here a variety of misfortunes assailed the Weber family. Major Franz Anton was unsuccessful in all his theatrical undertakings, and extreme poverty stared them all in the face. The gentle mother, too, whom Karl so dearly loved, sickened and died. This was a terrible blow to the affectionate boy, from which he did not soon recover.

The next resting-place in the pilgrimage of the Weber family was Munich, where Major Weber, who, however flagrant his shortcomings in other ways, was resolved that the musical powers of his son should be thoroughly trained, placed him under the care of the organist Kalcher for studies in composition.

For several years, Karl was obliged to lead the same shifting, nomadic sort of life, never stopping long, but dragged hither and thither in obedience to his father's vagaries and necessities, but always studying under the best masters who could be obtained. While under Kalcher, several masses, sonatas, trios, and an opera, "Die Macht der Liebe und des Weins" ("The Might of Love and Wine"), were written. Another opera, "Das Waldmädchen" ("The Forest Maiden"), was composed and produced when he was fourteen; and two years later in Salzburg he composed "Peter Schmoll und seine Nachbarn," an operetta, which exacted warm praise from Michael Haydn.

At the age of seventeen he became the pupil of the great teacher, Abbé Vogler, under whose charge also Meyerbeer was then studying. Our young composer worked with great assiduity under the able instruction of Vogler, who was of vast service in bringing the chaos of his previous contradictory teachings into order and light. All these musical *Wanderjahre*, however trying, had steeled Karl Maria into a stern self-reliance, and he found in his skill as an engraver the means to remedy his father's wastefulness and folly.

II.

A curious episode in Weber's life was his connection with the royal family of Würtemberg, where he found a dissolute, poverty-stricken court, and a whimsical, arrogant, half-crazy king. Here he remained four years in a half-official musical position, his nominal duty being that of secretary to the king's brother, Prince Ludwig. This part of his career was almost a sheer waste, full of dreary and irritating experiences, which Weber afterwards spoke of with disgust and regret. His spirit revolted from the capricious tyranny which he was obliged to undergo, but circumstances seem to have coerced him into a protracted endurance of the place. His letters tell us how bitterly he detested the king and his dull, pompous court, though Prince Ludwig in a way seemed to have been attached to his secretary. One of his biographers says:—

"Weber hated the king, of whose wild caprice and vices he witnessed daily scenes, before whose palace-gates he was obliged to slink bareheaded, and who treated him with unmerited ignominy. Sceptre and crown had never been imposing objects in his eyes, unless worn by a worthy man; and consequently he was wont, in the thoughtless levity of youth, to forget the dangers he ran, and to answer the king with a freedom of tone which the autocrat was all unused to hear. In turn he was detested by the monarch. As negotiator for the spendthrift Prince Ludwig, he was already obnoxious enough; and it sometimes happened that, by way of variety to the customary torrent of invective, the king, after keeping the secretary for hours in his antechamber, would receive him only to turn him rudely out of the room, without hearing a word he had to say."

At last Karl Maria's indignation burst over bounds at some unusual indignity; and he played a practical joke on the king. Meeting an old woman in the palace one day near the door of the royal sanctum, she asked him where she could find the court-washerwoman. "There," said the reckless Weber, pointing to the door of the king's cabinet. The king, who hated old women, was in a transport of rage, and, on her terror-stricken explanation of the intrusion, had no difficulty in fixing the mischief in the right quarter. Weber was thrown into prison, and had it not been for Prince Ludwig's intercession he would have remained there for several years. While confined he managed to compose one of his most beautiful songs, "Ein steter Kampf ist unser Leben." He had not long been released when he was again imprisoned on account of some of his father's wretched follies, that arrogant old gentleman being utterly reckless how he involved others, so long as he carried out his own selfish purposes and indulgence. His friend Danzi, director of the royal opera at Stuttgart, proved his good genius in this instance; for he wrangled with the king till his young friend was released.

Weber's only consolations during this dismal life in Stuttgart were the friendship of Danzi, and his love for a beautiful singer named Gretchen. Danzi was a true mentor and a devoted friend. He was wont to say to Karl—"To be a true artist, you must be a true man." But the lovely Gretchen, however she may have consoled his somewhat arid life, was not a beneficial influence, for she led him into many sad extravagances and an unwholesome taste for playing the cavalier.

In spite of his discouraging surroundings, Weber's creative power was active during this period, and showed how, perhaps unconsciously to himself, he was growing in power and depth of experience. He wrote the cantata, "Der erste

Ton," a large number of songs, the first of his great piano sonatas, several overtures and symphonies, and the opera "Sylvana" ("Das Waldmädchen" rewritten and enlarged), which, both in its music and libretto, seems to have been the precursor of his great works, "Der Freischütz" and "Euryanthe." At the first performance of "Sylvana" in Frankfort, September 16, 1810, he met Miss Caroline Brandt, who sang the principal character. She afterwards became his wife, and her love and devotion were the solace of his life.

Weber spent most of the year 1810 in Darmstadt, where he again met Vogler and Meyerbeer. Vogler's severe artistic instructions were of great value to Weber in curbing his extravagance, and impressing on him that restraint was one of the most valuable factors in art. What Vogler thought of Weber we learn from a letter in which he writes— "Had I been forced to leave the world before I found these two, Weber and Meyerbeer, I should have died a miserable man."

III.

It was about this time, while visiting Mannheim, that the idea of "Der Freischütz" first entered his mind. His friend the poet Kind was with him, and they were ransacking an old book, Apel's *Ghost Stories*. One of these dealt with the ancient legend of the hunter Bartusch, a woodland myth ranking high in German folk-lore. They were both delighted with the fantastic and striking story, full of the warm colouring of Nature, and the balmy atmosphere of the forest and mountain. They immediately arranged the framework of the libretto, afterwards written by Kind, and set to such weird and enchanting music by Weber.

In 1811 Weber began to give concerts, for his reputation was becoming known far and wide as a brilliant composer and virtuoso. For two years he played a round of concerts in Munich, Leipsic, Gotha, Weimar, Berlin, and other places. He was everywhere warmly welcomed. Lichtenstein, in his *Memoir of Weber*, writes of his Berlin reception—

"Young artists fell on their knees before him; others embraced him wherever they could get at him. All crowded around him, till his head was crowned, not with a chaplet of flowers, but a circlet of happy faces." The devotion of his friends, his happy family relations, the success of his published works, conspired to make Weber cheerful and joyous beyond his wont, for he was naturally of a melancholy and serious turn, disposed to look at life from its tragic side.

In 1813 he was called to Prague to direct the music of the German opera in that Bohemian capital. The Bohemians had always been a highly musical race, and their chief city is associated in the minds of the students of music as the place where many of the great operas were first presented to the public. Mozart loved Prague, for he found in its people the audiences who appreciated and honoured him the most. Its traditions were honoured in their treatment of Weber, for his three years there were among the happiest of his life.

Our composer wrote his opera of "Der Freischütz" in Dresden. It was first produced in the opera-house of that classic city, but it was not till 1821, when it was performed in Berlin, that its greatness was recognised. Weber can best tell the story of its reception himself. In his letter to his co-author, Kind, he writes:—

"The free-shooter has hit the mark. The second representation has succeeded as well as the first; there was the same enthusiasm. All the places in the house are taken for the third, which comes off to-morrow. It is the greatest triumph one can have. You cannot imagine what a lively interest your text inspires from beginning to end. How happy I should have been if you had only been present to hear it for yourself! Some of the scenes produced an effect which I was far from anticipating; for example, that of the young girls. If I see you again at Dresden, I will tell you all about it; for I cannot do it justice in writing. How much I am indebted to you for your magnificent poem! I embrace you with the sincerest emotion, returning to your muse the laurels I owe her. God grant that you may be happy. Love him who loves you with infinite respect.

"Your WEBER."

"Der Freischütz" was such a success as to place the composer in the front ranks of the lyric stage. The striking originality, the fire, the passion of his music, the ardent national feeling, and the freshness of treatment, gave a genuine shock of delight and surprise to the German world.

IV.

The opera of "Preciosa," also a masterpiece, was given shortly after with great *éclat*, though it failed to inspire the deep enthusiasm which greeted "Der Freischütz." In 1823, "Euryanthe" was produced in Berlin—a work on which Weber exhausted all the treasures of his musical genius. Without the elements of popular success which made his first great opera such an immediate favourite, it shows the most finished and scholarly work which Weber ever attained. Its symmetry and completeness, the elaboration of all the forms, the richness and variety of the orchestration, bear witness to the long and thoughtful labour expended on it. It gradually won its way to popular recognition, and has always remained one of the favourite works of the German stage.

The opera of "Oberon" was Weber's last great production. The celebrated poet Wieland composed the poem underlying the libretto, from the mediæval romance of Huon of Bordeaux. The scenes are laid in fairy-land, and it may be almost called a German "Midsummer-Night's Dream," though the story differs widely from the charming phantasy of our own Shakespeare. The opera of "Oberon" was written for Kemble, of the Covent Garden theatre, in London, and was produced by Weber under circumstances of failing health and great mental depression. The composer pressed every energy to the utmost to meet his engagement, and it was feared by his friends that he would not live to see it put on the stage. It did, indeed, prove the song of the dying swan, for he only lived four months after reaching London. "Oberon" was performed with immense success under the direction of Sir George Smart, and the fading days of the author were cheered by the acclamations of the English public; but the work cost him his life. He died in London, June 5, 1826. His last words were—"God reward you for all your kindness to me. —Now let me sleep."

Apart from his dramatic compositions, Weber is known for his many beautiful overtures and symphonies for the orchestra, and his various works for the piano, from sonatas to waltzes and minuets. Among his most pleasing piano-works are the "Invitation to the Waltz," the "Perpetual Rondo," and the "Polonaise in E major." Many of his songs rank among the finest German lyrics. He would have been recognised as an able composer had he not produced great operas; but the superior excellence of these cast all his other compositions in the shade.

Weber was fortunate in having gifted poets to write his dramas. As rich as he was in melodic affluence, his creative faculty seems to have had its tap-root in deep personal feelings and enthusiasms. One of the most poetic and picturesque of composers, he needed a powerful exterior suggestion to give his genius wings and fire. The Germany of his time was alive with patriotic ardour, and the existence of the nation gathered from its emergencies new strength and force. The heart of Weber beat strong with the popular life. Romantic and serious in his taste, his imagination fed on old German tradition and song, and drew from them its richest food. The whole life of the Fatherland, with its glow of love for home, its keen sympathies with the influences of Nature, its fantastic play of thought, its tendency to embody the primitive forces in weird myths, found in Weber an eloquent exponent; and we perceive in his music all the colour and vividness of these influences.

Weber's love of Nature was singularly keen. The woods, the mountains, the lakes, and the streams, spoke to his soul with voices full of meaning. He excelled in making these voices speak and sing; and he may, therefore, be entitled the father of the romantic and descriptive school in German operatic music. With more breadth and robustness, he expressed the national feelings of his people, even as Chopin did those of dying Poland. Weber's motives are generally caught from the immemorial airs which resound in every village and hamlet, and the fresh beat of the German heart sends its thrill through almost every bar of his music. Here is found the ultimate significance of his art-work, apart from the mere musical beauty of his compositions.

MENDELSSOHN.

I.

FEW careers could present more startling contrasts than those of Mozart and Mendelssohn, in many respects of similar genius, but utterly opposed in the whole surroundings of their lives. FELIX MENDELSSOHN-BARTHOLDY was the grandson of the celebrated philosopher, Moses Mendelssohn, and the son of a rich Hamburg banker. His uncles were distinguished in literary and social life. His friends from early childhood were eminent scholars, poets, painters, and musicians, and his family moved in the most refined and wealthy circles. He was nursed in the lap of luxury, and never knew the cold and hunger of life. All the good fairies and graces seemed to have smiled benignly on his birth, and to have showered on him their richest gifts. Many successful wooers of the muse have been, fortunately for themselves, the heirs of poverty, and became successful only to yield themselves to fat and slothful ease. But, with every incitement to an idle and contented life, Mendelssohn toiled like a galley-slave, and saw in his wealth only the means of a more exclusive consecration to his art. A passionate impulse to labour was the law of his life.

Many will recollect the brilliant novel, *Charles Auchester*, in which, under the names of Seraphael, Aronach, Charles Auchester, Julia Bennett, and Starwood Burney, are painted the characters of Mendelssohn, Zelter his teacher, Joachim the violinist, Jenny Lind, and Sterndale Bennett, the English composer. The brilliant colouring does not disguise nor flatter the lofty Christian purity, the splendid genius, and the great personal charm of the composer, who shares in largest measure the homage which the English public lays at the feet of Handel.

As child and youth Mendelssohn, born at Hamburg, February 3, 1809, displayed the same precocity of talent as was shown by Mozart. Sir Julius Benedict relates his first meeting with him. He was walking in Berlin with Von Weber, and the latter called his attention to a boy about eleven years old, who, perceiving the author of "Der Freischütz," gave him a hearty greeting. "'Tis Felix Mendelssohn," said Weber, introducing the marvellous boy. Benedict narrates his amazement to find the extraordinary attainments of this beautiful youth, with curling auburn hair, brilliant clear eyes, and lips smiling with innocence and candour. Five minutes after young Mendelssohn had astonished his English friend by his admirable performance of several of his own compositions, he forgot Weber, quartets, and counterpoint, to leap over the garden hedges and climb the trees like a squirrel. When scarcely twenty years old he had composed his octet, three quartets for the piano and strings, two sonatas, two symphonies, his first violin quartet, various operas, many songs, and the immortal overture of "A Midsummer-Night's Dream."

Mendelssohn received an admirable education, was an excellent classicist and linguist, and during a short residence at Düsseldorf showed such talent for painting as to excite much wonder. Before he was twenty he was the friend of Goethe and Herder, who delighted in a genius so rich and symmetrical. Some of Goethe's letters are full of charming expressions of praise and affection, for the aged Jupiter of German literature found in the promise of this young Apollo something of the many-sided power which made himself so remarkable.

II.

The Mendelssohn family had moved to Berlin when Felix was only three years old, and the Berliners always claimed him as their own. Strange to say, the city of his birth did not recognise his talent for many years. At the age of twenty he went to England, and the high breeding, personal beauty, and charming manner of the young musician gave him the *entrée* into the most fastidious and exclusive circles. His first symphony and the "Midsummer-Night's Dream" overture stamped his power with the verdict of a warm enthusiasm; for London, though cold and conservative, is prompt to recognise a superior order of merit.

His travels through Scotland inspired Mendelssohn with sentiments of great admiration. The scenery filled his mind with the highest suggestions of beauty and grandeur. He afterwards tells us that "he preferred the cold sky and the pines of the north to charming scenes in the midst of landscapes bathed in the glowing rays of the sun and azure light." The vague Ossianic figures that raised their gigantic heads in the fog-wreaths of clouded mountain-tops and lonely lochs had a peculiar fascination for him, and acted like wine on his imagination. The "Hebrides" overture was the fruit of this tour, one of the most powerful and characteristic of his minor compositions. His sister Fanny (Mrs. Hensel) asked him to describe the grey scenery of the north, and he replied in music by improvising his impressions. This theme was afterwards worked out in the elaborate overture.

We will not follow him in his various travels through France and Italy. Suffice it to say, that his keen and passionate mind absorbed everything in art which could feed the divine hunger, for he was ever discontented, and had his mind fixed on an absolute and determined ideal. During this time of travel he became intimate with the sculptor Thorwaldsen, and the painters Leopold Robert and Horace Vernet. This period produced "Walpurgis Night," the first of the "Songs without Words," the great symphony in A major, and the "Melusine" overture. He is now about to enter on the epoch which puts to the fullest test the varied resources of his genius. To Moscheles he writes, in answer to his old teacher's warm praise—"Your praise is better than three orders of nobility." For several years we see him busy in multifarious ways, composing, leading musical festivals, concert-giving, directing opera-houses, and yet finding time to keep up a busy correspondence with the most distinguished men in Europe ; for Mendelssohn seemed to find in letter-writing a rest for his over-taxed brain.

In 1835 he completed his great oratorio of "St. Paul," for Leipsic. The next year he received the title of Doctor of Philosophy and the Fine Arts; and in 1837 he married the charming Cécile Jeanrenaud, who made his domestic life so gentle and harmonious. It has been thought strange that Mendelssohn should have made so little mention of his lovely wife in his letters, so prone as he was to speak of affairs of his daily life. Be this as it may, his correspondence with Moscheles, Devrient, and others, as well as the general testimony of his friends, shows us unmistakably that his home-life was blessed in an exceptional degree with intellectual sympathy, and the tenderest and most thoughtful love.

In 1841 Mendelssohn became Kapellmeister of the Prussian court. He now wrote the "Athalie" music, the "Midsummer-Night's Dream," and a large number of lesser pieces, including the "Songs without Words," and piano sonatas, as well as much church music. The greatest work of this period was the "Hymn of Praise," a symphonic cantata for the Leipsic anniversary of the invention of printing, regarded by many as his finest composition.

Mendelssohn always loved England, and made frequent visits across the Channel; for he felt that among the English he was fully appreciated, both as man and composer.

His oratorio of "Elijah" was composed for the English public, and produced at the great Birmingham festival in 1846, under his own direction, with magnificent success. It was given a second time in April 1847, with his final refinements and revisions; and the event was regarded in England as one of the greatest since the days of Handel, to whom, as well as to Haydn and Beethoven, Mendelssohn showed himself a worthy rival in the field of oratorio composition. Of this visit to England Lampadius, his friend and biographer, writes—"Her Majesty, who as well as her husband was a great friend of art, and herself a distinguished musician, received the distinguished German in her own sitting-room, Prince Albert being the only one present besides herself. As he entered she asked his pardon for the somewhat disorderly state of the room, and began to re-arrange the articles with her own hands, Mendelssohn himself gallantly offering his assistance. Some parrots whose cages hung in the room she herself carried into the next room, in which Mendelssohn helped her also. She then requested her guest to play something, and afterwards sang some songs of his which she had sung at a court concert soon after the attack on her person. She was not wholly pleased, however, with her own performance, and said pleasantly to Mendelssohn, 'I can do better—ask Lablache if I cannot; but I am afraid of you!'"

This anecdote was related by Mendelssohn himself to show the graciousness of the English queen. It was at this time that Prince Albert sent to Mendelssohn the book of the oratorio "Elijah" with which he used to follow the performance, with the following autographic inscription :—

"To the noble artist, who, surrounded by the Baal worship of corrupted art, has been able by his genius and science to preserve faithfully like another Elijah the worship of true art, and once more to accustom our ear, lost in the whirl of an empty play of sounds, to the pure notes of expressive composition and legitimate harmony— to the great master, who makes us conscious of the unity of his conception through the whole maze of his creation, from the soft whispering to the mighty raging of the elements: Written in token of grateful remembrance by

"ALBERT.

"BUCKINGHAM PALACE, *April* 24, 1847."

An occurrence at the Birmingham festival throws a clear light on Mendelssohn's presence of mind, and on his faculty of instant concentration. On the last day, among other things, one of Handel's anthems was given. The concert was already going on, when it was discovered that the short recitative which precedes the "Coronation Hymn," and which the public had in the printed text, was lacking in the voice parts. The directors were perplexed. Mendelssohn, who was sitting in an ante-room of the hall, heard of it, and said, "Wait, I will help you." He sat down directly at a table, and composed the music for the recitative and the orchestral accompaniment in about half an hour. It was at once transcribed, and given without any rehearsal, and went very finely.

On returning to Leipsic he determined to pass the summer in Vevay, Switzerland, on account of his failing health, which had begun to alarm himself and his friends. His letters from Switzerland at this period show how the shadow of rapidly approaching death already threw a deep gloom over his habitually cheerful nature. He returned to Leipsic, and resumed hard work. His operetta entitled "Return from among Strangers" was his last production, with the exception of some lively songs and a few piano pieces of the "Lieder ohne Worte," or "Songs without Words," series. Mendelssohn was seized with an apoplectic attack on October 9, 1847. Second and third seizures quickly followed, and he died November 4th, aged thirty-eight years.

All Germany and Europe sorrowed over the loss of this great musician, and his funeral was attended by many of the most distinguished persons from all parts of the land, for the loss was felt to be something like a national calamity.

III.

Mendelssohn was one of the most intelligent and scholarly composers of the century. Learned in various branches of knowledge, and personally a man of unusual accomplishments, his career was full of manly energy, enlightened enthusiasm, and severe devotion to the highest forms of the art of music. Not only his great oratorios, "St. Paul" and "Elijah," but his music for the piano, including the "Songs without Words," sonatas, and many occasional pieces, have won him a high place among his musical brethren. As an orchestral composer, his overtures are filled with strikingly original thoughts and elevated conceptions, expressed with much delicacy of instrumental colouring. He was brought but little in contact with the French and Italian schools, and there is found in his works a severity of art-form which shows how closely he sympathised with Bach and Handel in his musical tendencies. He died while at the very zenith of his powers, and we may well believe that a longer life would have developed much richer beauty in his compositions. Short as his career was, however, he left a great number of magnificent works, which entitle him to a place among the Titans of music.

RICHARD WAGNER.

I.

It is curious to note how often art-controversy has become edged with a bitterness rivalling even the gall and venom of religious dispute. Scholars have not yet forgotten the fiery war of words which raged between Richard Bentley and his opponents concerning the authenticity of the *Epistles of Phalaris,* nor how literary Germany was divided into two hostile camps by Wolf's attack on the personality of Homer. It is no less fresh in the minds of critics how that modern Jupiter, Lessing, waged a long and bitter battle with the Titans of the French classical drama, and finally crushed them with the thunderbolt of the *Dramaturgie;* nor what acrimony sharpened the discussion between the rival theorists in music, Gluck and Piccini, at Paris. All of the intensity of these art-campaigns, and many of the conditions of the last, enter into the contest between Richard Wagner and the *Italianissimi* of the present day.

The exact points at issue were for a long time so befogged by the smoke of the battle that many of the large class who are musically interested, but never had an opportunity to study the question, will find an advantage in a clear and comprehensive sketch of the facts and principles involved. Until recently there were still many people who thought of Wagner as a youthful and eccentric enthusiast, all afire with misdirected genius, a mere carpet-knight on the sublime battle-field of art, a beginner just sowing his wild-oats in works like "Lohengrin," "Tristan and Iseult," or the "Rheingold." It is a revelation full of suggestive value for these to realise that he is a musical thinker, ripe with sixty years of labour and experience; that he represents the rarest and choicest fruits of modern culture, not only as musician, but as poet and philosopher; that he is one of the few examples in the history of the art where massive scholarship and the power of subtile analysis have been united, in a pre-eminent degree, with great creative genius. Preliminary to a study of what Wagner and his disciples entitled the "Art-work of the Future," let us take a swift survey of music as a medium of expression for the beautiful, and some of the forms which it has assumed.

This Ariel of the fine arts sends its messages to the human soul by virtue of a fourfold capacity—Firstly, the imitation of the voices of Nature, such as the winds, the waves, and the cries of animals; secondly, its potential delight as melody, modulation, rhythm, harmony—in other words, its simple worth as a "thing of beauty," without regard to cause or consequence; thirdly, its force of boundless suggestion; fourthly, that affinity for union with the more definite and exact forms of the imagination (poetry), by which the intellectual context of the latter is raised to a far higher power of grace, beauty, passion, sweetness, without losing individuality of outline—like, indeed, the hazy aureole which painters set on the brow of the man Jesus, to fix the seal of the ultimate Divinity. Though several or all of these may be united in the same composition, each musical work may be characterised in the main as descriptive, sensuous, suggestive, or dramatic, according as either element contributes most largely to its purpose. Simple melody or harmony appeals mostly to the sensuous love of sweet sounds. The symphony does this in an enlarged and complicated sense, but is still more marked by the marvellous suggestive energy with which it unlocks all the secret raptures of fancy, floods the border-lands of thought with a glory not to be found on sea or land, and paints ravishing pictures, that come and go like dreams, with colours drawn from the "twelve-tinted tone-spectrum." Shelley describes this peculiar influence of music in his "Prometheus Unbound," with exquisite beauty and truth—

> " My soul is an enchanted boat,
> Which, like a sleeping swan, doth float
> Upon the silver waves of thy sweet singing;

> And thine doth like an angel sit
> Beside the helm conducting it,
> While all the waves with melody are ringing.
> It seems to float ever, for ever,
> Upon that many-winding river,
> Between mountains, woods, abysses,
> A paradise of wildernesses."

As the symphony best expresses the suggestive potency in music, the operatic form incarnates its capacity of definite thought, and the expression of that thought. The term "lyric," as applied to the genuine operatic conception, is a misnomer. Under the accepted operatic form, however, it has relative truth, as the main musical purpose of opera seems, hitherto, to have been less to furnish expression for exalted emotions and thoughts, or exquisite sentiments, than to grant the vocal *virtuoso* opportunity to display phenomenal qualities of voice and execution. But all opera, however it may stray from the fundamental idea, suggests this dramatic element in music, just as mere lyricism in the poetic art is the blossom from which is unfolded the full-blown perfection of the word-drama, the highest form of all poetry.

II.

That music, by and of itself, cannot express the intellectual element in the beautiful dream-images of art with precision, is a palpable truth. Yet, by its imperial dominion over the sphere of emotion and sentiment, the connection of the latter with complicated mental phenomena is made to bring into the domain of tone vague and shifting fancies and pictures. How much further music can be made to assimilate to the other arts in directness of mental suggestion, by wedding to it the noblest forms of poetry, and making each the complement of the other, is the knotty problem which underlies the great art-controversy about which this article concerns itself. On the one side we have the claim that music is the all-sufficient law unto itself; that its appeal to sympathy is through the intrinsic sweetness of harmony and tune, and the intellect must be satisfied with what it may accidentally glean in this harvest-field; that, in the rapture experienced in the sensuous apperception of its beauty, lies the highest phase of art-sensibility. Therefore, concludes the syllogism, it matters nothing as to the character of the libretto or poem to whose words the music is arranged, so long as the dramatic framework suffices as a support for the flowery festoons of song, which drape its ugliness and beguile attention by the fascinations of bloom and grace. On the other hand, the apostles of the new musical philosophy insist that art is something more than a vehicle for the mere sense of the beautiful, an exquisite provocation wherewith to startle the sense of a selfish, epicurean pleasure; that its highest function—to follow the idea of the Greek Plato, and the greatest of his modern disciples, Schopenhauer—is to serve as the incarnation of the true and the good; and, even as Goethe makes the Earth-Spirit sing in "Faust"—

" 'Tis thus ever at the loom of Time I ply,
And weave for God the garment thou seest him by "—

so the highest art is that which best embodies the immortal thought of the universe as reflected in the mirror of man's consciousness; that music, as speaking the most spiritual language of any of the art-family, is burdened with the most pressing responsibility as the interpreter between the finite and the infinite; that all its forms must be measured by the earnestness and success with which they teach and suggest what is best in aspiration and truest in thought; that music, when wedded to the highest form of poetry (the drama), produces the consummate art-result, and sacrifices to some extent its power of suggestion, only to acquire a greater glory and influence, that of investing definite intellectual images with spiritual raiment, through which they shine on the supreme altitudes of ideal thought; that to make this marriage perfect as an art-form and fruitful in result, the two partners must come as equals, neither one the drudge of the other; that in this organic fusion music and poetry contribute, each its best, to emancipate art from its thraldom to that which is merely trivial, commonplace, and accidental, and make it a revelation of all that is most exalted in thought, sentiment, and purpose. Such is the æsthetic theory of Richard Wagner's art-work.

III.

It is suggestive to note that the earliest recognised function of music, before it had learned to enslave itself to mere sensuous enjoyment, was similar in spirit to that which its latest reformer demands for it in the art of the future. The glory of its birth then shone on its brow. It was the handmaid and minister of the religious instinct. The imagination became afire with the mystery of life and Nature, and burst into the flames and frenzies of rhythm. Poetry was born, but instantly sought the wings of music for a higher flight than the mere word would permit. Even the great epics of the "Iliad" and "Odyssey" were originally sung or chanted by the Homeridæ, and the same essential union seems to have been in some measure demanded afterwards in the Greek drama, which, at its best, was always inspired with the religious sentiment. There is every reason to believe that the chorus of the drama of Æschylus, Sophocles, and Euripides uttered their comments on the action of the play with such a prolongation and variety of pitch in the rhythmic intervals as to constitute a sustained and melodic recitative. Music at this time was an essential part of the drama. When the creative genius of Greece had set towards its ebb, they were divorced, and music was only set to lyric forms. Such remained the status of the art till, in the Italian Renaissance, modern opera was born in the reunion of music and the drama. Like the other arts, it assumed at the outset to be a mere revival of antique traditions. The great poets of Italy had then passed away, and it was left for music to fill the void.

The muse, Polyhymnia, soon emerged from the stage of childish stammering. Guittone di Arezzo taught her to fix her thoughts in indelible signs, and two centuries of training culminated in the inspired composers, Orlando di Lasso and Palestrina. Of the gradual degradation of the operatic art as its forms became more elaborate and fixed; of the arbitrary transfer of absolute musical forms like the aria, duet, finale, etc., into the action of the opera without regard to poetic propriety; of the growing tendency to treat the human voice like any other instrument, merely to show its resources as an organ; of the final utter bondage of the poet to the musician, till opera became little more than a congeries of musico-gymnastic forms, wherein the vocal soloists could display their art, it needs not to speak at length, for some of these vices have not yet disappeared. In the language of Dante's guide through the Inferno, at one stage of their wanderings, when the sights were peculiarly mournful and desolate—

"Non raggioniam da lor, ma guarda e passa."

The loss of all poetic verity and earnestness in opera furnished the great composer Gluck with the motive of the bitter and protracted contest which he waged with varying success throughout Europe, though principally in Paris. Gluck boldly affirmed, and carried out the principle in his compositions, that the task of dramatic music was to accompany the different phases of emotion in the text, and give them their highest effect of spiritual intensity. The singer must be the mouthpiece of the poet, and must take extreme care in giving the full poetical burden of the song. Thus, the declamatory music became of great importance, and Gluck's recitative reached an unequalled degree of perfection.

The critics of Gluck's time hurled at him the same charges which are familiar to us now as coming from the mouths and pens of the enemies of Wagner's music. Yet Gluck, however conscious of the ideal unity between music and poetry, never thought of bringing this about by a sacrifice of any of the forms of his own peculiar art. His influence, however, was very great, and the traditions of the great *maestro's* art have been kept alive in the works of his no less great disciples, Méhul, Cherubini, Spontini, and Meyerbeer.

Two other attempts to ingraft new and vital power on the rigid and trivial sentimentality of the Italian forms of opera were those of Rossini and Weber. The former was gifted with the greatest affluence of pure melodiousness ever given to a composer. But even his sparkling originality and freshness did little more than reproduce the old forms under a more attractive guise. Weber, on the other hand, stood in the van of a movement which had its fountain-head in the strong romantic and national feeling, pervading the whole of society and literature. There was a general revival of mediæval and popular poetry, with its balmy odour of the woods, and fields, and streams. Weber's melody was the direct offspring of the tunefulness of the German *Volkslied*, and so it expressed, with wonderful freshness and beauty, all the range of passion and sentiment within the limits of this pure and simple language. But the boundaries were far too narrow to build upon them the ultimate union of music and poetry, which should express the perfect harmony of the two arts. While it is true that all of the great German composers protested, by their works, against the spirit and character of the Italian school of music, Wagner claims that the first abrupt and strongly-defined departure towards a radical reform in art is found in Beethoven's Ninth Symphony with chorus. Speaking of this remarkable leap from instrumental to vocal music in a professedly symphonic composition, Wagner, in his *Essay on Beethoven*, says— "We declare that the work of art, which was formed and quickened entirely by that deed, must present the most perfect artistic form, *i.e.*, that form in which, as for the drama, so also and especially for music, every conventionality would be abolished." Beethoven is asserted to have founded the new musical school, when he admitted, by his recourse to the vocal cantata in the greatest of his symphonic works, that he no longer recognised absolute music as sufficient unto itself.

In Bach and Handel, the great masters of fugue and counterpoint; in Rossini, Mozart, and Weber, the consummate creators of melody—then, according to this view, we only recognise thinkers in the realm of pure music. In Beethoven, the greatest of them all, was laid the basis of the new epoch of tone-poetry. In the immortal songs of Schubert, Schumann, Mendelssohn, Liszt, and Franz, and the symphonies of the first four, the vitality of the reformatory idea is richly illustrated. In the music-drama of Wagner, it is claimed by his disciples, is found the full flower and development of the art-work.

WILLIAM RICHARD WAGNER, the formal projector of the great changes whose details are yet to be sketched, was born at Leipsic in 1813. As a child he displayed no very marked artistic tastes, though his ear and memory for music were quite remarkable. When admitted to the Kreuzschule of Dresden, the young student, however, distinguished himself by his very great talent for literary composition and the classical languages. To this early culture, perhaps, we are indebted for the great poetic power which has enabled him to compose the remarkable libretti which have furnished the basis of his music. His first creative attempt was a blood-thirsty drama, where forty-two characters are killed, and the few survivors are haunted by the ghosts. Young Wagner soon devoted himself to the study of music, and, in 1833, became a pupil of Theodor Weinlig, a distinguished teacher of harmony and counterpoint. His four years of study at this time were also years of activity in creative experiment, as he composed four operas.

His first opera of note was "Rienzi," with which he went to Paris in 1837. In spite of Meyerbeer's efforts in its favour, this work was rejected, and laid aside for some years. Wagner supported himself by musical criticism and other literary work, and soon was in a position to offer another opera, "Der fliegende Holländer," to the authorities of the Grand Opera-House. Again the directors refused the work, but were so charmed with the beauty of the libretto that they bought it to be reset to music. Until the year 1842, life was a trying struggle for the indomitable young musician. "Rienzi" was then produced at Dresden, so much to the delight of the King of Saxony that the composer was made royal Kapellmeister and leader of the orchestra. The production of "Der fliegende Holländer" quickly followed; next came "Tanhäuser" and "Lohengrin," to be swiftly succeeded by the "Meistersinger von Nürnberg." This period of our *maestro's* musical activity also commenced to witness the development of his theories on the philosophy of his art, and some of his most remarkable critical writings were then given to the world.

Political troubles obliged Wagner to spend seven years of exile in Zurich; thence he went to London, where he remained till 1861 as conductor of the London Philharmonic Society. In 1861 the exile returned to his native country, and spent several years in Germany and Russia—there having arisen quite a *furore* for his music in the latter country. The enthusiasm awakened in the breast of King Louis of Bavaria by "Der fliegende Holländer" resulted in a summons to Wagner to settle at Munich, and with the glories of the Royal Opera-House in that city his name has been principally connected. The culminating art-splendour of his life, however, was the production of his stupendous tetralogy, the "Ring der Niebelungen," at the great opera-house at Bayreuth, in the summer of the year 1876.

IV.

The first element to be noted in Wagner's operatic forms is the energetic protest against the artificial and conventional in music. The utter want of dramatic symmetry and fitness in the operas we have been accustomed to hear could only be overlooked by the force of habit, and the tendency to submerge all else in the mere enjoyment of the music. The utter variance of music and poetry was to Wagner the stumbling-block which, first of all, must be removed. So he crushed at one stroke all the hard, arid forms which existed in the lyrical drama as it had been known. His opera, then, is no longer a congeries of separate musical numbers, like duets, arias, chorals, and finales, set in a flimsy web of formless recitative, without reference to dramatic economy. His great purpose is lofty dramatic truth, and to this end he sacrifices the whole framework of accepted musical forms, with the exception of the chorus, and this he remodels. The musical energy is concentrated in the dialogue as the main factor of the dramatic problem, and fashioned entirely according to the requirements of the action. The continuous flow of beautiful melody takes the place alike of the dry recitative and the set musical forms which characterise the accepted school of opera. As the dramatic *motif* demands, this "continuous melody" rises into the highest ecstasies of the lyrical fervour, or ebbs into a chant-like swell of subdued feeling, like the ocean after the rush of the storm. If Wagner has destroyed musical forms, he has also added a positive element. In place of the aria we have the *logos*. This is the musical expression of the principal passion underlying the action of the drama. Whenever, in the course of the development of the story, this passion comes into ascendency, the rich strains of the *logos* are heard anew, stilling all other sounds. Gounod has, in part, applied this principle in "Faust." All opera-goers will remember the intense dramatic effect arising from the recurrence of the same exquisite lyric outburst from the lips of Marguerite.

The peculiar character of Wagner's word-drama next arouses critical interest and attention. The composer is his own poet, and his creative genius shines no less here than in the world of tone. The musical energy flows entirely from the dramatic conditions, like the electrical current from the cups of the battery; and the rhythmical structure of the *melos* (tune) is simply the transfiguration of the poetical basis. The poetry, then, is all-important in the music-drama. Wagner has rejected the forms of blank verse and rhyme as utterly unsuited to the lofty purposes of music, and has gone to the metrical principle of all the Teutonic and Slavonic poetry. This rhythmic element of alliteration, or *staffrhyme*, we find magnificently illustrated in the Scandinavian Eddas, and even in our own Anglo-Saxon fragments of the days of Cædmon and Alcuin. By the use of this new form, verse and melody glide together in one exquisite rhythm, in which it seems impossible to separate the one from the other. The strong accent of the alliterating syllables supply the music with firmness, while the low-toned syllables give opportunity for the most varied *nuances* of declamation.

The first radical development of Wagner's theories we see in "The Flying Dutchman." In "Tanhäuser" and "Lohengrin" they find full sway. The utter revolt of his mind from the trivial and commonplace sentimentalities of Italian opera led him to believe that the most heroic and lofty motives alone should furnish the dramatic foundation of opera. For a while he oscillated between history and legend, as best adapted to furnish his material. In his selection of the dream-land of myth and legend, we may detect another example of the profound and *exigeant* art-instincts which have ruled the whole of Wagner's life. There could be no question as to the utter incongruity of any dramatic picture of ordinary events, or ordinary personages, finding expression in musical utterance. Genuine and profound art must always be consistent with itself, and what we recognise as general truth. Even characters set in the comparatively near background of history are too closely related to our own familiar surroundings of thought and mood to be regarded as artistically natural in the use of music as the organ of the every-day life of emotion and sentiment. But with the dim and heroic shapes that haunt the border-land of the supernatural, which we call legend, the case is far different. This is the drama of the demigods, living in a different atmosphere from our own, however akin to ours may be their passions and purposes. For these we are no longer compelled to regard the medium of music as a forced and untruthful expression, for do they not dwell in the magic lands of the imagination? All sense of dramatic inconsistency instantly vanishes, and the conditions of artistic illusion are perfect.

> " 'Tis distance lends enchantment to the view,
> And clothes the mountains with their azure hue."

Thus all of Wagner's works, from "Der fliegende Holländer" to the "Ring der Niebelungen," have been located in the world of myth, in obedience to a profound art-principle. The opera of "Tristan and Iseult," first performed in 1865, announced Wagner's absolute emancipation, both in the construction of music and poetry, from the time-honoured and time-corrupted canons, and, aside from the last great work, it may be received as the most perfect representation of his school.

The third main feature in the Wagner music is the wonderful use of the orchestra as a factor in the solution of the art-problem. This is no longer a mere accompaniment to the singer, but translates the passion of the play into a grand symphony, running parallel and commingling with the vocal music. Wagner, as a great master of orchestration, has had few equals since Beethoven; and he uses his power with marked effect to heighten the dramatic intensity of the action, and at the same time to convey certain meanings which can only find vent in the vague and indistinct forms of pure music. The romantic conception of the mediæval love, the shudderings and raptures of Christian revelation, have certain phases that absolute music alone can express. The orchestra, then, becomes as much an integral part of the music-drama, in its actual current movement, as the chorus or the leading performers. Placed on the stage, yet out of sight, its strains might almost be fancied the sound of the sympathetic communion of good and evil spirits, with whose presence mystics formerly claimed man was constantly surrounded. Wagner's use of the orchestra may be illustrated from the opera of "Lohengrin."

The ideal background, from which the emotions of the human actors in the drama are reflected with supernatural light, is the conception of the "Holy Graal," the mystic symbol of the Christian faith, and its descent from the skies, guarded by hosts of seraphim. This is the subject of the orchestral prelude, and never have the sweetnesses and terrors of the Christian ecstasy been more potently expressed. The prelude opens with long-drawn chords of the violins, in the highest octaves, in the most exquisite *pianissimo*. The inner eye of the spirit discerns in this the suggestion of shapeless white clouds, hardly discernible from the aërial blue of the sky. Suddenly the strings seem to sound from the farthest distance, in continued *pianissimo*, and the melody, the Graal-motive, takes shape. Gradually, to the fancy, a group of angels seem to reveal themselves, slowly descending from the heavenly heights, and bearing in their midst the *Sangréal*. The modulations throb through the air, augmenting in richness and sweetness, till the *fortissimo* of the full orchestra reveals the sacred mystery. With this climax of spiritual ecstasy the harmonious waves gradually recede and ebb away in dying sweetness, as the angels return to their heavenly abode. This orchestral movement recurs in the opera, according to the laws of dramatic fitness, and its melody is heard also in the *logos* of Lohengrin, the knight of the Graal, to express certain phases of his action. The immense power which music is thus made to have in dramatic effect can easily be fancied.

A fourth prominent characteristic of the Wagner music-drama is that, to develop its full splendour, there must be a co-operation of all the arts, painting, sculpture, and architecture, as well as poetry and music. Therefore, in realising its effects, much importance rests in the visible beauties of action, as they may be expressed by the painting of scenery and the grouping of human figures. Well may such a grand conception be called the "Art-work of the Future."

Wagner for a long time despaired of the visible execution of his ideas. At last the celebrated pianist, Tausig, suggested an appeal to the admirers of the new music throughout the world for means to carry out the composer's great ideas—viz., to perform the "Niebelungen" at a theatre to be erected for the purpose, and by a select company, in the manner of a national festival, and before an audience entirely removed from the atmosphere of vulgar theatrical shows After many delays Wagner's hopes were attained, and in the summer of 1876 a gathering of the principal celebrities of Europe was present to criticise the fully perfected fruit of the composer's theories and genius. This festival was so recent, and its events have been the subject of such elaborate comment, that further description will be out of place here.

As a great musical poet, rather epic than dramatic in his powers, there can be no question as to Wagner's rank. The performance of the "Niebelungenring," covering "Rheingold," "Die Walküren," "Siegfried," and "Götterdämmerung," was one of the epochs of musical Germany. However deficient Wagner's skill in writing for the human voice, the power and symmetry of his conceptions, and his genius in embodying them in massive operatic forms, are such as to storm even the prejudices of his opponents. The poet-musician rightfully claims that in his music-drama is found that wedding of two of the noblest of the arts, pregnantly suggested by Shakespeare :—

> "If Music and sweet Poetry both agree,
> As they must needs, the sister and the brother;
> . . . . . .
> One God is God of both, as poets feign."

NOTE BY THE EDITOR.—The knowledge of Wagner's music in England originated chiefly with the masterly playing of Herr Von Büloz, with the concerts given by Messrs. Dannreuther and Bache, and later on by the Wagner festival held at the Albert Hall in 1877, where Wagner himself presided at the performance of the music of his *Ring des Niebelungen*. He was not quite satisfied with its reception; but this is not altogether to be wondered at when we consider that the work was divorced from its scenic adjuncts, and that in his operas—in accordance with his own theory—the plastic arts as well as poetry and music are equally required to produce a well-balanced result. None the less, this festival greatly increased the interest in "the Music of the Future;" and in 1880 *The Ring des Niebelungen* was performed at Covent Garden, while his other operas were given in their proper sequence at Drury Lane. In 1882 his last great work, *Parsifal*, was performed with striking eclat at Bayreuth. On the 18th of February 1883 he died of heart disease at Venice, whither he had gone to recruit his health. A personal friend has recorded that Wagner's body was laid in the coffin by the widow herself, who—as a last token of her love and admiration—cut off the beautiful hair her husband had so admired, and placed it on a red cushion under the head of the departed. The body of the great musician was taken to Bayreuth and buried, in accordance with the wishes he had himself expressed, in the garden of his own house, "Vahnfried." A large wreath from the King of Bavaria lay on the coffin, bearing the appropriate inscription—"To the Deathless One." On the 24th of July in the same year, *Parsifal* was again performed at Bayreuth—a fitting requiem service over the great master. *Parsifal* is the culmination of Wagner's epic work. In it he completes the cycle of myths by which he strove to express the varied and fervent aspirations of humanity; and in particular "the two burning questions of the day—1. The Tremendous Empire of the Senses. 2. The Immense Supremacy of Soul; and how to reconcile them."

The Legend of the Sangrail, the *motif* of his last work, is "the most poetic and pathetic form of transubstantiation; . . . it possesses the true legendary power of attraction and assimilation." In Mr. Haweis' words, "The *Tannhäuser* and the *Lohengrin* are the two first of the legendary dramas which serve to illustrate the Christian Chivalry and religious aspirations of the middle ages, in conflict on the one side with the narrow ideals of Catholicism, and on the other with the free instincts of human nature. *Parsifal* forms with them a great Trilogy of Christian legends, as the *Ring of the Niebelungen* forms a Tetralogy of Pagan, Rhine, and Norse legends. Both series of sacred and profane myths in the hands of Wagner, whilst striking the great key-notes, Paganism and Catholicism, become the fitting and appropriate vehicles for the display of the ever-recurrent struggles of the human heart—now in the grip of inexorable fate, now passion-tossed, at war with itself and with time—soothed with spaces of calm—flattered with the dream of ineffable joys—filled with sublime hopes ; and content at last with far-off glimpses of God."

ITALIAN AND FRENCH COMPOSERS.

PALESTRINA.

I.

THE Netherlands share other glories than that of having nursed the most indomitable spirit of liberty known to mediæval Europe. The fine as well as the industrial arts found among this remarkable people, distinguished by Erasmus as possessed of the *patientia laboris*, an eager and passionate culture. The early contributions of the Low Countries to the growth of the pictorial art are well known to all. But to most it will be a revelation that the Belgian school of music was the great fructifying influence of the fifteenth century, to which Italy and Germany owe a debt not easily measured. The art of interweaving parts and that science of sound known as counterpoint were placed by this school of musical scholars and workers on a solid basis, which enabled the great composers who came after them to build their beautiful tone fabrics in forms of imperishable beauty and symmetry. For a long time most of the great Italian churches had Belgian chapel-masters, and the value of their example and teachings was vital in its relation to Italian music.

The last great master among the Belgians, and, after Palestrina, the greatest of the sixteenth century, was

Orlando di Lasso, born in Hainault, in the year 1520. His life of a little more than three score years and ten was divided between Italy and Germany. He left the deep imprint of his severe style, though but a young man, on his Italian *confrères*, and the young Palestrina owed to him much of the largeness and beauty of form through which he poured his genius in the creation of such works as have given him so distinct a place in musical history. The pope created Orlando di Lasso Knight of the Golden Spur, and sought to keep him in Italy. Unconcerned as to fame, the gentle, peaceful musician lived for his art alone, and the flattering expressions of the great were not so much enjoyed as endured by him. A musical historian, Heimsoeth, says of him—"He is the brilliant master of the North, great and sublime in sacred composition, of inexhaustible invention, displaying much breadth, variety, and depth in his treatment; he delights in full and powerful harmonies, yet, after all—owing to an existence passed in journeys, as well as service at court, and occupied at the same time with both sacred and secular music—he came short of that lofty, solemn tone which pervades the works of the great master of the South, Palestrina, who, with advancing years, restricted himself more and more to church music." Of the celebrated penitential psalms of Di Lasso, it is said that Charles IX. of France ordered them to be written "in order to obtain rest for his soul after the terrible massacre of St. Bartholomew." Aside from his works, this musician has a claim on fame through his lasting improvements in musical form and method. He illuminated, and at the same time closed, the great epoch of Belgian ascendancy, which had given three hundred musicians of great science to the times in which they lived. So much has been said of Orlando di Lasso, for he was the model and Mentor of the greatest of early church composers, Palestrina.

II.

The melodious and fascinating style, soon to give birth to the characteristic genius of the opera, was as yet unborn, though dormant. In Rome, the chief seat of the Belgian art, the exclusive study of technical skill had frozen music to a mere formula. The Gregorian chant had become so overladen with mere embellishments as to make the prescribed church-form difficult of recognition in its borrowed garb, for it had become a mere jumble of sound. Musicians, indeed, carried their profanation so far as to take secular melodies as the themes for masses and motetts. These were often called by their profane titles. So the name of a love-sonnet or a drinking-song would sometimes be attached to a *miserere*. The Council of Trent, in 1562, cut at these evils with sweeping axe, and the solemn anathemas of the church fathers roused the creative powers of the subject of this sketch, who raised his art to an independent national existence, and made it rank with sculpture and painting, which had already reached their zenith in Leonardo Da Vinci, Raphael, Correggio, Titian, and Michel Angelo. Henceforth Italian music was to be a vigorous, fruitful stock.

GIOVANNI PERLUIGUI ALOISIO DA PALESTRINA was born at Palestrina, the ancient Præneste, in 1524.* The memorials of his childhood are scanty. We know but little except that his parents were poor peasants, and that he learned the rudiments of literature and music as a choir-singer, a starting-point so common in the lives of great composers. In 1540 he went to Rome and studied in the school of Goudimel, a stern Huguenot Fleming, tolerated in the papal capital on account of his superior science and method of teaching, and afterwards murdered at Lyons on the day of the Paris massacre. Palestrina grasped the essential

---

* Our composer, as was common with artists and scholars in those days, took the name of his natal town, and by this he is known to fame. Old documents also give him the old Latin name of the town with the personal ending.

doctrines of the school without adopting its mannerisms. At the age of thirty he published his first compositions, and dedicated them to the reigning pontiff, Julius III. In the formation of his style, which moved with such easy, original grace within the old prescribed rules, he learned much from the personal influence and advice of Orlando di Lasso, his warm friend and constant companion during these earlier days.

Several of his compositions, written at this time, are still performed in Rome on Good Friday, and Goethe and Mendelssohn have left their eloquent tributes to the impression made on them by music alike simple and sublime. The pope was highly pleased with Palestrina's noble music, and appointed him one of the papal choristers, then regarded as a great honour. But beyond Rome the new light of music was but little known. The Council of Trent, in their first indignation at the abuse of church music, had resolved to abolish everything but the simple Gregorian chants, but the remonstrances of the Emperor Ferdinand and the Roman cardinals stayed the austere fiat. The final decision was made to rest on a new composition of Palestrina, who was permitted to demonstrate that the higher forms of musical art were consistent with the solemnities of church worship.

All eyes were directed to the young musician, for the very existence of his art was at stake. The motto of his first mass, "Illumina oculos meos," shows the pious enthusiasm with which he undertook his labours. Instead of one, he composed three six-part masses. The third of these excited such admiration that the pope exclaimed in raptures, "It is John who gives us here in this earthly Jerusalem a foretaste of that new song which the holy Apostle John realised in the heavenly Jerusalem in his prophetic trance." This is now known as the "mass of Pope Marcel," in honour of a former patron of Palestrina.

A new pope, Paul IV., on ascending the pontifical throne, carried his desire of reforming abuses to fanaticism. He insisted on all the papal choristers being clerical.

Palestrina had married early in life a Roman lady, of whom all we know is that her name was Lucretia. Four children had blessed the union, and the composer's domestic happiness became a bar to his temporal preferment. With two others he was dismissed from the chapel because he was a layman, and a trifling pension allowed him. Two months afterwards, though, he was appointed chapel-master of St. John Lateran. His works now succeeded each other rapidly, and different collections of his masses were dedicated to the crowned heads of Europe. In 1571 he was appointed chapel-master of the Vatican, and Pope Gregory XIII. gave special charge of the reform of sacred music to Palestrina.

The death of the composer's wife, whom he idolised, in 1580, was a blow from which he never recovered. In his latter days he was afflicted with great poverty, for the positions he held were always more honourable than lucrative. Mental depression and physical weakness burdened the last few years of his pious and gentle life, and he died after a lingering and severe illness. The register of the pontifical chapel contains this entry—"February 2, 1594. This morning died the most excellent musician, Signor Giovanni Palestrina, our dear companion and *maestro di capella* of St. Peter's church, whither his funeral was attended not only by all the musicians of Rome, but by an infinite concourse of people, when his own 'Libera me, Domine' was sung by the whole college."

Such are the simple and meagre records of the life of the composer who carved and laid the foundation of the superstructure of Italian music; who, viewed in connection with his times and their limitations, must be regarded as one of the great creative minds in his art; who shares with Sebastian Bach the glory of having built an imperishable base for the labours of his successors.

III.

Palestrina left a great mass of compositions, all glowing with the fire of genius, only part of which have been published. His simple life was devoted to musical labour, and passed without romance, diversion, or excitement. His works are marked by utter absence of contrast and colour. Without dramatic movement, they are full of melody and majesty—a majesty serene, unruffled by the slightest suggestion of human passion. Voices are now and then used for individual expression, but either in unison or harmony. As in all great church music, the chorus is the key of the work. The general judgment of musicians agrees that repose and enjoyment are more characteristic of this music than that of any other master. The choir of the Sistine chapel, by the inheritance of long-cherished tradition, is the most perfect exponent of the Palestrina music. During the annual performance of the "Improperie" and "Lamentations," the altar and walls are despoiled of their pictures and ornaments, and everything is draped in black. The cardinals dressed in serge, no incense, no candles: the whole scene is a striking picture of trouble and desolation. The faithful come in two by two and bow before the cross, while the sad music reverberates through the chapel arches. This powerful appeal to the imagination, of course, lends greater power to the musical effect. But all minds who have felt the lift and beauty of these compositions have acknowledged how far they soar above words and creeds, and the picturesque framework of a liturgy.

Mendelssohn, in a letter to Zelter on the Palestrina music as heard in the Sistine chapel, says that nothing could exceed the effect of the blending of the voices, the prolonged tones gradually merging from one note and chord to another, softly swelling, decreasing, at last dying out. "They understand," he writes, "how to bring out and place each trait in the most delicate light, without giving it undue prominence; one chord gently melts into another.

The ceremony at the same time is solemn and imposing; deep silence prevails in the chapel, only broken by the re-echoing Greek 'holy,' sung with unvarying sweetness and expression." The composer Paër was so impressed with the wonderful beauty of the music and the performance, that he exclaimed, "This is indeed divine music, such as I have long sought for, and my imagination was never able to realise, but which, I knew, must exist."

Palestrina's versatility and genius enabled him to lift ecclesiastical music out of the rigidity and frivolity characterising on either hand the opposing ranks of those that preceded him, and to embody the religious spirit in works of the highest art. He transposed the ecclesiastical melody (*canto fermo*) from the tenor to the soprano (thus rendering it more intelligible to the ear), and created that glorious thing choir song, with its refined harmony, that noble music of which his works are the models, and the papal chair the oracle. No individual pre-eminence is ever allowed to disturb and weaken the ideal atmosphere of the whole work. However Palestrina's successors have aimed to imitate his effects, they have, with the exception of Cherubini, failed for the most part; for every peculiar genus of art is the result of innate genuine inspiration, and the spontaneous growth of the age which produces it. As a parent of musical form he was the protagonist of Italian music, both sacred and secular, and left an admirable model, which even the new school of opera so soon to rise found it necessary to follow in the construction of harmony. The splendid and often licentious music of the theatre built its most worthy effects on the work of the pious composer, who lived, laboured, and died in an atmosphere of almost anchorite sanctity.

The great disciples of his school, Nannini and Allegri, continued his work, and the splendid "Miserere" of the latter was regarded as such an inestimable treasure that no copy of it was allowed to go out of the Sistine chapel, till the infant prodigy, Wolfgang Mozart, wrote it out from the memory of a single hearing.

PICCINI, PAISIELLO, AND CIMAROSA.

I.

Music, as speaking the language of feeling, emotion, and passion, found its first full expansion in the operatic form. There had been attempts to represent drama with chorus, founded on the ancient Greek drama, but it was soon discovered that dialogue and monologue could not be embodied in choral forms without involving an utter absurdity. The spirit of the renaissance had freed poetry, statuary, and painting from the monopolising claims of the church. Music, which had become a well-equipped and developed science, could not long rest in a similar servitude. Though it is not the aim of the author to discuss operatic history, a brief survey of the progress of opera from its birth cannot be omitted.

The oldest of the entertainments which ripened into Italian opera belongs to the last years of the fifteenth century, and was the work of the brilliant Politian, known as one of the revivalists of Greek learning attached to the court of Cosmo de' Medici and his son Lorenzo. This was the musical drama of "Orfeo." The story was written in Latin, and sung in music principally choral, though a few solo phrases were given to the principal characters. It was performed at Rome with great magnificence, and Vasari tells us that Peruzzi, the decorator of the papal theatre, painted such scenery for it that even the great Titian was so struck with the *vraisemblance* of the work that he was not satisfied until he had touched the canvas to be sure of its not being in relief. We may fancy indeed that the scenery was one great attraction of the representation. In spite of spasmodic encouragement by the more liberally-minded pontiffs, the general weight of church influence was against the new musical tendency, and the most skilled composers were at first afraid to devote their talents to further its growth.

What musicians did not dare undertake out of dread of the thunderbolts of the church, a company of *literati* at Florence commenced in 1580. The primary purpose was the revival of Greek art, including music. This association, in conjunction with the Medicean Academy, laid down the rule that distinct individuality of expression in music was to be sought for. As results, quickly came musical drama with recitative (modern form of the Greek chorus) and solo melody for characteristic parts of the legend or story. Out of this beginning swiftly grew the opera. Composers in the new form sprung up in various parts of Italy, though Naples, Venice, and Florence continued to be its centres.

Between 1637 and 1700 there were performed three hundred operas at Venice alone. An account of the performance of "Berenice," composed by Domenico Freschi, at Padua, in 1680, dwarfs all our present ideas of spectacular splendour. In this opera there were choruses of a hundred virgins and a hundred soldiers; a hundred horsemen in steel armour; a hundred performers on trumpets, cornets, sackbuts, drums, flutes, and other instruments, on horseback and on foot; two lions led by two Turks, and two elephants led by two Indians; Berenice's triumphal car drawn by four horses, and six other cars with spoils and prisoners, drawn by twelve horses. Among the scenes in the first act was a vast plain with two triumphal arches; another with pavilions and tents; a square prepared for the entrance of the triumphal procession, and a forest for the chase. In the second act there were the royal apartments of Berenice's temple of vengeance, a spacious court with view of the prison and a covered way with long lines of chariots. In the third act there were the royal dressing-room, the stables with a hundred live horses, porticoes adorned with tapestry, and a great palace in the perspective. In the course of the piece there were representations of the hunting of the boar, the stag, and the lions. The whole concluded with a huge globe descending from the skies, and dividing itself in lesser globes of fire, on which stood allegorical figures of fame, honour, nobility, virtue, and glory. The theatrical manager had princes and nobles for bankers and assistants, and they lavished their treasures of art and money to make such spectacles as the modern stagemen of London and Paris cannot approach.

In Evelyn's diary there is an entry describing opera at Venice in 1645:—"This night, having with my lord Bruce taken our places before, we went to the opera, where comedies and other plays are represented in recitative musiq by the most excellent musicians, vocal and instrumental, with variety of scenes painted and contrived with no lesse art of perspective, and machines for flying in the aire, and other wonderful motions; taken together it is one of the most magnificent and expensive diversions the wit of man can invent. The history was Hercules in Lydia. The sceanes changed thirteen times. The famous voices, Anna Rencia, a Roman, and reputed the best treble of women; but there was a Eunuch who in my opinion surpassed her; also a Genoise that in my judgment sung an incomparable base. They held us by the eyes and ears till two o'clock i' the morning." Again he writes of the carnival of 1646:—"The comedians have liberty and the operas are open; witty pasquils are thrown about, and the mountebanks have their stages at every corner. The diversion which chiefly took me up was three noble operas, where were most excellent voices and music, the most celebrated of which was the famous and beautiful Anna Rencia, whom we invited to a fish dinner after four daies in Lent, when they had given over at the theatre." Old Evelyn then narrates how he and his noble friend took the lovely diner out on a junketing, and got shot at with blunderbusses from the gondola of an infuriated rival.

Opera progressed towards a fixed status with a swiftness hardly paralleled in the history of any art. The soil was rich and fully prepared for the growth, and the fecund root, once planted, shot into a luxuriant beauty and symmetry, which nothing could check. The Church wisely gave up its opposition, and henceforth there was nothing to impede the progress of a product which spread and naturalised itself in

England, France, and Germany. The inventive genius of Monteverde, Carissimi, Scarlatti (the friend and rival of Handel), Durante, and Leonardo Leo, perfected the forms of the opera nearly as we have them to-day. A line of brilliant composers in the school of Durante and Leo brings us down through Pergolesi, Derni, Terradiglias, Jomelli, Traetta, Ciccio di Majo, Galuppi, and Giuglielmi, to the most distinguished of the early Italian composers, Niccolo Piccini, who, mostly forgotten in his works, is principally known to modern fame as the rival of the mighty Gluck in that art controversy which shook Paris into such bitter factions. Yet, overshadowed as Piccini was in the greatness of his rival, there can be no question of his desert as the most brilliant ornament and exponent of the early operatic school. No greater honour could have been paid to him than that he should have been chosen as their champion by the *Italianissimi* of his day in the battle royal with such a giant as Gluck, an honour richly deserved by a composer distinguished by multiplicity and beauty of ideas, dramatic insight, and ardent conviction.

II.

NICCOLO PICCINI, who was not less than fifty years of age when he left Naples for the purpose of outrivalling Gluck, was born at Bari, in the kingdom of Naples, in 1728. His father, also a musician, had destined him for holy orders, but Nature made him an artist. His great delight even as a little child was playing on the harpsichord, which he quickly learned. One day the bishop of Bari heard him playing, and was amazed at the power of the little *virtuoso*. "By all means send him to a conservatory of music," he said to the elder Piccini. "If the vocation of the priesthood brings trials and sacrifices, a musical career is not less beset with obstacles. Music demands great perseverance and incessant labour. It exposes one to many chagrins and toils."

By the advice of the shrewd prelate, the precocious boy

was placed at the school of St. Onofrio at the age of fourteen. At first confided to the care of an inferior professor, he revolted from the arid teachings of a mere human machine. Obeying the dictates of his daring fancy, though hardly acquainted with the rudiments of composition, he determined to compose a mass. The news got abroad that the little Niccolo was working on a grand mass, and the great Leo, the chief of the conservatory, sent for the trembling culprit.

"You have written a mass?" he commenced.

"Excuse me, sir, I could not help it," said the timid boy.

"Let me see it."

Niccolo brought him the score and all the orchestral parts, and Leo immediately went to the concert-room, assembled the orchestra, and gave them the parts. The boy was ordered to take his place in front and conduct the performance, which he went through with great agitation.

"I pardon you this time," said the grave *maestro*, at the end; "but, if you do such a thing again, I will punish you in such a manner that you will remember it as long as you live. Instead of studying the principles of your art, you give yourself up to all the wildness of your imagination; and, when you have tutored your ill-regulated ideas into something like shape, you produce what you call a mass, and no doubt think you have produced a masterpiece."

When the boy burst into tears at this rebuke, Leo clasped him in his arms, told him he had great talent, and after that took him under his special instruction. Leo was succeeded by Durante, who also loved Piccini, and looked forward to a future greatness for him. He was wont to say the others were his pupils, but Piccini was his son. After twelve years spent in the conservatory, Piccini commenced an opera. The director of the principal Neapolitan theatre said to Prince Vintimille, who introduced the young musician, that his work was sure to be a failure.

"How much can you lose by his opera," the prince replied,

"supposing it to be a perfect fiasco?" The manager named the sum.

"There is the money, then," replied Piccini's generous patron, handing him a purse. "If the 'Dorme Despetose'" (the name of the opera) "should fail, you may keep the money, but otherwise return it to me."

The friends of Lagroscino, the favourite composer of the day, were enraged when they heard that the next new work was to be from an obscure youth, and they determined to hiss the performance. So great, however, was the delight of the public with the freshness and beauty of Piccini's music, that even those who came to condemn remained to applaud. The reputation of the composer went on increasing until he became the foremost name of musical Italy, for his fertility of production was remarkable; and he gave the theatres a brilliant succession of comic and serious works. In 1758 he produced at Rome his "Alessandro nell' Indie," whose success surpassed all that had preceded it, and two years later a still finer masterpiece, "La Buona Figluola," written to a text furnished by the poet Goldoni, and founded on the story of Richardson's "Pamela." This opera was produced at every playhouse on the Italian peninsula in the course of a few years.

A pleasant *mot* by the Duke of Brunswick is worth preserving in this connection. Piccini had married a beautiful singer named Vicenza Sibilla, and his home was very happy. One day the German prince visited Piccini, and found him rocking the cradle of his youngest child, while the eldest was tugging at the paternal coat-tails. The mother, being *en déshabille*, ran away at the sight of a stranger. The duke excused himself for his want of ceremony, and added, "I am delighted to see so great a man living in such simplicity, and that the author of 'La Bonne Fille' is such a good father." Piccini's placid and pleasant life was destined, however, to pass into stormy waters.

His sway over the stage and the popular preference continued until 1773, when a clique of envious rivals at

Rome brought about his first disaster. The composer was greatly disheartened, and took to his bed, for he was ill alike in mind and body. The turning-point in his career had come, and he was to enter into an arena which taxed his powers in a contest such as he had not yet dreamed of. His operas having been heard and admired in France, their great reputation inspired the royal favourite, Mdme. du Barry, with the hope of finding a successful competitor to the great German composer, patronised by Marie Antoinette. Accordingly, Piccini was offered an indemnity of six thousand francs, and a residence in the hotel of the Neapolitan ambassador. When the Italian arrived in Paris, Gluck was in full sway, the idol of the court and public, and about to produce his "Armide."

Piccini was immediately commissioned to write a new opera, and he applied to the brilliant Marmontel for a libretto. The poet rearranged one of Quinault's tragedies, "Roland," and Piccini undertook the difficult task of composing music to words in a language as yet unknown to him. Marmontel was his unwearied tutor, and he writes in his "Memoirs" of his pleasant yet arduous task—"Line by line, word by word, I had everything to explain; and, when he had laid hold of the meaning of a passage, I recited it to him, marking the accent, the prosody, and the cadence of the verses. He listened eagerly, and I had the satisfaction to know that what he heard was carefully noted. His delicate ear seized so readily the accent of the language and the measure of the poetry, that in his music he never mistook them. It was an inexpressible pleasure to me to see him practice before my eyes an art of which before I had no idea. His harmony was in his mind. He wrote his airs with the utmost rapidity, and when he had traced its designs, he filled up all the parts of the score, distributing the traits of harmony and melody, just as a skilful painter would distribute on his canvas the colours, lights, and shadows of his picture. When all this was done, he opened his harpsichord, which he had been using as his writing-table; and then I heard an air, a duet, a chorus, complete in all its parts, with a truth of expression, an intelligence, a unity of design, a magic in the harmony, which delighted both my ear and my feelings."

Piccini's arrival in Paris had been kept a close secret while he was working on the new opera, but Abbé du Rollet ferreted it out, and acquainted Gluck, which piece of news the great German took with philosophical disdain. Indeed, he attended the rehearsal of " Roland ; " and when his rival, in despair over his ignorance of French and the stupidity of the orchestra, threw down the baton in despair, Gluck took it up, and by his magnetic authority brought order out of chaos and restored tranquillity, a help as much, probably, the fruit of condescension and contempt as of generosity.

Still Gluck was not easy in mind over this intrigue of his enemies, and wrote a bitter letter, which was made public, and aggravated the war of public feeling. Epigrams and accusations flew back and forth like hailstones.*

"Do you know that the Chevalier (Gluck's title) has an Armida and Orlando in his portfolio ?" said Abbé Arnaud to a Piccinist.

"But Piccini is also at work on an Orlando," was the retort.

"So much the better," returned the abbé, "for then we shall have an Orlando and also an Orlandino," was the keen answer.

The public attention was stimulated by the war of pamphlets, lampoons, and newspaper articles. Many of the great *literati* were Piccinists, among them Marmontel, La Harpe, D'Alembert, etc. Suard du Rollet and Jean Jacques Rousseau fought in the opposite ranks. Although the nation was trembling on the verge of revolution, and the French had just lost their hold on the East Indies ; though Mirabeau was thundering in the tribune, and Jacobin clubs were commencing their baleful work, soon to drench Paris in blood, all factions and discords were forgotten. The question was no longer, "Is he a Jansenist, a Molinist, an Encyclopædist, a philosopher, a free-thinker ?" One

* *See* article on Gluck in " Great German Composers."

question only was thought of, " Is he a Gluckist or Piccinist?" and on the answer often depended the peace of families and the cement of long-established friendships.

Piccini's opera was a brilliant success with the fickle Parisians, though the Gluckists sneered at it as pretty concert music. The retort was that Gluck had no gift of melody, though they admitted he had the advantage over his rival of making more noise. The poor Italian was so much distressed by the fierce contest that he and his family were in despair on the night of the first representation. He could only say to his weeping wife and son, " Come, my children, this is unreasonable. Remember that we are not among savages; we are living with the politest and kindest nation in Europe. If they do not like me as a musician, they will at all events respect me as a man and a stranger." To do justice to Piccini, a mild and timid man, he never took part in the controversy, and always spoke of his opponent with profound respect and admiration.

III.

Marie Antoinette, whom Mdme. du Barry and her clique looked on as Piccini's enemy, astonished both cabals by appointing Piccini her singing-master—an unprofitable honour, for he received no pay, and was obliged to give costly copies of his compositions to the royal family. He might have quoted from the Latin poet in regard to this favour from Marie Antoinette, whose faction in music, among other names, was known as the Greek party, " *Timeo Danaos et dona ferentes.*"* Beaumarchais, the brilliant author of " Figaro," had found the same inconvenience when acting as court teacher to the daughters of Louis XV. The French kings were parsimonious except when lavishing money on their vices.

The action of the dauphiness, however, paved the way for a reconciliation between Piccini and Gluck. Berton, the manager of the opera, gave a luxurious banquet, and the musicians, side by side, pledged each other in libations

* I fear the Greeks, though offering gifts.

of champagne. Gluck got confidential in his cups. "These French," he said, "are good enough people, but they make me laugh. They want us to write songs for them, and they can't sing." In fact, the quarrel was not between the musicians but their adherents. In his own heart Piccini knew his inferiority to Gluck.

De Vismes, Berton's successor, proposed that both should write operas on the same subject, "Iphigenia in Tauris," and gave him a libretto. "The French public will have for the first time," he said, "the pleasure of hearing two operas on the same theme, with the same incidents, the same characters, but composed by two great masters of totally different schools."

"But," objected the alarmed Italian, "if Gluck's opera is played first, the public will be so delighted that they will not listen to mine."

"To avoid that catastrophe," said the director, "we will play yours first."

"But Gluck will not permit it."

"I give you my word of honour," said De Vismes, "that your opera shall be put in rehearsal and brought out as soon as it is finished."

Before Piccini had finished his opera, he heard that his rival was back from Germany with his "Iphigenia" completed, and that it was in rehearsal. The director excused himself on the plea of its being a royal command. Gluck's work was his masterpiece, and produced an unparalleled sensation among the Parisians. Even his enemies were silenced, and La Harpe said it was the *chef d'œuvre* of the world. Piccini's work, when produced, was admired, but it stood no chance with the profound, serious, and wonderfully dramatic composition of his rival.

On the night of the first performance Mdlle. Laguerre, to whom Piccini had trusted the rôle of Iphigenia, could not stand straight from intoxication. "This is not 'Iphigenia in Tauris,'" said the witty Sophie Arnould, "but 'Iphigenia in champagne.'" She compensated afterwards, though, by singing the part with exquisite effect.

While the Gluck-Piccini battle was at its height, an amateur who was disgusted with the contest returned to the country and sang the praises of the birds and their gratuitous performances in the following epigram:—

> "La n'est point d'art, d'ennui scientifique ;
> Piccini, Gluck, n'ont point noté les airs.
> Nature seule en dicta la musique,
> Et Marmontel n'en a pas fait les vers."

The sentiment of this was probably applauded by the many who were wearied of the bitter recriminations, which degraded the art which they professed to serve.

During the period when Gluck and Piccini were composing for the French opera, its affairs flourished liberally under the sway of De Vismes. Gluck, Piccini, and Rameau wrote serious operas, while Piccini, Sacchini, Anfossi, and Paisiello composed comic operas. The ballet flourished with unsurpassed splendour, and on the whole it may be said that never has the opera presented more magnificence at Paris than during the time France was on the eve of the Reign of Terror. The gay capital was thronged with great singers, the traditions of whose artistic ability compare favourably with those of a more recent period.

The witty and beautiful Sophie Arnould, who had a train of princes at her feet, was the principal exponent of Gluck's heroines, while Mdlle. Laguerre was the mainstay of the Piccinists. The rival factions made the names of these charming and capricious women their war-cries not less than those of the composers. The public bowed and cringed before these idols of the stage. Gaetan Vestris, the first of the family, known as the "*Dieu de la Danse*" and who held that there were only three great men in Europe, Frederick the Great of Prussia, Voltaire, and himself, dared to dictate even to Gluck. "Write me the music of a chaconne, Monsieur Gluck," said the god of dancing.

"A chaconne!" said the enraged composer. "Do you think the Greeks, whose manners we are endeavouring to depict, knew what a chaconne was?"

"Did they not?" replied Vestris, astonished at this news,

and in a tone of compassion continued, "then they are much to be pitied."

Vestris did not obtain his ballet music from the obdurate German; but, when Piccini's rival "*Iphigénie en Tauride*" was produced, such beautiful dance measures were furnished by the Italian composer as gave Vestris the opportuity for one of his greatest triumphs.

IV.

The contest between Gluck and Piccini, or rather the cabals who adopted the two musicians as their figure-heads, was brought to an end by the death of the former. An attempt was made to set up Sacchini in his place, but it proved unavailing, as the new composer proved to be quite as much a follower of the prevailing Italian method as of the new school of Gluck. The French revolution swept away Piccini's property, and he retired to Italy. Bad fortune pursued him, however. Queen Caroline of Naples conceived a dislike to him, and used her influence to injure his career, out of a fit of wounded vanity.

"Do you not think I resemble my sister, Marie Antoinette?" queried the somewhat ill-favoured queen. Piccini, embarrassed but truthful, replied, "Your majesty, there may be a family likeness, but no resemblance." A fatality attended him even to Venice. In 1792 he was mobbed and his house burned, because the populace regarded him as a republican, for he had a French son-in-law. Some partial musical successes, however, consoled him, though they flattered his *amour propre* more than they benefited his purse. On his return to Naples he was subjected to a species of imprisonment during four years, for royal displeasure in those days did not confine itself merely to lack of court favour. Reduced to great poverty, the composer who had been the favourite of the rich and great for so many years knew often the actual pangs of hunger, and eked out his subsistence by writing conv ntual psalms, as payment for the broken food doled out by the monks.

At last he was released, and the tenor, David, sent him funds to pay his journey to Paris. Napoleon, the first consul, received him cordially in the Luxembourg palace.

"Sit down," said he to Piccini, who remained standing, "a man of your greatness stands in no one's presence." His reception in Paris was, in fact, an ovation. The manager of the opera gave him a pension of twenty-four hundred francs, a government pension was also accorded, and he was appointed sixth inspector at the Conservatory. But the benefits of this pale gleam of wintry sunshine did not long remain. He died at Passy in the year 1800, and was followed to the grave by a great throng of those who loved his beautiful music and admired his gentle life.

In the present day Gluck appears to have vanquished Piccini, because occasionally an opera of the former is performed, while Piccini's works are only known to the musical antiquarian. But even the marble temples of Gluck are moss-grown and neglected, and that great man is known to the present day rather as one whose influence profoundly coloured and changed the philosophy of opera, than through any immediate acquaintance with his productions. The connoisseurs of the eighteenth century found Piccini's melodies charming, but the works that endure as masterpieces are not those which contain the greatest number of beauties, but those of which the form is the most perfect. Gluck had larger conceptions and more powerful genius than his Italian rival, but the latter's sweet spring of melody gave him the highest place which had so far been attained in the Italian operatic school.

"Piccini," says M. Genguéné, his biographer, "was under the middle size, but well made, with considerable dignity of carriage. His countenance was very agreeable. His mind was acute, enlarged, and cultivated. Latin and Italian literature was familiar to him when he went to France, and afterwards he became almost as well acquainted with French literature. He spoke and wrote Italian with great purity, but among his countrymen he preferred the Neapolitan dialect, which he considered the most expressive, the most difficult, and the most figurative of all languages. He used it principally in narration, with a gaiety, a truth, and a pantomimic expression after the manner of his country, which delighted all his friends, and made his stories intelligible even to those who knew Italian but slightly."

As a musician Piccini was noticeable, according to the judgment of his best critics, for the purity and simplicity of his style. He always wished to preserve the supremacy of the voice, and, though he well knew how to make his instrumentation rich and effective, he was a resolute opponent to the florid and complex accompaniments which were coming into vogue in his day. His recorded opinion on this subject may have some interest for the musicians of the present day:—

"Were the employment which Nature herself assigns to the instruments of an orchestra preserved to them, a variety of effects and a series of infinitely diversified pictures would be produced. But they are all thrown in at once and used incessantly, and they thus overpower and indurate the ear, without presenting any picture to the mind, to which the ear is the passage. I should be glad to know how they will arouse it when it is accustomed to this uproar, which will soon happen, and of what new witchcraft they will avail themselves. . . . It is well known what occurs to palates blunted by the use of spirituous liquors. In a few months everything may be learned which is necessary to produce these exaggerated effects, but it requires much time and study to be able to excite genuine emotion." Piccini followed strictly the canons of the Italian school; and, though far inferior in really great qualities to his rival Gluck, his compositions had in them so much of fluent grace and beauty as to place him at the head of his predecessors. Some curious critics have indeed gone so far as to charge that many of the finest arias of Rossini, Donizetti, and Bellini owe their paternity to this composer, an indictment not uncommon in music, for most of the great composers have rifled the sweets of their predecessors without scruple.

V.

Paisiello and Cimarosa, in their style and processes of work, seem to have more nearly caught the mantle of Piccini than any others, though they were contemporaries as well as successors. GIOVANNI PAISIELLO, born in 1741, was educated, like many other great musicians, at the Conservatory of San Onofrio. During his early life he produced a great number of pieces for the Italian theatres, and in 1776 accepted the invitation of Catherine to become the court composer at St. Petersburgh, where he remained nine years, and produced several of his best operas, chief among them, "Il Barbiere di Seviglia" (a different version of Beaumarchais's celebrated comedy from that afterwards used by Rossini).

The empress was devotedly attached to him, and showed her esteem in many signal ways. On one occasion, while Paisiello was accompanying her in a song, she observed that he shuddered with the bitter cold. On this Catherine took off her splendid ermine cloak, decorated with clasps of brilliants, and threw it over her tutor's shoulders. In a quarrel which Paisiello had with Marshal Beloseloky, the temporary favourite of the Russian Messalina, her favour was shown in a still more striking way. The marshal had given the musician a blow, on which Paisiello, a very large, athletic man, drubbed the Russian general most unmercifully. The latter demanded the immediate dismissal of the composer for having insulted a dignitary of the empire. Catherine's reply was similar to the one made by Francis the First of France in a parallel case about Leonardo da Vinci—

"I neither can nor will attend to your request; you forgot your dignity when you gave an unoffending man and a great artist a blow. Are you surprised that he should have forgotten it too? As for rank, it is in my power to make fifty marshals, but not one Paisiello."

Some years after his return to Italy, he was engaged by Napoleon as chapel-master; for that despot ruled the art and literature of his times as autocratically as their politics. Though Paisiello did not wish to obey the mandate, to refuse was ruin. The French ruler had already shown his favour by giving him the preference over Cherubini in several important musical contests, for the latter had always displayed stern independence of courtly favour. On Paisiello's arrival in Paris, several lucrative appointments indicated the sincerity of Napoleon's intentions. The composer did not hesitate to stand on his rights as a musician on all occasions. When Napoleon complained of the inefficiency of the chapel service, he said, courageously, "I can't blame people for doing their duty carelessly, when they are not justly paid." The cunning Italian knew how to flatter, though, when occasion served. He once addressed his master as "Sire."

"'Sire,' what do you mean?" answered the first consul. "I am a general and nothing more."

"Well, General," continued the composer, "I have come to place myself at your majesty's orders."

"I must really beg you," rejoined Napoleon, "not to address me in this manner."

"Forgive me, General," said Paisiello. "But I cannot give up the habit I have contracted in addressing sovereigns, who, compared with you, are but pigmies. However, I will not forget your commands, and, if I have been unfortunate enough to offend, I must throw myself on your majesty's indulgence."

Paisiello received ten thousand francs for the mass written for Napoleon's coronation, and one thousand for all others. As he produced masses with great rapidity, he could very well afford to neglect operatic writing during this period. His masses were pasticcio work made up of pieces selected from his operas and other compositions. This could be easily done, for music is arbitrary in its associations. Love songs of a passionate and sentimental cast were quickly made religious by suitable words. Thus the same melody will depict equally well the rage of a baffled conspirator, the jealousy of an injured husband, the grief of lovers about to part, the despondency of a man bent on suicide, the devotion of the nun, or the rapt adoration of worship. A different text and a slight change in time effect the marvel, and hardly a composer has disdained to borrow from one work to enrich another. His only opera composed in Paris, "Proserpine," was not successful.

Failure of health obliged Paisiello to return to Naples, when he again entered the service of the king. Attached to the fortunes of the Bonaparte family, his prosperity fell with theirs. He had been crowned with honours by all the musical societies of the world, but his pensions and emoluments ceased with the fall of Joachim Murat from the Neapolitan throne. He died June 5, 1816, and the court, which neglected him living, gave him a magnificent funeral.

"Paisiello," says the Chevalier Le Sueur, "was not only a great musician, but possessed a large fund of general information. He was well versed in the dead languages, acquainted with all branches of literature, and on terms of friendship with the most distinguished persons of the age. His mind was noble and above all mean passions; he neither knew envy nor the feeling of rivalry. . . . He composed," says the same writer, "seventy-eight operas, of which twenty-seven were serious, and fifty-one comic, eight *intermezzi*, and an immense number of cantatas, oratorios, masses, etc.; seven symphonies for King Joseph of Spain, and many miscellaneous pieces for the court of Russia."

Paisiello's style, according to Fétis, was characterised by great simplicity and apparent facility. His few and unadorned notes, full of grace, were yet deep and varied in their expression. In his simplicity was the proof of his abundance. It was not necessary for him to have recourse to musical artifice and complication to conceal poverty of invention. His accompaniments were similar in character, clear and picturesque, without pretence of elaboration. The latter not only relieved and sustained the voice, but were full of original effects, novel to his time. He was the author, too, of important improvements in instrumental composition. He introduced the viola, clarionet, and bassoon into the orchestra of the Italian opera. Though voluminous both in serious and comic opera, it was in the latter that he won his chief laurels. His "Pazza per Amore" was one of the great Pasta's favourites, and Catalani added largely to her reputation in the part of *La Frascatana*. Several of Paisiello's comic operas still keep a dramatic place on the German stage, where excellence is not sacrificed to novelty.

VI.

A still higher place must be assigned to another disciple and follower of the school perfected by Piccini, DOMINIC CIMAROSA, born in Naples in 1749. His life down to his latter years was an uninterrupted flow of prosperity. His mother, a humble washerwoman, could do little for her fatherless child, but an observant priest saw the promise of the lad, and taught him till he was old enough to enter the Conservatory of St. Maria di Loretto. His early works showed brilliant invention and imagination, and the young Cimarosa, before he left the Conservatory, had made himself a good violinist and singer. He worked hard, during a musical apprenticeship of many years, to lay a solid foundation for the fame which his teachers prophesied for him from the onset. Like Paisiello, he was for several years attached to the court of Catherine II. of Russia. He had already produced a number of pleasing works, both serious and comic, for the Italian theatres, and his faculty of production was equalled by the richness and variety of his scores. During a period of four years spent at the imperial court of the North, Cimarosa produced nearly five hundred works, great and small, and only left the service of his magnificent patroness, who was no less passionately fond of art than she was great as a ruler and dissolute as a woman, because the severe climate affected his health, for he was a typical Italian in his temperament.

He was arrested in his southward journey by the urgent persuasions of the Emperor Leopold, who made him chapel-master, with a salary of twelve thousand florins. The taste for the Italian school was still paramount at the musical capital of Austria. Though such composers as Haydn, Salieri, and young Mozart, who had commenced to be welcomed as an unexampled prodigy, were in Vienna, the court preferred the suave and shallow beauties of Italian music to their own serious German school, which was commencing to send down such deep roots into the popular heart.

Cimarosa produced "Il Matrimonio Segreto" (The Secret Marriage), his finest opera, for his new patron. The libretto was founded on a forgotten French operetta, which again was adapted from Garrick and Colman's "Clandestine Marriage." The emperor could not attend the first representation, but a brilliant audience hailed it with delight. Leopold made amends, though, on the second night, for he stood in his box, and said, aloud—

"Bravo, Cimarosa, bravissimo! The whole opera is admirable, delightful, enchanting! I did not applaud, that I might not lose a single note of this masterpiece. You have heard it twice, and I must have the same pleasure before I go to bed. Singers and musicians, pass into the next room. Cimarosa will come, too, and preside at the banquet prepared for you. When you have had sufficient rest, we will begin again. I encore the whole opera, and in the meanwhile let us applaud it as it deserves."

The emperor gave the signal, and, midst a thunderstorm of plaudits, the musicians passed into their midnight feast. There is no record of any other such compliment, except that to the Latin dramatist, Plautus, whose "Eunuchus" was performed twice on the same day.

Yet the same Viennese public, six years before, had actually hissed Mozart's "Nozze di Figaro," which shares with Rossini's "Il Barbiere" the greatest rank in comic opera, and has retained, to this day, its perennial freshness and interest. Cimarosa himself did not share the opinion of his admirers in respect to Mozart. A certain Viennese painter attempted to flatter him, by decrying Mozart's music in comparison with his own. The following retort shows the nobility of genius—"I, sir? What would you call the man who would seek to assure you that you were superior to Raphael?" Another acute rejoinder, on the respective merits of Mozart and Cimarosa, was made by the French composer, Grétry, in answer to a criticism by Napoleon, when first consul, that great man affecting to be a *dilettante* in music—

"Sire, Cimarosa puts the statue on the theatre and the pedestal in the orchestra, instead of which Mozart puts the statue in the orchestra and the pedestal on the theatre."

The composer's hitherto brilliant career was doomed to a gloomy close. On returning to Naples, at the Emperor Leopold's death, Cimarosa produced several of his finest works, among which musical students place first—"Il Matrimonio per Susurro," "La Penelope," "L'Olimpiade," "Il Sacrificio d'Abrama," "Gli Amanti Comici," and "Gli Orazi." These were performed almost simultaneously in the theatres of Paris, Naples, and Vienna. Cimarosa attached himself warmly to the French cause in Italy, and when the Bourbons finally triumphed the musician suffered their bitterest resentment. He narrowly escaped with his life, and languished for a long time in a dungeon, so closely immured that it was for a long time believed by his friends that his head had fallen on the block.

At length released, he quitted the Neapolitan territory, only to die at Venice in a few months, "in consequence," Stendhal says, in his *Life of Rossini*, "of the barbarous treatment he had met with in the prison into which he had been thrown by Queen Caroline." He died January 11, 1801.

Cimarosa's genius embraced both the tragic and comic schools of composition. He may be specially called a genuine master of musical comedy. He was the finest example of the school perfected by Piccini, and was indeed the link between the old Italian opera and the new development of which Rossini is such a brilliant exponent. Schluter, in his *History of Music*, says of him—"Like

Mozart, he excels in those parts of an opera which decide its merits as a work of art, the *ensembles* and *finale*. His admirable and by no means antiquated opera, 'Il Matrimonio Segreto' (the charming offspring of his 'secret marriage' with the Mozart opera) is a model of exquisite and graceful comedy. The overture bears a striking resemblance to that of 'Figaro,' and the instrumentation of the whole opera is highly characteristic, though not so prominent as in Mozart. Especially delightful are the secret love-scenes, written evidently *con amore*, the composer having practised them many a time in his youth."

This opera is still performed in many parts of Europe to delighted audiences, and is ranked by competent critics as the third finest comic opera extant, Mozart and Rossini only surpassing him in their masterpieces. It was a great favourite with Lablache, and its magnificent performance by Grisi, Mario, Tamburini, and the king of bassos, is a gala reminiscence of English and French opera-goers.

We quote an opinion also from another able authority— "The drama of 'Gli Orazi' is taken from Corneille's tragedy, 'Les Horaces.' The music is full of noble simplicity, beautiful melody, and strong expression. In the airs dramatic truth is never sacrificed to vocal display, and the concerted pieces are grand, broad, and effective. Taken as a whole, the piece is free from antiquated and obsolete forms; and it wants nothing but an orchestral score of greater fullness and variety to satisfy the modern ear. It is still frequently performed in Germany, though in France and England, and even in its native country, it seems to be forgotten."

Cardinal Consalvi, Cimarosa's friend, caused splendid funeral honours to be paid to him at Rome. Canova executed a marble bust of him, which was placed in the gallery of the Capitol.

ROSSINI.

I.

The "Swan of Pesaro" is a name linked with some of the most charming musical associations of this age. Though forty years silence made fruitless what should have been the richest creative period of Rossini's life, his great works, poured forth with such facility, and still retaining their grasp in spite of all changes in public opinion, stamp him as being the most gifted composer ever produced by a country so fecund in musical geniuses. The old set forms of Italian opera had already yielded in large degree to the energy and pomp of French declamation, when Rossini poured into them afresh such exhilaration and sparkle as again placed his country in the van of musical Europe. With no pretension to the grand, majestic, and severe, his fresh and delightful melodies, flowing without stint, excited alike the critical and the unlearned into a species of artistic craze, a mania which has not yet subsided. The stiff and stately Oublicheff confesses, with many compunctions of conscience, that, when listening for the first time to one of Rossini's operas, he forgot for the time being all that he had ever known, admired, played, or sung, for he was musically drunk, as if with champagne. Learned Germans might shake their heads and talk about shallowness and contrapuntal rubbish, his *crescendo* and *stretto* passages, his tameness and uniformity even in melody, his want of artistic finish; but, as Richard Wagner, his direct antipodes, frankly confesses in his "Oper und Drama," such objections were dispelled by Rossini's opera-airs as if they were mere delusions of the fancy. Essentially different from Beethoven, Bach, Mozart, Haydn, or even Weber, with whom he has some affinities, he stands a unique figure in the history of art, an original both as man and musician.

Gioacchino Rossini was the son of a town-trumpeter and an operatic singer of inferior rank, born in Pesaro, Romagna, February 29, 1792. The child attended the itinerant couple in their visits to fairs and musical gatherings, and was in danger, at the age of seven, of becoming a thorough-paced little vagabond, when maternal alarm trusted his education to the friendly hands of the music-master, Prinetti. At this tender age even he had been introduced to the world of art, for he sang the part of a child at the Bologna opera. "Nothing," said Mdme. Georgi-Righetti, "could be imagined more tender, more touching, than the voice and action of this remarkable child."

The young Rossini, after a year or two, came under the notice of the celebrated teacher Tesei, of Bologna, who gave him lessons in pianoforte playing and the voice, and obtained him a good place as boy-soprano at one of the churches. He now attracted the attention of the Countess Perticari, who admired his voice, and she sent him to the Lyceum to learn fugue and counterpoint at the feet of a very strict Gamaliel, Padre Mattei. The youth was no dull student, and, in spite of his capricious indolence, which vexed the soul of his tutor, he made such rapid progress that at the age of sixteen he was chosen to write the cantata, annually awarded to the most promising student. Success greeted the juvenile effort, and thus we see Rossini fairly launched as a composer. Of the early operas which he poured out for five years it is not needful to speak, except that one of them so pleased the austere Marshal Massena that he exempted the composer from conscription. The first opera which made Rossini's name famous through Europe was "Tancredi," written for the Venetian public. To this opera belongs the charming "Di tanti palpiti," written under the following circumstances:—Mdme. Melanotte, the *prima donna*, took the whim during the final rehearsal that she would not sing the opening air, but must have another. Rossini went home in sore disgust, for the whole opera was likely to be put off by this caprice. There were but two hours before the performance. He sat waiting for his macaroni, when an exquisite air came into his head, and it was written in five minutes.

After his great success he received offers from almost every town in Italy, each clamouring to be served first. Every manager was required to furnish his theatre with an opera from the pen of the new idol. For these earlier essays he received a thousand francs each, and he wrote five or six a year. Stendhall, Rossini's spirited biographer, gives a picturesque account of life in the Italian theatres at this time, a status which remains in some of its features to-day—

"The mechanism is as follows:—The manager is frequently one of the most wealthy and considerable persons of the little town he inhabits. He forms a company, consisting of *prima donna*, *tenoro*, *basso cantante*, *basso buffo*, a second female singer, and a third *basso*. The *libretto*, or poem, is purchased for sixty or eighty francs from some unlucky son of the muses, who is generally a half-starved abbé, the hanger-on of some rich family in the neighbourhood. The character of the parasite, so admirably painted by Terence, is still to be found in all its glory in Lombardy, where the smallest town can boast of some five or six families of some wealth. A *maestro*, or composer, is then engaged to write a new opera, and he is obliged to adapt his own airs to the voices and capacity of the company. The manager intrusts the care of the financial department to a *registrario*, who is generally some pettifogging attorney, who holds the position of his steward. The next thing that generally happens is that the manager falls in love with the *prima donna*; and the progress of this important amour gives ample employment to the curiosity of the gossips.

"The company thus organised at length gives its first representation, after a month of cabals and intrigues, which furnish conversation for the town. This is an event in the simple annals of the town, of the importance of which the residents of large places can form no idea. During months together a population of eight or ten thousand people do nothing but discuss the merit of the forthcoming music and singers with the eager impetuosity which belongs to the

Italian character and climate. The first representation, if successful, is generally followed by twenty or thirty more of the same piece, after which the company breaks up. . . . From this little sketch of theatrical arrangements in Italy some idea may be formed of the life which Rossini led from 1810 to 1816." Between these years he visited all the principal towns, remaining three or four months at each, the idolised guest of the *dilettanti* of the place. Rossini's idleness and love of good cheer always made him procrastinate his labours till the last moment, and placed him in dilemmas from which only his fluency of composition extricated him. His biographer says:—

"The day of performance is fast approaching, and yet he cannot resist the pressing invitations of these friends to dine with them at the tavern. This, of course, leads to a supper, the champagne circulates freely, and the hour of morning steals on apace. At length a compunctious vision shoots across the mind of the truant composer. He rises abruptly; his friends insist on seeing him home; and they parade the silent streets bareheaded, shouting in chorus whatever comes uppermost, perhaps a portion of a *miserere*, to the great scandal of pious Catholics tucked snugly in their beds. At length he reaches his lodging, and shutting himself up in his chamber is, at this, to every-day mortals, most ungenial hour, visited by some of his most brilliant inspirations. These he hastily scratches down on scraps of paper, and next morning arranges them, or, in his own phrase, instruments them, amid the renewed interruptions of his visitors. At length the important night arrives. The *maestro* takes his place at the pianoforte. The theatre is overflowing, people having flocked to the town from ten leagues distance. Every inn is crowded, and those unable to get other accomodations encamp around the theatre in their various vehicles. All business is suspended, and, during the performances, the town has the appearance of a desert. The passions, the anxieties, the very life of a whole population are centered in the theatre."

Rossini would preside at the first three representations,

and, after receiving a grand civic banquet, set out for the next place, his portmanteau fuller of music-paper than of other effects, and perhaps a dozen sequins in his pocket. His love of jesting during these gay Bohemian wanderings made him perpetrate innumerable practical jokes, not sparing himself when he had no more available food for mirth. On one occasion, in travelling from Ancona to Reggio, he passed himself off for a musical professor, a mortal enemy of Rossini, and sang the words of his own operas to the most execrable music, in a cracked voice, to show his superiority to that donkey, Rossini. An unknown admirer of his was in such a rage that he was on the point of chastising him for slandering the great musician, about whom Italy raved.

Our composer's earlier style was quite simple and unadorned, a fact difficult for the present generation, only acquainted with the florid beauties of his later works, to appreciate. Rossini only followed the traditions of Italian music in giving singers full opportunity to embroider the naked score at their own pleasure. He was led to change this practice by the following incident. The tenor-singer Velluti was then the favourite of the Italian theatres, and indulged in the most unwarrantable tricks with his composers. During the first performance of "L'Aureliano," at Naples, the singer loaded the music with such ornaments that Rossini could not recognise the offspring of his own brains. A fierce quarrel ensued between the two, and the composer determined thereafter to write music of such a character that the most stupid singer could not suppose any adornment needed. From that time the Rossini music was marked by its florid and brilliant embroidery. Of the same Velluti, spoken of above, an incident is told, illustrating the musical craze of the country and the period. A Milanese gentleman, whose father was very ill, met his friend in the street—"Where are you going?" "To the Scala, to be sure." "How! your father lies at the point of death." "Yes! yes! I know, but Velluti sings to-night."

II.

An important step in Rossini's early career was his connection with the widely known impresario of the San Carlo, Naples, Barbaja. He was under contract to produce two new operas annually, to rearrange all old scores, and to conduct at all of the theatres ruled by this manager. He was to receive two hundred ducats a month, and a share in the profits of the bank of the San Carlo gambling-saloon. His first opera composed here was "Elisabetta, Regina d'Inghilterra," which was received with a genuine Neapolitan *furore*. Rossini was fêted and caressed by the ardent *dilettanti* of this city to his heart's content, and was such an idol of the "fickle fair" that his career on more than one occasion narrowly escaped an untimely close, from the prejudices of jealous spouses. The composer was very vain of his handsome person, and boasted of his *escapades d'amour*. Many, too, will recall his *mot*, spoken to a beauty standing between himself and the Duke of Wellington—"Madame, how happy should you be to find yourself placed between the two greatest men in Europe!"

One of Rossini's adventures at Naples has in it something of romance. He was sitting in his chamber, humming one of his own operatic airs, when the ugliest Mercury he had ever seen entered and gave him a note, then instantly withdrew. This, of course, was a tender invitation, and an assignation at a romantic spot in the suburb. On arriving Rossini sang his *aria* for a signal, and from the gate of a charming park surrounding a small villa appeared his beautiful and unknown inamorata. On parting it was agreed that the same messenger should bring notice of the second appointment. Rossini suspected that the lady, in disguise, was her own envoy, and verified the guess by following the light-footed page. He then discovered that she was the wife of a wealthy Sicilian, widely noted for her beauty, and one of the reigning toasts. On renewing his visit, he barely arrived at the gate of the park, when a carbine-bullet grazed his head, and two masked assailants sprang toward him with drawn rapiers, a proceeding which left Rossini no option but to take to his heels, as he was unarmed.

During the composer's residence at Naples he was made acquainted with many of the most powerful princes and nobles of Europe, and his name became a recognised factor in European music, though his works were not widely known outside of his native land. His reputation for genius spread by report, for all who came in contact with the brilliant, handsome Rossini were charmed. That which placed his European fame on a solid basis was the production of "Il Barbiere di Seviglia" at Rome during the carnival season of 1816.

Years before Rossini had thought of setting the sparkling comedy of Beaumarchais to music, and Sterbini, the author of the *libretto* used by Paisiello, had proposed to rearrange the story. Rossini, indeed, had been so complaisant as to write to the older composer for permission to set fresh music to the comedy; a concession not needed, for the plays of Metastasio had been used by different musicians without scruple. Paisiello intrigued against the new opera, and organised a conspiracy to kill it on the first night. Sterbini made the libretto totaly different from the other, and Rossini finished the music in thirteen days, during which he never left the house. "Not even did I get shaved," he said to a friend. "It seems strange that through the 'Barber' you should have gone without shaving." "If I had shaved," Rossini exclaimed, "I should have gone out; and, if I had gone out, I should not have come back in time."

The first performance was a curious scene. The Argentina Theatre was packed with friends and foes. One of the greatest of tenors, Garcia, the father of Malibran and Pauline Viardot, sang Almaviva. Rossini had been weak enough to allow Garcia to sing a Spanish melody for a serenade, for the latter urged the necessity of vivid national and local colour. The tenor had forgotten to tune his guitar, and in the operation on the stage a string broke. This gave the signal for a tumult of ironical laughter and hisses. The same hostile atmosphere continued during the evening. Even Madame Georgi-Righetti, a great favourite of the Romans, was coldly received by the audience. In short, the opera seemed likely to be damned.

When the singers went to condole with Rossini, they found him enjoying a luxurious supper with the gusto of the *gourmet* that he was. Settled in his knowledge that he had written a masterpiece, he could not be disturbed by unjust clamour. The next night the fickle Romans made ample amends, for the opera was concluded amid the warmest applause, even from the friends of Paisiello.

Rossini's "Il Barbiere," within six months, was performed on nearly every stage in Europe, and received universally with great admiration. It was only in Paris, two years afterwards, that there was some coldness in its reception. Every one said that after Paisiello's music on the same subject it was nothing, when it was suggested that Paisiello's should be revived. So the St. Petersburg "Barbiere" of 1788 was produced, and beside Rossini's it proved so dull, stupid, and antiquated that the public instantly recognised the beauties of the work which they had persuaded themselves to ignore. Yet for this work, which placed the reputation of the young composer on a lofty pedestal, he received only two thousand francs.

Our composer took his failures with great phlegm and good-nature, based, perhaps, on an invincible self-confidence. When his "Sigismonde" had been hissed at Venice, he sent his mother a *fiasco* (bottle). In the last instance he sent her, on the morning succeeding the first performance, a letter with a picture of a *fiaschetto* (little bottle).

III.

The same year (1816) was produced at Naples the opera of "Otello," which was an important point of departure in the reforms introduced by Rossini on the Italian stage. Before speaking further of this composer's career, it is necessary to admit that every valuable change furthered by him had already been inaugurated by Mozart, a musical genius so great that he seems to have included all that went before, all that succeeded him. It was not merely that Rossini enriched the orchestration to such a degree, but, revolting from the delay of the dramatic movement, caused by the great number of arias written for each character, he gave large prominence to the concerted pieces, and used them where monologue had formerly been the rule. He developed the basso and baritone parts, giving them marked importance in serious opera, and worked out the choruses and finales with the most elaborate finish.

Lord Mount-Edgcumbe, a celebrated connoisseur and admirer of the old school, wrote of these innovations, ignoring the fact that Mozart had given the weight of his great authority to them before the daring young Italian composer:—

"The construction of these newly-invented pieces is essentially different from the old. The dialogue, which used to be carried on in recitative, and which, in Metastasio's operas, is often so beautiful and interesting, is now cut up (and rendered unintelligible if it were worth listening to) into *pezzi concertati*, or long singing conversations, which present a tedious succession of unconnected, ever-changing motives, having nothing to do with each other; and if a satisfactory air is for a moment introduced, which the ear would like to dwell upon, to hear modulated, varied, and again returned to, it is broken off, before it is well understood, by a sudden transition in an entirely different melody, time, and key, and recurs no more, so that no impression can be made, or recollection of it preserved. Single songs are almost exploded. . . . Even the *prima donna*, who formerly would have complained at having less than three or four airs allotted to her, is now satisfied with having one single *cavatina* given to her during the whole opera."

In "Otello," Rossini introduced his operatic changes to the Italian public, and they were well received; yet great opposition was manifested by those who clung to the time-honoured canons. Sigismondi, of the Naples Conservatory, was horror-stricken on first seeing the score of this opera. The clarionets were too much for him, but on seeing third and fourth horn-parts, he exclaimed, "What does the man want? The greatest of our composers have always been contented with two. Shades of Pergolesi, of Leo, of Jomelli! How they must shudder at the bare thought! Four horns! Are we at a hunting-party? Four horns! Enough to blow us to perdition!" Donizetti, who was Sigismondi's pupil, also tells an amusing incident of his preceptor's disgust. He was turning over a score of "Semiramide" in the library, when the *maestro* came in and asked him what music it was. "Rossini's," was the answer. Sigismondi glanced at the page and saw 1. 2. 3. trumpets, being the first, second, and third trumpet parts. Aghast, he shouted, stuffing his fingers in his ears, "One hundred and twenty-three trumpets! *Corpo di Cristo!* the world's gone mad, and I shall go mad too!" And so he rushed from the room, muttering to himself about the hundred and twenty-three trumpets.

The Italian public, in spite of such criticism, very soon accepted the opera of "Otello" as the greatest serious opera ever written for their stage. It owed much, however, to the singers who illustrated its rôles. Mdme. Colbran, afterwards Rossini's wife, sang Desdemona, and Davide, Otello. The latter was the predecessor of Rubini as the finest singer of the Rossinian music. He had the prodigious compass of three octaves; and M. Bertin, a French critic, says of this singer, so honourably linked with the career of our composer, "He is full of warmth, *verve*, energy, expression, and musical sentiment; alone he can fill up and give life to a scene; it is impossible for another singer to carry away an audience as he does, and, when he will only be simple, he is admirable. He is the Rossini of song; he is the greatest singer I ever heard." Lord Byron, in one of his letters to Moore, speaks of the first production at Milan, and praises the music enthusiastically, while condemning the libretto as a degradation of Shakespeare.

"La Cenerentola" and "La Gazza Ladra" were written in quick succession for Naples and Milan. The former of these works, based on the old Cinderella myth, was the last opera written by Rossini to illustrate the beauties of the contralto voice, and Madame Georgi-Righetti, the early friend and steadfast patroness of the musician during his early days of struggle, made her last great appearance in it before retiring from the stage. In this composition, Rossini, though one of the most affluent and rapid of composers, displays that economy in art which sometimes characterised him. He introduced in it many of the more beautiful airs from his earlier and less successful works. He believed on principle that it was folly to let a good piece of music be lost through being married to a weak and faulty libretto. The brilliant opera of "La Gazza Ladra," set to the story of a French melodrama, "La Pie Voleuse," aggravated the quarrel between Paer, the director of the French opera, and the gifted Italian. Paer had designed to have written the music himself, but his librettist slyly turned over the poem to Rossini, who produced one of his masterpieces in setting it. The audience at La Scala received the work with the noisiest demonstrations, interrupting the progress of the drama with constant cries of "*Bravo! Maestro!*" "*Viva Rossini!*" The composer afterwards said that acknowledging the calls of the audience fatigued him much more than the direction of the opera. When the same work was produced four years after in London, under Mr. Ebers's management, an incident related by that *impresario* in his *Seven Years of the King's Theatre*, shows how eagerly it was received by an English audience:—

"When I entered the stage door, I met an intimate friend, with a long face and uplifted eyes. 'Good God! Ebers, I pity you from my soul. This ungrateful public,' he continued. 'The wretches! Why! my dear sir, they have not left you a seat in you own house.' Relieved from the fears he had created, I joined him in his laughter, and proceeded, assuring him that I felt no ill towards the public for their conduct towards me."

Passing over "Armida," written for the opening of the new San Carlo at Naples, "Adelaida di Borgogna," for the Roman Carnival of 1817, and "Adina," for a Lisbon theatre, we come to a work which is one of Rossini's most solid claims on musical immortality, "Mosé in Egitto," first produced at the San Carlo, Naples, in 1818. In "Mosé," Rossini carried out still further than ever his innovations, the two principal rôles—*Mosé* and *Faraoni*—being assigned to basses. On the first representation, the crossing of the Red Sea moved the audience to satirical laughter, which disconcerted the otherwise favourable reception of the piece, and entirely spoiled the final effects. The manager was at his wit's end, till Tottola, the librettist, suggested a prayer for the Israelites before and after the passage of the host through the cleft waters. Rossini instantly seized the idea, and, springing from bed in his night-shirt, wrote the music with almost inconceivable rapidity, before his embarrassed visitors recovered from their surprise. The same evening the magnificent *Dal tuo stellato soglio* ("To thee, Great Lord") was performed with the opera.

Let Stendhall, Rossini's biographer, tell the rest of the story—"The audience was delighted as usual with the first act, and all went well till the third, when, the passage of the Red Sea being at hand, the audience as usual prepared to be amused. The laughter was just beginning in the pit, when it was observed that Moses was about to sing. He began his solo, the first verse of a prayer, which all the people repeat in chorus after Moses. Surprised at this novelty, the pit listened and the laughter entirely ceased. The chorus, exceedingly fine, was in the minor. Aaron continues, followed by the people. Finally, Eleia addresses to Heaven the same supplication, and the people respond. Then all fall on their knees and repeat the prayer with enthusiasm; the miracle is performed, the sea is opened to leave a path for the people protected by the Lord. This last part is in the major. It is impossible to imagine the thunders of applause that resounded through the house;

one would have thought it was coming down. The spectators in the boxes, standing up and leaning over, called out at the top of their voices, '*Bello, bello ! O che bello !*' I never saw so much enthusiasm nor such a complete success, which was so much the greater, inasmuch as the people were quite prepared to laugh. . . . I am almost in tears when I think of this prayer. This state of things lasted a long time, and one of its effects was to make for its composer the reputation of an assassin, for Dr. Cottogna is said to have remarked—'I can cite to you more than forty attacks of nervous fever or violent convulsions on the part of young women, fond to excess of music, which have no other origin than the prayer of the Hebrews in the third act, with its superb change of key.'" Thus, by a stroke of genius, a scene which first impressed the audience as a piece of theatrical burlesque, was raised to sublimity by the solemn music written for it.

M. Bochsa some years afterwards produced "Mosé" as an oratorio in London, and it failed. A new libretto, however, "Pietro L'Eremito,"* again transformed the music into an opera. Ebers tells us that Lord Sefton, a distinguished connoisseur, only pronounced the general verdict in calling it the greatest of serious operas, for it was received with the greatest favour. A gentleman of high rank was not satisfied with assuring the manager that he had deserved well of his country, but avowed his determination to propose him for membership at the most exclusive of aristocratic clubs—White's.

"La Donna del Lago," Rossini's next great work, also first produced at the San Carlo during the Carnival of 1820, though splendidly performed, did not succeed well the first night. The composer left Naples the same night for Milan, and coolly informed every one *en route* that the opera was very successful, which proved to be true when he reached his journey's end, for the Neapolitans on the second night

* The same music was set to a poem founded on the first crusade, all the most effective situations being dramatically utilised for the Christian legend.

reversed their decision into an enthusiasm as marked as their coldness had been.

Shortly after this Rossini married his favourite *prima donna*, Madame Colbran. He had just completed two of his now forgotten operas, "Bianca e Faliero" and "Matilda di Shabran," but did not stay to watch their public reception. He quietly took away the beautiful Colbran, and at Bologna was married by the archbishop. Thence the freshly-wedded couple visited Vienna, and Rossini there produced his "Zelmira," his wife singing the principal part. One of the most striking of this composer's works in invention and ingenious development of ideas, Carpani says of it—"It contains enough to furnish not one but four operas. In this work, Rossini, by the new riches which he draws from his prodigious imagination, is no longer the author of 'Otello,' 'Tancredi,' 'Zoraide,' and all his preceding works; he is another composer, new, agreeable, and fertile, as much as at first, but with more command of himself, more pure, more masterly, and, above all, more faithful to the interpretation of the words. The forms of style employed in this opera, according to circumstances, are so varied, that now we seem to hear Gluck, now Traetta, now Sacchini, now Mozart, now Handel; for the gravity, the learning, the naturalness, the suavity of their conceptions, live and blossom again in 'Zelmira.' The transitions are learned, and inspired more by considerations of poetry and sense than by caprice and a mania for innovation. The vocal parts, always natural, never trivial, give expression to the words without ceasing to be melodious. The great point is to preserve both. The instrumentation of Rossini is really incomparable by the vivacity and freedom of the manner, by the variety and justness of the colouring." Yet it must be conceded that, while this opera made a deep impression on musicians and critics, it did not please the general public. It proved languid and heavy with those who could not relish the science of the music and the skill of the combinations. Such instances as this are the best answer to that school of critics, who have never ceased clamouring that Rossini could write nothing but beautiful tunes to tickle the vulgar and uneducated mind.

"Semiramide," first performed at the Fenice theatre in Venice on February 3, 1823, was the last of Rossini's Italian operas, though it had the advantage of careful rehearsals and a noble caste. It was not well received at first, though the verdict of time places it high among the musical masterpieces of the century. In it were combined all of Rossini's ideas of operatic reform, and the novelty of some of the innovations probably accounts for the inability of his earlier public to appreciate its merits. Mdme. Rossini made her last public appearance in this great work.

IV.

Henceforward the career of the greatest of the Italian composers, the genius who shares with Mozart the honour of having impressed himself more than any other on the style and methods of his successors, was to be associated with French music, though never departing from his characteristic quality as an original and creative mind. He modified French music, and left great disciples on whom his influence was radical, though perhaps we may detect certain reflex influences in his last and greatest opera, "William Tell." But of this more hereafter.

Before finally settling in the French capital, Rossini visited London, where he was received with great honours. "When Rossini entered,"* says a writer in a London paper of that date, "he was received with loud plaudits, all the persons in the pit standing on the seats to get a better view of him. He continued for a minute or two to bow respectfully to the audience, and then gave the signal for the overture to begin. He appeared stout and somewhat be'ow the middle height, with rather a heavy air, and a countenance which, though intelligent, betrayed none of the vivacity

* His first English appearance in public was at the King's Theatre, on the 24th of January 1824, when he conducted his own opera, "Zelmira."

which distinguishes his music; and it was remarked that he had more of the appearance of a sturdy beef-eating Englishman than a fiery and sensitive native of the south."

The king, George IV., treated Rossini with peculiar consideration. On more than one occasion he walked with him arm-in-arm through a crowded concert-hall to the conductor's stand. Yet the composer, who seems not to have admired his English Majesty, treated the monarch with much independence, not to say brusqueness, on one occasion, as if to signify his disdain of even royal patronage. At a grand concert at St. James's Palace, the king said, at the close of the programme, "Now, Rossini, we will have one piece more, and that shall be the *finale*." The other replied, "I think, sir, we have had music enough for one night," and made his bow.

He was an honoured guest at the most fashionable houses, where his talents as a singer and player were displayed with much effect in an unconventional, social way. Auber, the French composer, was present on one of these occasions, and indicates how great Rossini could have been in executive music had he not been a king in the higher sphere. "I shall never forget the effect," writes Auber, "produced by his lightning-like execution. When he had finished I looked mechanically at the ivory keys. I fancied I could see them smoking." Rossini was richer by seven thousand pounds by this visit to the English metropolis. Though he had been under engagement to produce a new opera as well as to conduct those which had already made him famous, he failed to keep this part of his contract. Passages in his letters at this time would seem to indicate that Rossini was much piqued because the London public received his wife, to whom he was devotedly attached, with coldness. Notwithstanding the beauty of her face and figure, and the greatness of her style both as actress and singer, she was pronounced *passée* alike in person and voice, with a species of brutal frankness not uncommon in English criticism.

When Rossini arrived in Paris he was almost immediately appointed director of the Italian Opera by the Duc de Lauriston. With this and the Académie he remained connected till the revolution of 1830. "Le Siége de Corinthe," adapted from his old work, "Maometto II.," was the first opera presented to the Parisian public, and, though admired, did not become a favourite. The French *amour propre* was a little stung when it was made known that Rossini had simply modified and reshaped one of his early and immature productions as his first attempt at composition in French opera. His other works for the French stage were "Il Viaggio a Rheims," "Le Comte Ory," and "Guillaume Tell."

The last-named opera, which will ever be Rossini's crown of glory as a composer, was written with his usual rapidity while visiting the château of M. Aguado, a country-seat some distance from Paris. This work, one of the half-dozen greatest ever written, was first produced at the Académie Royale on August 3, 1829. In its early form of libretto it had a run of fifty-six representations, and was then withdrawn from the stage; and the work of remodelling from five to three acts, and other improvements in the dramatic framework, was thoroughly carried out. In its new form the opera blazed into an unprecedented popularity, for of the greatness of the music there had never been but one judgment. Fétis, the eminent critic, writing of it immediately on its production, said—"The work displays a new man in an old one, and proves that it is in vain to measure the action of genius," and follows with—"This production opens a new career to Rossini," a prophecy unfortunately not to be realised, for Rossini was soon to retire from the field in which he had made such a remarkable career, while yet in the very prime of his powers.

"Guillaume Tell" is full of melody, alike in the solos and the massive choral and ballet music. It runs in rich streams through every part of the composition. The overture is better known to the general public than the opera itself, and is one of the great works of musical art. The opening andante in triple time for the five violoncelli and double basses at once carries the hearer to the regions of the upper Alps, where, amid the eternal snows, Nature sleeps in a peaceful dream. We perceive the coming of the sunlight, and the hazy atmosphere clearing away before the new-born day. In the next movement the solitude is all dispelled. The raindrops fall thick and heavy, and a thunderstorm bursts. But the fury is soon spent, and the clouds clear away. The shepherds are astir, and from the mountain-sides come the peculiar notes of the " Ranz des Vaches " from their pipes. Suddenly all is changed again. Trumpets call to arms, and with the mustering battalions the music marks the quickstep, as the shepherd patriots march to meet the Austrian chivalry. A brilliant use of the violins and reeds depicts the exultation of the victors on their return, and closes one of the grandest sound-paintings in music.

The original cast of "Guillaume Tell" included the great singers then in Paris, and these were so delighted with the music, that the morning after the first production they assembled on the terrace before his house and performed selections from it in his honour.

With this last great effort Rossini, at the age of thirty-seven, may be said to have retired from the field of music, though his life was prolonged for forty years. True, he composed the "Stabat Mater" and the "Messe Solennelle," but neither of these added to the reputation won in his previous career. The "Stabat Mater," publicly performed for the first time in 1842, has been recognised, it is true, as a masterpiece; but its entire lack of devotional solemnity, its brilliant and showy texture, preclude its giving Rossini any rank as a religious composer.

He spent the forty years of his retirement partly at Bologna, partly at Passy, near Paris, the city of his adoption. His hospitality welcomed the brilliant men from all parts of Europe who loved to visit him, and his relations with other great musicians were of the most kindly and cordial character. His sunny and genial nature never knew envy, and he was quick to recognise the merits of schools opposed to his own. He died, after intense suffering, on November 13, 1868. He had been some time ill, and four of the greatest physicians in Europe were his almost constant attendants. The funeral of "The Swan of Pesaro," as he was called by his compatriots, was attended by an immense concourse, and his remains rest in Père-Lachaise.

V.

Moscheles, the celebrated pianist, gives us some charming pictures of Rossini in his home at Passy, in his diary of 1860. He writes—"Felix [his son] had been made quite at home in the villa on former occasions. To me the *parterre salon*, with its rich furniture, was quite new, and before the *maestro* himself appeared we looked at his photograph in a circular porcelain frame, on the sides of which were inscribed the names of his works. The ceiling is covered with pictures illustrating scenes out of Palestrina's and Mozart's lives; in the middle of the room stands a Pleyel piano. When Rossini came in he gave me the orthodox Italian kiss, and was effusive of expressions of delight at my reappearance, and very complimentary on the subject of Felix. In the course of our conversation he was full of hard-hitting truths on the present study and method of vocalisation. 'I don't want to hear anything more of it,' he said; 'they scream. All I want is a resonant, full-toned voice, not a screeching voice. I care not whether it be for speaking or singing, everything ought to sound melodious.'" So, too, Rossini assured Moscheles that he hated the new school of piano-players, saying the piano was horribly maltreated, for the performers thumped the keys as if they had some vengeance to wreak on them. When the great player improvised for Rossini, the latter says, "It is music that flows from the fountain-head. There is reservoir water and spring water. The former only runs when you turn the cock, and is always redolent of the vase; the latter always gushes forth fresh and limpid. Nowadays people confound the simple and the trivial; a *motif* of Mozart they would call trivial, if they dared."

On other occasions Moscheles plays to the *maestro*, who insists on having discovered barriers in the "humoristic variations," so boldly do they seem to raise the standard of musical revolution; his title of the "Grand Valse" he finds too unassuming. "Surely a waltz with some angelic creature must have inspired you, Moscheles, with this composition, and *that* the title ought to express. Titles, in fact, should pique the curiosity of the public." "A view uncongenial to me," adds Moscheles; "however, I did not discuss it. . . . A dinner at Rossini's is calculated for the enjoyment of a 'gourmet,' and he himself proved to be the one, for he went through the very select *menu* as only a connoisseur would. After dinner he looked through my album of musical autographs with the greatest interest, and finally we became very merry, I producing my musical jokes on the piano, and Felix and Clara figuring in the duet which I had written for her voice and his imitation of the French horn. Rossini cheered lustily, and so one joke followed another till we received the parting kiss and 'good night.' . . . At my next visit, Rossini showed me a charming 'Lied ohne Worte,' which he composed only yesterday; a graceful melody is embodied in the well-known technical form. Alluding to a performance of 'Semiramide,' he said, with a malicious smile, 'I suppose you saw the beautiful decorations in it?' He has not received the Sisters Marchisio for fear they should sing to him, nor has he heard them in the theatre; he spoke warmly of Pasta, Lablache, Rubini, and others, then he added that I ought not to look with jealousy upon his budding talent as a pianoforte-player, but that, on the contrary, I should help to establish his reputation as such in Leipsic. He again questioned me with much interest about my intimacy with Clementi, and, calling me that master's worthy successor, he said he should like to visit me in Leipsic, if it were not for those dreadful railways, which he would never travel by. All this in his bright and lively way; but when we came to discuss Chevet, who wishes to supplant musical notes by ciphers, he maintained, in an earnest and dogmatic tone, that the system of notation, as it had developed itself since Pope Gregory's time, was sufficient for all musical requirements. He certainly could not withhold some appreciation for Chevet, but refused to indorse the certificate granted by the Institute in his favour ; the system he thought impracticable.

"The never-failing stream of conversation flowed on until eleven o'clock, when I was favoured with the inevitable kiss, which on this occasion was accompanied by special farewell blessings."

Shortly after Moscheles had left Paris, his son forwarded to him most friendly messages from Rossini, and continues thus—"Rossini sends you word that he is working hard at the piano, and, when you next come to Paris, you shall find him in better practice. . . . The conversation turning upon German music, I asked him 'which was his favourite among the great masters?' Of Beethoven he said, 'I take him twice a-week, Haydn four times, and Mozart every day. You will tell me that Beethoven is a Colossus who often gives you a dig in the ribs, while Mozart is always adorable; it is that the latter had the chance of going very young to Italy, at a time when they still sang well.' Of Weber he says, 'He has talent enough, and to spare' (*Il a du talent à revendre, celui-là*). He told me in reference to him, that, when the part of 'Tancred' was sung at Berlin by a bass voice, Weber had written violent articles not only against the management, but against the composer, so that, when Weber came to Paris, he did not venture to call on Rossini, who, however, let him know that he bore him no grudge for having made these attacks; on receipt of that message Weber called and they became acquainted.

"I asked him if he had met Byron in Venice? 'Only in a restaurant,' was the answer, 'where I was introduced to him ; our acquaintance, therefore, was very slight ; it seems he has spoken of me, but I don't know what he says.' I translated for him, in a somewhat milder form, Byron's words, which happened to be fresh in my memory—'They have been crucifying Othello into an opera; the music good but lugubrious, but, as for the words, all the real scenes with Iago cut out, and the greatest nonsense instead, the handkerchief turned into a billet-doux, and the first singer would not black his face—singing, dresses, and music very good.' The *maestro* regretted his ignorance of the English language, and said, 'In my day I gave much time to the study of our Italian literature. Dante is the man I owe most to; he taught me more music than all my music-masters put together, and when I wrote my 'Otello,' I would introduce those lines of Dante—you know the song of the gondolier. My librettist would have it that gondoliers never sang Dante, and but rarely Tasso, but I answered him, 'I know all about that better than you, for I have lived in Venice and you haven't. Dante I must and will have.'"

VI.

An ardent disciple of Wagner sums up his ideas of the mania for the Rossini music, which possessed Europe for fifteen years, in the following—"Rossini, the most gifted and spoiled of her sons [speaking of Italy] sallied forth with an innumerable army of Bacchantic melodies to conquer the world, the Messiah of joy, the breaker of thought and sorrow. Europe, by this time, had tired of the empty pomp of French declamation. It lent but too willing an ear to the new gospel, and eagerly quaffed the intoxicating potion, which Rossini poured out in inexhaustible streams." This very well expresses the delight of all the countries of Europe in music which for a long time almost monopolised the stage.

The charge of being a mere tune-spinner, the denial of invention, depth, and character, have been common watchwords in the mouths of critics wedded to other schools. But Rossini's place in music stands unshaken by all assaults. The vivacity of his style, the freshness of his melodies, the richness of his combinations, made all the Italian music that preceded him pale and colourless. No other writer revels in such luxury of beauty, and delights the ear with such a succession of delicious surprises in melody.

Henry Chorley, in his *Thirty Years' Musical Recollections*, rebukes the bigotry which sees nothing good but in its own kind—"I have never been able to understand why this [referring to the Rossinian richness of melody] should be contemned as necessarily false and meretricious— why the poet may not be allowed the benefit of his own period and time—why a lover of architecture is to be compelled to swear by the *Dom* at Bamberg, or by the Cathedral at Monreale—that he must abhor and denounce Michael Angelo's church or the Baths of Diocletian at Rome—why the person who enjoys 'Il Barbiere' is to be denounced as frivolously faithless to Mozart's 'Figaro'— and as incapable of comprehending 'Fidelio,' because the last act of 'Otello' and the second of 'Guillaume Tell' transport him into as great an enjoyment of its kind as do the duet in the cemetery between Don Juan and Leporello and the 'Prisoners' Chorus.' How much good, genial pleasure has not the world lost in music, owing to the pitting of styles one against the other! Your true traveller will be all the more alive to the beauty of Nuremberg because he has looked out over the 'Golden Shell' at Palermo; nor delight in Rhine and Danube the less because he has seen the glow of a southern sunset over the broken bridge at Avignon."

As grand and true as are many of the essential elements in the Wagner school of musical composition, the bitterness and narrowness of spite with which its upholders have pursued the memory of Rossini is equally offensive and unwarrantable. Rossini, indeed, did not revolutionise the forms of opera as transmitted to him by his predecessors, but he reformed and perfected them in various notable ways. Both in comic and serious opera, music owes much to Rossini. He substituted genuine singing for the endless recitative of which the Italian opera before him largely consisted; he brought the bass and baritone voices to the front, banished the pianoforte from the orchestra, and laid down the principle that the singer should deliver the notes written for him without additions of his own. He gave the chorus a much more important part than before, and elaborated the concerted music, especially in the *finales*, to a degree of artistic beauty before unknown in the Italian opera. Above all, he made the operatic orchestra what it is to-day. Every new instrument that was invented Rossini found a place for in his brilliant scores, and thereby incurred the warmest indignation of all writers of the old school. Before him the orchestras had consisted largely of strings, but Rossini added an equally imposing element of the brasses and reeds. True, Mozart had forestalled Rossini in many if not all these innovations, a fact which the Italian cheerfully admitted; for, with the simple frankness characteristic of the man, he always spoke of his obligations to and his admiration of the great German. To an admirer who was one day burning incense before him, Rossini said, in the spirit of Cimarosa quoted elsewhere, "My 'Barber' is only a bright farce, but in Mozart's 'Marriage of Figaro' you have the finest possible masterpiece of musical comedy."

With all concessions made to Mozart as the founder of the forms of modern opera, an equally high place must be given to Rossini for the vigour and audacity with which he made these available, and impressed them on all his contemporaries and successors. Though Rossini's self-love was flattered by constant adulation, his expressions of respect and admiration for such composers as Mozart, Gluck, Beethoven, and Cherubini, display what a catholic and generous nature he possessed. The judgment of Ambros, a severe critic, whose bias was against Rossini, shows what admiration was wrung from him by the last opera of the composer—"Of all that particularly characterises Rossini's early operas nothing is discoverable in 'Tell;' there is none of his usual mannerism; but, on the contrary, unusual richness of form and careful finish of detail, combined with grandeur of outline. Meretricious embellishment, shakes, runs, and cadences are carefully avoided in this work, which is natural and characteristic throughout; even the melodies have not the stamp and style of Rossini's earlier times, but only their graceful charm and lively colouring."

Rossini must be allowed to be unequalled in genuine comic opera, and to have attained a distinct greatness in serious opera, to be the most comprehensive, and, at the same time, the most national composer of Italy—to be, in short, the Mozart of his country. After all has been admitted and regretted—that he gave too little attention to musical science; that he often neglected to infuse into his work the depth and passion of which it was easily capable; that he placed too high a value on merely brilliant effects *ad captandum vulgus*—there remains the fact that his operas embody a mass of imperishable music, which will live with the art itself. Musicians of every country now admit his wondrous grace, his fertility and freshness of invention, his matchless treatment of the voice, his effectiveness in arrangement of the orchestra. He can never be made a model, for his genius had too much spontaneity and individuality of colour. But he impressed and modified music hardly less than Gluck, whose tastes and methods were entirely antagonistic to his own. That he should have retired from the exercise of his art while in the full flower of his genius is a perplexing fact. No stranger story is recorded in the annals of art with respect to a genius who filled the world with his glory, and then chose to vanish, " not unseen." On finishing his crowning stroke of genius and skill in " William Tell," he might have said with Shakespeare's enchanter, Prospero—

". . . . But this magic
I here abjure; and when I have required
Some heavenly music (which even now I do)
To work mine end upon their senses that
This airy charm is for, I'll break my staff—
Bury it certain fathoms in the earth,
And, deeper than did ever plummet sound,
I'll drown my book."

DONIZETTI AND BELLINI.

I.

A BRIGHT English critic, whose style is as charming as his judgments are good, says, in his study of the Donizetti music, "I find myself thinking of his music as I do of Domenichino's pictures of 'St. Agnes' and the 'Rosario' in the Bologna gallery, of the 'Diana' in the Borghese Palace at Rome, as pictures equable and skilful in the treatment of their subjects, neither devoid of beauty of form nor of colour, but which make neither the pulse quiver nor the eye wet; and then such a sweeping judgment is arrested by a work like the 'St. Jerome' in the Vatican, from which a spirit comes forth so strong and so exalted, that the beholder, however trained to examine and compare and collect, finds himself raised above all recollections of manner by the sudden ascent of talent into the higher world of genius. Essentially a second-rate composer,* Donizetti struck out some first-rate things in a happy hour, such as the last act of 'La Favorita.'"

Both Donizetti and Bellini, though far inferior to their master in richness of resources, in creative faculty and instinct for what may be called dramatic expression in pure musical form, were disciples of Rossini in their ideas and methods of work. Milton sang of Shakespeare—

> "Sweetest Shakespeare, Fancy's child,
> Warbles his native wood-notes wild!"

In a similar spirit, many learned critics have written of Rossini, and if it can be said of him in a musical sense that he had "little Latin and less Greek," still more true is it of the two popular composers whose works have filled so

---

* Mr. Chorley probably means "second-rate" as compared with the few very great names, which can be easily counted on the fingers.

large a space in the opera-house of the last thirty years, for their scores are singularly thin, measured by the standard of advanced musical science. Specially may this be said of Bellini, in many respects the greater of the two. There is scarcely to be found in music a more signal example to show that a marked individuality may rest on a narrow base. In justice to him, however, it may be said that his early death prevented him from doing full justice to his powers, for he had in him the material out of which the great artist is made. Let us first sketch the career of Donizetti, the author of sixty-four operas, besides a mass of other music, such as cantatas, ariettas, duets, church music, etc., in the short space of twenty-six years.

GAETANO DONIZETTI was born at Bergamo, 25th September 1798, his father being a man of moderate fortune.* Receiving a good classical education, the young Gäetano had three careers open before him: the bar, to which the will of his father inclined; architecture, indicated by his talent for drawing; and music, to which he was powerfully impelled by his own inclinations. His father sent him, at the age of seventeen, to Bologna to benefit by the instruction of Padre Mattei, who had also been Rossini's master. The young man showed no disposition for the heights of musical science as demanded by religious composition, and, much to his father's disgust, avowed his determination to write dramatic music. Paternal anger, for the elder Donizetti

---

* Admirers of the author of "Don Pasquale" and "Lucia" may be interested in knowing that Donizetti was of Scotch descent. His grandfather was a native of Perthshire, named Izett. The young Scot was beguiled by the fascinating tongue of a recruiting-sergeant into his Britannic majesty's service, and was taken prisoner by General La Hoche during the latter's invasion of Ireland. Already tired of a private's life, he accepted the situation, and was induced to become the French general's private secretary. Subsequently he drifted to Italy, and married an Italian lady of some rank, denationalising his own name into Donizetti. The Scottish predilections of our composer show themselves in the music of "Don Pasquale," noticeably in "Com' e gentil;" and the score of "Lucia" is strongly flavoured by Scottish sympathy and minstrelsy.

seems to have had a strain of Scotch obstinacy and austerity, made the youth enlist as a soldier, thinking to find time for musical work in the leisure of barrack-life. His first opera, "Enrico di Borgogna," was so highly admired by the Venetian manager, to whom it was offered, that he induced friends of his to release young Donizetti from his military servitude. He now pursued musical composition with a facility and industry which astonished even the Italians, familiar with feats of improvisation. In ten years twenty-eight operas were produced. Such names as "Olivo e Pasquale," "La Convenienze Teatrali," "Il Borgomaestro di Saardam," "Gianni di Calais," "L'Esule di Roma," "Il Castello di Kenilworth," "Imelda di Lambertazzi," have no musical significance, except as belonging to a catalogue of forgotten titles. Donizetti was so poorly paid that need drove him to rapid composition, which could not wait for the true afflatus.

It was not till 1831 that the evidence of a strong individuality was given, for hitherto he had shown little more than a slavish imitation of Rossini. "Anna Bolena" was produced at Milan and gained him great credit, and even now, though it is rarely sung even in Italy, it is much respected as a work of art as well as of promise. It was first interpreted by Pasta and Rubini, and Lablache won his earliest London triumph in it. "Marino Faleiro" was composed for Paris in 1835, and "L'Elisir d'Amore," one of the most graceful and pleasing of Donizetti's works, for Milan in 1832. "Lucia di Lammermoor," based on Sir Walter Scott's novel, was given to the public in 1835, and has remained the most popular of the composer's operas. Edgardo was written for the great French tenor, Duprez, Lucia for Persiani.

Donizetti's kindness of heart was illustrated by the interesting circumstances of his saving an obscure Neapolitan theatre from ruin. Hearing that it was on the verge of suspension and the performers in great distress, the composer sought them out and supplied their immediate wants. The manager said a new work from the pen of Donizetti would be his salvation. "You shall have one within a week," was the answer.

Lacking a subject, he himself rearranged an old French vaudeville, and within the week the libretto was written, the music composed, the parts learned, the opera performed, and the theatre saved. There could be no greater proof of his generosity of heart and his versatility of talent. In these days of bitter quarrelling over the rights of authors in their works, it may be amusing to know that Victor Hugo contested the rights of Italian librettists to borrow their plots from French plays. When "Lucrezia Borgia," composed for Milan in 1834, was produced at Paris in 1840, the French poet instituted a suit for an infringement of copyright. He gained his action, and "Lucrezia Borgia" became "La Rinegata," Pope Alexander the Sixth's Italians being metamorphosed into Turks.*

"Lucrezia Borgia," which, though based on one of the most dramatic of stories and full of beautiful music, is not dramatically treated by the composer, seems to mark the distance about half-way between the styles of Rossini and Verdi. In it there is but little recitative, and in the treatment of the chorus we find the method which Verdi afterwards came to use exclusively. When Donizetti revisited Paris in 1840, he produced in rapid succession "I Martiri," "La Fille du Regiment," and "La Favorita." In the second of these works Jenny Lind, Sontag, and Alboni won bright triumphs at a subsequent period.

---

* Victor Hugo did the same thing with Verdi's "Ernani," and other French authors followed with legal actions. The matter was finally arranged on condition of an indemnity being paid to the original French dramatists. The principle involved had been established nearly two centuries before. In a privilege granted to St. Amant in 1653 for the publication of his "Moïse Sauvé," it was forbidden to extract from that epic materials for a play or poem. The descendants of Beaumarchais fought for the same concession, and not very long ago it was decided that the translators and arrangers of "Le Nozze di Figaro" for the Théâtre Lyrique must share their receipts with the living representatives of the author of "Le Mariage de Figaro."

II.

"La Favorita," the story of which was drawn from "L'Ange de Nigida," and founded in the first instance on a French play, "Le Comte de Commingues," was put on the stage at the Académie with a magnificent cast and scenery, and achieved a success immediately great, for as a dramatic opera it stands far in the van of all the composer's productions. The whole of the grand fourth act, with the exception of one cavatina, was composed in three hours. Donizetti had been dining at the house of a friend, who was engaged in the evening to go to a ball. On leaving the house his host, with profuse apologies, begged the composer to stay and finish his coffee, of which Donizetti was inordinately fond. The latter sent out for music paper, and, finding himself in the vein for composition, went on writing till the completion of the work. He had just put the final stroke to the celebrated "Viens dans un autre patrie" when his friend returned at one in the morning to congratulate him on his excellent method of passing the time, and to hear the music sung for the first time from Donizetti's own lips.

After visiting Rome, Milan, and Vienna, for which last city he wrote "Linda di Chamouni," our composer returned to Paris, and in 1843 wrote "Don Pasquale" for the Théâtre Italien, and "Don Sebastian" for the Académie. Its lugubrious drama was fatal to the latter, but the brilliant gaiety of "Don Pasquale," rendered specially delightful by such a cast as Grisi, Mario, Tamburini, and Lablache, made it one of the great art attractions of Paris, and a Fortunatus purse for the manager. The music of this work, perhaps, is the best ever written by Donizetti, though it lacks the freshness and sentiment of his "Elisir d'Amore," which is steeped in rustic poetry and tenderness like a rose wet with dew. The production of "Maria di Rohan" in Vienna the same year, an opera with some powerful dramatic effects and bold music, gave Ronconi the opportunity to prove himself not merely a fine buffo singer, but a noble tragic actor. In this work Donizetti displays that rugged earnestness and vigour so characteristic of Verdi; and, had his life been greatly prolonged, we might have seen him ripen into a passion and power at odds with the elegant frivolity which for the most part tainted his musical quality. Donizetti's last opera, "Catarina Comaro," the sixty-third one represented, was brought out at Naples in the year 1844, without adding aught to his reputation. Of this composer's long list of works only ten or eleven retain any hold on the stage, his best serious operas being "La Favorita," "Linda," "Anna Bolena," "Lucrezia Borgia," and "Lucia;" the finest comic works, "L'Elisir d'Amore," "La Fille du Regiment," and "Don Pasquale."

In composing Donizetti never used the pianoforte, writing with great rapidity and never making corrections. Yet curious to say, he could not do anything without a small ivory scraper by his side, though never using it. It was given him by his father when commencing his career, with the injunction that, as he was determined to become a musician, he should make up his mind to write as little rubbish as possible, advice which Donizetti sometimes forgot.

The first signs of the malady, which was the cause of the composer's death, had already shown themselves in 1845. Fits of hallucination and all the symptoms of approaching derangement displayed themselves with increasing intensity. An incessant worker, overseer of his operas on twenty stages, he had to pay the tax by which his fame became his ruin. It is reported that he anticipated the coming scourge, for during the rehearsals of "Don Sebastian" he said, "I think I shall go mad yet." Still he would not put the bridle on his restless activity. At last paralysis seized him, and in January 1846 he was placed under the care of the celebrated Dr. Blanche at Ivry. In the hope that the mild influence of his native air might heal his distempered brain, he was sent to Bergamo, in 1848, but died in his brother's arms April 8th. The inhabitants of the Peninsula were then at war with Austria, and the bells that sounded the knell of Donizetti's departure mingled their solemn peals with the roar of the cannon fired to celebrate the victory of Goïto.

His faithful valet, Antoine, wrote to Adolphe Adam, describing his obsequies:—"More than four thousand persons," he relates, "were present at the ceremony. The procession was composed of the numerous clergy of Bergamo, the most illustrious members of the community and its environs, and of the civic guard of the town and the suburbs. The discharge of musketry, mingled with the light of three or four thousand torches, presented a fine effect; the whole was enhanced by the presence of three military bands and the most propitious weather it was possible to behold. The young gentlemen of Bergamo insisted on bearing the remains of their illustrious fellow-townsman, although the cemetery was a league and a-half from the town. The road was crowded its whole length by people who came from the surrounding country to witness the procession; and to give due praise to the inhabitants of Bergamo, never, hitherto, had such great honours been bestowed upon any member of that city."

III.

The future author of "Norma" and "La Sonnambula," Bellini, took his first lessons in music from his father, an organist at Catania.* He was sent to the Naples Conservatory by the generosity of a noble patron, and there was the fellow-pupil of Mercadante, a composer who blazed into a temporary lustre which threatened to outshine his fellows, but is now forgotten except by the antiquarian and the lover of church music. Bellini's early works, for he composed three before he was twenty, so pleased Barbaja, the manager of the San Carlo and La Scala, that he intrusted the youth with the libretto "Il Pirata," to be composed for representation at Florence. The tenor part was written for

* Bellini was born in 1802, nine years after his contemporary and rival, Donizetti, and died in 1835, thirteen years before.

the great singer, Rubini, whose name has no peer among artists since male sopranos were abolished by the outraged moral sense of society. Rubini retired to the country with Bellini, and studied, as they were produced, the simple touching airs with which he so delighted the public on the stage.

La Scala rang with plaudits when the opera was produced, and Bellini's career was assured. "I Capuletti" was his next successful opera, performed at Venice in 1829, but it never became popular out of Italy.

The significant period of Bellini's life was in the year 1831, which produced "La Sonnambula," to be followed by "Norma" the next season. Both these were written for and introduced before the Neapolitan public. In these works he reached his highest development, and by them he is best known to fame. The opera-story of "La Sonnambula," by Romani, an accomplished writer and scholar, is one of the most artistic and effective ever put into the hands of a composer. M. Scribe had already used the plot, both as the subject of a vaudeville and a choregraphic drama; but in Romani's hands it became a symmetrical story full of poetry and beauty. The music of this opera, throbbing with pure melody and simple emotion, as natural and fresh as a bed of wild flowers, went to the heart of the universal public, learned and unlearned; and, in spite of its scientific faults, it will never cease to delight future generations, as long as hearts beat and eyes are moistened with human tenderness and sympathy. And yet, of this work an English critic wrote, on its first London presentation:—

"Bellini has soared too high; there is nothing of grandeur, no touch of true pathos in the commonplace workings of his mind. He cannot reach the *opera semi-seria*; he should confine his powers to the musical drama, the one-act *opera buffa*." But the history of art-criticism is replete with such instances.

"Norma" was also a grand triumph for the young composer from the outset, especially as the lofty character of the Druid priestess was sung by that unapproachable lyric tragedienne, the Siddons of the opera, Madame Pasta. Bellini is said to have had this queen of dramatic song in his mind in writing the opera, and right nobly did she vindicate his judgment, for no European audience afterwards but was thrilled and carried away by her masterpiece of acting and singing in this part.

Bellini himself considered "Norma" his *chef d'œuvre*. A beautiful Parisienne attempted to extract from his reluctant lips his preference of his own works. The lady finally overcame his evasions by the query, "But if you were out at sea, and should be shipwrecked——" "Ah!" he cried, without allowing her to finish. "I would leave all the rest and try to save 'Norma.'"

"I Puritani" was composed for and performed at Paris in 1834, by that splendid quartette of artists, Grisi, Rubini, Tamburini, and Lablache. Bellini compelled the singers to execute after *his* style. While Rubini was rehearsing the tenor part, the composer cried out in rage, "You put no life into your music. Show some feeling. Don't you know what love is?" Then changing his tone, "Don't you know your voice is a gold-mine that has not been fully explored? You are an excellent artist, but that is not sufficient. You must forget yourself and represent Gualtiero. Let's try again." The tenor, stung by the admonition, then gave the part magnificently. After the success of "I Puritani," the composer received the Cross of the Legion of Honour, an honour then not often bestowed. The "Puritani" season is still remembered, it is said, with peculiar pleasure by the older connoisseurs of Paris and London, as the enthusiasm awakened in musical circles has rarely been equalled.

Bellini had placed himself under contract to write two new works immediately, one for Paris, the other for Naples, and retired to the villa of a friend at Puteaux to insure the more complete seclusion. Here, while pursuing his art with almost sleepless ardour, he was attacked by his fatal malady, intestinal fever.

"From his youth up," says his biographer Mould,

"Vincenzo's eagerness in his art was such as to keep him at the piano night and day, till he was obliged forcibly to leave it. The ruling passion accompanied him through his short life, and by the assiduity with which he pursued it brought on the dysentery which closed his brilliant career, peopling his last hours with the figures of those to whom his works owed so much of their success. During the moments of delirium which preceded his death, he was constantly speaking of Lablache, Tamburini, and Grisi; and one of his last recognisable impressions was that he was present at a brilliant representation of his last opera at the Salle Favart. His earthly career closed September 23, 1835, at the age of thirty-three.

On the eve of his interment, the Théâtre Italien reopened with the "Puritani." It was an occasion full of solemn gloom. Both the musicians and audience broke from time to time into sobs. Tamburini, in particular, was so oppressed by the death of his young friend that his vocalisation, generally so perfect, was often at fault, while the faces of Grisi, Rubini, and Lablache too plainly showed their aching hearts.

Rossini, Cherubini, Paer, and Carafa had charge of the funeral, and M. Habeneck, *chief d' orchestre* of the Académie Royale, of the music. The next remarkable piece on the funeral programme was a *Lacrymosa* for four voices without accompaniment, in which the text of the Latin hymn was united to the beautiful tenor melody in the third act of the "Puritani." This was executed by Rubini, Ivanoff, Tamburini, and Lablache. The services were performed at the Church of the Invalides, and the remains were interred in Père Lachaise.

Rossini had ever shown great love for Bellini, and Rosario Bellini, the stricken father, wrote to him a touching letter, in which, after speaking of his grief and despair, the old man said—

"You always encouraged the object of my eternal regret in his labours; you took him under your protection, you neglected nothing that could increase his glory and his welfare. After my son's death, what have you not done to honour my son's name and render it dear to posterity? I learned this from the newspapers; and I am penetrated with gratitude for your excessive kindness as well as for that of a number of distinguished artists, which also I shall never forget. Pray, sir, be my interpreter, and tell these artists that the father and family of Bellini, as well as of our compatriots of Catania, will cherish an imperishable recollection of this generous conduct. I shall never cease to remember how much you did for my son. I shall make known everywhere, in the midst of my tears, what an affectionate heart belongs to the great Rossini, and how kind, hospitable, and full of feeling are the artists of France."

Bellini was affable, sincere, honest, and affectionate. Nature gave him a beautiful and ingenuous face, noble features, large, clear blue eyes, and abundant light hair. His countenance instantly won on the regards of all that met him. His disposition was melancholy; a secret depression often crept over his most cheerful hours. We are told there was a tender romance in his earlier life. The father of the lady he loved, a Neapolitan judge, refused his suit on account of his inferior social position. When Bellini became famous the judge wished to make amends, but Bellini's pride interfered. Soon after the young lady, who loved him unalterably, died, and it is said the composer never recovered from the shock.

IV.

Donizetti and Bellini were peculiarly moulded by the great genius of Rossini, but in their best works they show individuality, colour, and special creative activity. The former composer, one of the most affluent in the annals of music, seemed to become more fresh in his fancies with increased production. He is an example of how little the skill and touch, belonging to unceasing work, should be despised in comparison with what is called inspiration.

Donizetti arrived at his freshest creations at a time when there seemed but little left for him except the trite and threadbare. There are no melodies so rich and well fancied as those to be found in his later works; and in sense of dramatic form and effective instrumentation (always a faulty point with Donizetti) he displayed great progress at the last. It is, however, a noteworthy fact, that the latest Italian composers have shown themselves quite weak in composing expressly for the orchestra. No operatic overture since "William Tell" has been produced by this school of music, worthy to be rendered in a concert-room.

Donizetti lacked the dramatic instinct in conceiving his music. In attempting it he became hollow and theatric; and beautiful as are the melodies and concerted pieces in "Lucia," where the subject ought to inspire a vivid dramatic nature with such telling effects, it is in the latter sense one of the most disappointing of operas.

He redeemed himself for the nonce, however, in the fourth act of "La Favorita," where there is enough musical and dramatic beauty to condone the sins of the other three acts. The solemn and affecting church chant, the passionate romance for the tenor, the great closing duet in which the ecstasy of despair rises to that of exaltation, the resistless sweep of the rhythm—all mark one of the most effective single acts ever written. He showed himself here worthy of companionship with Rossini and Meyerbeer.

In his comic operas, "L'Elisir d'Amore," "La Fille du Regiment," and "Don Pasquale," there is a continual well-spring of sunny, bubbling humour. They are slight, brilliant, and catching, everything that pedantry condemns, and the popular taste delights in. Mendelssohn, the last of the German classical composers, admired "L'Elisir," so much that he said he would have liked to have written it himself. It may be said that while Donizetti lacks grand conceptions, or even great beauties for the most part, his operas contain so much that is agreeable, so many excellent opportunities for vocal display, such harmony between sound and situation, that he will probably retain a hold on the stage when much greater composers are only known to the general public by name.

Bellini, with less fertility and grace, possessed far more picturesqueness and intensity. His powers of imagination transcended his command over the working tools of his art. Even more lacking in exact and extended musical science than Donizetti, he could express what came within his range with a simple vigour, grasp, and beauty, which make him a truly dramatic composer. In addition to this, a matter which many great composers ignore, Bellini had extraordinary skill in writing music for the voice, not that which merely gave opportunity for executive trickery and embellishment, but the genuine accents of passion, pathos, and tenderness, in forms best adapted to be easily and effectively delivered.

He had no flexibility, no command over mirthful inspiration, such as we hear in Mozart, Rossini, or even Donizetti. But his monotone is in subtle *rapport* with the graver aspects of nature and life. Chorley sums up this characteristic of Bellini in the following words:—

"In spite of the inexperience with which the instrumental score is filled up, the opening scene of 'Norma' in the dim druidical wood bears the true character of ancient sylvan antiquity. There is daybreak again—a fresh tone of reveille—in the prelude to 'I Puritani.' If Bellini's genius was not versatile in its means of expression, if it had not gathered all the appliances by which science fertilises Nature, it beyond all doubt included appreciation of truth, no less than instinct for beauty."

VERDI.

I.

In 1872 the Khédive of Egypt, an oriental ruler, whose love of western art and civilisation has since tangled him in economic meshes to escape from which has cost him his independence, produced a new opera with barbaric splendour of appointments, at Grand Cairo. The spacious theatre blazed with fantastic dresses and showy uniforms, and the curtain rose on a drama which gave a glimpse to the Arabs, Copts, and Franks present of the life and religion, the loves and hates of ancient Pharaonic times, set to music by the most celebrated of living Italian composers.

That an eastern prince should have commissioned Giuseppe Verdi to write "Aida" for him, in his desire to emulate western sovereigns as a patron of art, is an interesting fact, but not wonderful or significant.

The opera itself was freighted, however, with peculiar significance as an artistic work, far surpassing that of the circumstances which gave it origin, or which saw its first production in the mysterious land of the Nile and Sphinx.

Originally a pupil, thoroughly imbued with the method and spirit of Rossini, though never lacking in original quality, Verdi as a young man shared the suffrages of admiring audiences with Donizetti and Bellini. Even when he diverged widely from his parent stem and took rank as the representative of the melodramatic school of music, he remained true to the instincts of his Italian training.

The remarkable fact is that Verdi, at the age of fifty-eight, when it might have been safely assumed that his theories and preferences were finally crystallised, produced an opera in which he clasped hands with the German enthusiast, who preached an art system radically opposed to his own, and lashed with scathing satire the whole musical cult of the Italian race.

In "Aida" and the "Manzoni Mass," written in 1873, Verdi, the leader among living Italian composers, practically conceded that, in the long, bitterly fought battle between Teuton and Italian in music, the former was the victor. In the opera we find a new departure, which, if not embodying all the philosophy of the "new school," is stamped with its salient traits—viz., the subordination of all the individual effects to the perfection and symmetry of the whole; a lavish demand on all the sister arts to contribute their rich gifts to the heightening of the illusion; a tendency to enrich the harmonic value in the choruses, the concerted pieces, and the instrumentation, to the great sacrifice of the solo pieces; the use of the heroic and mythical element as a theme.

Verdi, the subject of this interesting revolution, has filled a very brilliant place in modern musical art, and his career has been in some ways as picturesque as his music.

Verdi's parents were literally hewers of wood and drawers of water, earning their bread, after the manner of Italian peasants, at a small settlement called La Roncali, near Busseto, where the future composer was born on October 9, 1813.

His earliest recollections were with the little village church, where the little Giuseppe listened with delight to the church organ, for, as with all great musicians, his fondness for music showed itself at a very early age. The elder Verdi, though very poor, gratified the child's love of music when he was about eight by buying a small spinet, and placing him under the instruction of Provesi, a teacher in Busseto. The boy entered on his studies with ardour, and made more rapid progress than the slender facilities which were allowed him would ordinarily justify.

An event soon occurred which was destined to wield a lasting influence on his destiny. He one day heard a skilful performance on a fine piano, while passing by one of the better houses of Busseto. From that time a constant fascination drew him to the house; for day after day he lingered and seemed unwilling to go away lest he should perchance lose some of the enchanting sounds which so enraptured him. The owner of the premises was a rich merchant, one Antonio Barezzi, a cultivated and high-minded man, and a passionate lover of music withal. 'Twas his daughter whose playing gave the young Verdi such pleasure.

Signor Barezzi had often seen the lingering and absorbed lad, who stood as if in a dream, oblivious to all that passed around him in the practical work-a-day world. So one day he accosted him pleasantly and inquired why he came so constantly and stayed so long doing nothing.

"I play the piano a little," said the boy, "and I like to come here and listen to the fine playing in your house."

"Oh! if that is the case, come in with me that you may enjoy it more at your ease, and hereafter you are welcome to do so whenever you feel inclined."

It may be imagined the delighted boy did not refuse the kind invitation, and the acquaintance soon ripened into intimacy, for the rich merchant learned to regard the bright young musician with much affection, which it is needless to say was warmly returned. Verdi was untiring in study and spent the early years of his youth in humble quiet, in the midst of those beauties of nature which have so powerful an influence in moulding great susceptibilities. At his seventeenth year he had acquired as much musical knowledge as could be acquired at a place like Busseto, and he became anxious to go to Milan to continue his studies. The poverty of his family precluding any assistance from this quarter, he was obliged to find help from an eleemosynary fund then existing in his native town. This was an institution called the Monte di Pietà, which offered yearly to four young men the sum of twenty-five *lire* a-month each, in order to help them to an education; and Verdi, making an application and sustained by the influence of his friend the rich merchant, was one of the four whose good fortune it was to be selected.

The allowance thus obtained, with some assistance from Barezzi, enabled the ambitious young musician to go to Milan, carrying with him some of his compositions. When he presented himself for examination at the Conservatory, he was made to play on the piano, and his compositions examined. The result fell on his hopes like a thunderbolt. The pedantic and narrow-minded examiners not only scoffed at the state of his musical knowledge, but told him he was incapable of becoming a musician. To weaker souls this would have been a terrible discouragement, but to his ardour and self-confidence it was only a challenge. Barezzi had equal confidence in the abilities of his *protégé*, and warmly encouraged him to work and hope. Verdi engaged an excellent private teacher and pursued his studies with unflagging energy, denying himself all but the barest necessities, and going sometimes without sufficient food.

A stroke of fortune now fell in his way; the place of organist fell vacant at the Busseto church, and Verdi was appointed to fill it. He returned home, and was soon afterwards married to the daughter of the benefactor to whom he owed so much. He continued to apply himself with great diligence to the study of his art, and completed an opera early in 1839. He succeeded in arranging for the production of this work, "L'Oberto, Conte de San Bonifacio," at La Scala, Milan; but it excited little comment and was soon forgotten, like the scores of other shallow or immature compositions so prolifically produced in Italy.

The impresario, Merelli, believed in the young composer though, for he thought he discovered signs of genius. So he gave him a contract to write three operas, one of which was to be an *opera buffa*, and to be ready in the following autumn. With hopeful spirits Verdi set to work on the opera, but that year of 1840 was to be one of great trouble and trial. Hardly had he set to work all afire with eagerness and hope, when he was seized with severe illness. His recovery was followed by the successive sickening of his two children, who died, a terrible blow to the father's fond heart. Fate had the crowning stroke though still to give, for the young mother, agonised by this loss, was seized with a fatal inflammation of the brain. Thus within a brief period Verdi was bereft of all the sweet consolations of home, and his life became a burden to him. Under these conditions he was to write a comic opera, full of sparkle, gaiety, and humour. Can we wonder that his work was a failure? The public came to be amused by bright, joyous music, for it was nothing to them that the composer's heart was dead with grief at his afflictions. The audience hissed " Un Giorno di Regno," for it proved a funereal attempt at mirth. So Verdi sought to annul the contract.

To this the impresario replied—

"So be it, if you wish ; but, whenever you want to write again on the same terms, you will find me ready."

To tell the truth, the composer was discouraged by his want of success, and wholly broken down by his numerous trials. He now withdrew from all society, and, having hired a small room in an out-of-the-way part of Milan, passed most of his time in reading the worst books that could be found, rarely going out, unless occasionally in the evening, never giving his attention to study of any kind, and never touching the piano. Such was his life from October 1840 to January 1841. One evening, early in the new year, while out walking, he chanced to meet Merelli, who took him by the arm; and, as they sauntered towards the theatre, the impresario told him that he was in great trouble, Nicolai, who was to write an opera for him, having refused to accept a *libretto* entitled "Nabucco."

To this Verdi replied—

"I am glad to be able to relieve you of your difficulty. Don't you remember the libretto of 'Il Proscritto,' which you procured for me, and for which I have never composed the music? Give that to Nicolai in place of 'Nabucco."

Merelli thanked him for his kind offer, and, as they reached the theatre, asked him to go in, that they might ascertain whether the manuscript of "Il Proscritto" was really there. It was at length found, and Verdi was on the point of leaving, when Merelli slipped into his pocket the book of "Nabucco," asking him to look it over. For want of something to do, he took up the drama the next morning and read it through, realising how truly grand it was in conception. But, as a lover forces himself to feign indifference to his coquettish *innamorata*, so he, disregarding his inclinations, returned the manuscript to Merelli that same day.

"Well?" said Merelli, inquiringly.

"*Musicabilissimo!*" he replied; "full of dramatic power and telling situations!"

"Take it home with you, then, and write the music for it."

Verdi declared that he did not wish to compose, but the worthy impresario forced the manuscript on him, and persisted that he should undertake the work. The composer returned home with the libretto, but threw it on one side without looking at it, and for the next five months continued his reading of bad romances and yellow-covered novels.

The impulse of work soon came again, however. One beautiful June day the manuscript met his eye, while looking listlessly over some old papers. He read one scene and was struck by its beauty. The instinct of musical creation rushed over him with irresistible force; he seated himself at the piano, so long silent, and began composing the music. The ice was broken. Verdi soon entered into the spirit of the work, and in three months "Nabucco" was entirely completed. Merelli gladly accepted it, and it was performed at La Scala in the spring of 1842. As a result Verdi was besieged with petitions for new works from every impresario in Italy.

II

From 1842 to 1851 Verdi's busy imagination produced a series of operas, which disputed the palm of popularity with the foremost composers of his time. "I Lombardi," brought out at La Scala in 1843; "Ernani," at Venice in 1844; "I Due Foscari," at Rome in 1844; "Giovanna D'Arco," at Milan, and "Alzira," at Naples in 1845; "Attila," at Venice in 1846; and "Macbetto," at Florence in 1847, were—all of them—successful works. The last created such a genuine enthusiasm that he was crowned with a golden laurel-wreath and escorted home from the theatre by an enormous crowd. "I Masnadieri" was written for Jenny Lind, and performed first in London in 1847 with that great singer, Gardoni, and Lablache, in the cast. His next productions were "Il Corsaro," brought out at Trieste in 1848; "La Battaglia di Legnano" at Rome in 1849; "Luisa Miller" at Naples in the same year; and "Stiffelio" at Trieste in 1850. By this series of works Verdi impressed himself powerfully on his age, but in them he preserved faithfully the colour and style of the school in which he had been trained. But he had now arrived at the commencement of his transition period. A distinguished French critic marks this change in the following summary:—"When Verdi began to write, the influences of foreign literature and new theories on art had excited Italian composers to seek a violent expression of the passions, and to leave the interpretation of amiable and delicate sentiments for that of sombre flights of the soul. A serious mind gifted with a rich imagination, Verdi became chief of the new school. His music became more intense and dramatic; by vigour, energy, *verve*, a certain ruggedness and sharpness, by powerful effects of sound, he conquered an immense popularity in Italy, where success had hitherto been attained only by the charm, suavity, and abundance of the melodies produced."

In "Rigoletto," produced in Venice in 1851, the full flowering of his genius into the melodramatic style was signally shown. The opera story adapted from Victor Hugo's "Le Roi s'amuse" is itself one of the most dramatic of plots, and it seemed to have fired the composer into music singularly vigorous, full of startling effects and novel treatment. Two years afterwards were brought out at Rome and Venice respectively two operas, stamped with the same salient qualities, "Il Trovatore" and "La Traviata," the last a lyric adaptation of Dumas *fils's* "Dame aux Camélias." These three operas have generally been considered his masterpieces, though it is more than possible that the riper judgment of the future will not sustain this claim. Their popularity was such that Verdi's time was absorbed for several years in their production at various opera-houses, utterly precluding new compositions. Of his later operas may be mentioned "Les Vêpres Siciliennes," produced in Paris in 1855; "Un Ballo in Maschera," performed at Rome in 1859; "La Forza del Destino," written for St. Petersburg, where it was sung in 1863; "Don Carlos," produced in London in 1867; and "Aida" in Grand Cairo in 1872. When the latter work was finished, Verdi had composed twenty-nine operas, besides lesser works, and attained the aged of fifty-seven.

Verdi's energies have not been confined to music. An ardent patriot, he has displayed the deepest interest in the affairs of his country, and taken an active part in its tangled politics. After the war of 1859 he was chosen a member of the Assembly of Parma, and was one of the most influential advocates for the annexation to Sardinia. Italian unity found in him a passionate advocate, and, when the occasion came, his artistic talent and earnestness proved that they might have made a vigorous mark in political oratory as well as in music.

The cry of "Viva Verdi" often resounded through Sardinia and Italy, and it was one of the war-slogans of the Italian war of liberation. This enigma is explained in the fact that the five letters of his name are the initials of those of Vittorio Emanuele Rè D'Italia. His private resources were liberally poured forth to help the national cause, and in 1861 he was chosen a deputy in Parliament from Parma. Ten years later he was appointed by the Minister of Public Instruction to superintend the reorganisation of the National Musical Institute.

The many decorations and titular distinctions lavished on him show the high esteem in which he is held. He is a member of the Legion of Honour, corresponding member of the French Academy of Fine Arts, grand cross of the Prussian order of St. Stanislaus, of the order of the Crown of Italy, and of the Egyptian order of Osmanli. He divides his life between a beautiful residence at Genoa, where he overlooks the waters of the sparkling Mediterranean, and a country villa near his native Busseto, a house of quaint artistic architecture, approached by a venerable, moss-grown stone bridge, at the foot of which are a large park and artificial lake. When he takes his evening walks, the peasantry, who are devotedly attached to him, unite in singing choruses from his operas.

In Verdi's bedroom, where alone he composes, is a fine piano—of which instrument, as well as of the violin, he is a master—a modest library, and an oddly-shaped writing-desk. Pictures and statuettes, of which he is very fond, are thickly strewn about the whole house. Verdi is a man of vigorous and active habits, taking an ardent interest in agriculture. But the larger part of his time is taken up in composing, writing letters, and reading works on philosophy, politics, and history. His personal appearance is very distinguished. A tall figure with sturdy limbs and square shoulders, surmounted by a finely-shaped head; abundant hair, beard, and moustache, whose black is sprinkled with grey; dark-grey eyes, regular features, and an earnest, sometimes intense, expression make him a noticeable-looking man. Much sought after in the brilliant society of Florence, Rome, and Paris, our composer spends most of his time in the elegant seclusion of home.

III.

Verdi is the most nervous, theatric, sensuous composer of the present century. Measured by the highest standard, his style must be criticised as often spasmodic, tawdry, and meretricious. He instinctively adopts a bold and eccentric treatment of musical themes; and, though there are always to be found stirring movements in his scores as well as in his opera stories, he constantly offends refined taste by sensation and violence.

With a redundancy of melody, too often of the cheap and shallow kind, he rarely fails to please the masses of opera-goers, for his works enjoy a popularity not shared at present by any other composer. In Verdi a sudden blaze of song, brief spirited airs, duets, trios, etc., take the place of the elaborate and beautiful music, chiselled into order and symmetry, which characterises most of the great composers of the past. Energy of immediate impression is thus gained at the expense of that deep, lingering power, full of the subtile side-lights and shadows of suggestion, which is the crowning benison of great music. He stuns the ear and captivates the senses, but does not subdue the soul.

Yet, despite the grievous faults of these operas, they blaze with gems, and we catch here and there true swallow-flights of genius, that the noblest would not disown. With all his puerilities there is a mixture of grandeur. There are passages in "Ernani," "Rigoletto," "Traviata," "Trovatore," and "Aida," so strong and dignified, that it provokes a wonder that one with such capacity for greatness should often descend into such bathos.

To better illustrate the false art which mars so much of Verdi's dramatic method, a comparison between his "Rigoletto," so often claimed as his best work, and Rossini's "Otello" will be opportune. The air sung by Gilda in the "Rigoletto," when she retires to sleep on the eve of the outrage, is an empty, sentimental yawn; and in the quartet of the last act, a noble dramatic opportunity, she ejects a chain of disconnected, unmusical sobs, as offensive as Violetta's consumptive cough. Desdemona's agitated air, on the other hand, under Rossini's treatment, though broken short in the vocal phrase, is magnificently sustained by the orchestra, and a genuine passion is made consistently musical; and then the wonderful burst of bravura, where despair and resolution run riot without violating the bounds of strict beauty in music—these are master-strokes of genius restrained by art.

In Verdi, passion too often misses intensity and becomes hysterical. He lacks the elements of tenderness and humour, but is frequently picturesque and charming by his warmth and boldness of colour. His attempts to express the gay and mirthful, as for instance in the masquerade music of "Traviata" and the dance music of "Rigoletto," are dreary, ghastly, and saddening; while his ideas of tenderness are apt to take the form of mere sentimentality. Yet generalities fail in describing him, for occasionally he attains effects strong in their pathos, and artistically admirable; as, for example, the slow air for the heroine, and the dreamy song for the gipsy mother in the last act of "Trovatore." An artist who thus contradicts himself is a perplexing problem, but we must judge him by the habitual, not the occasional.

Verdi is always thoroughly in earnest, never frivolous. He walks on stilts indeed, instead of treading the ground or cleaving the air, but is never timid or tame in aim or execution. If he cannot stir the emotions of the soul he subdues and absorbs the attention against even the dictates of the better taste; while genuine beauties gleaming through picturesque rubbish often repay the true musician for what he has undergone.

So far this composer has been essentially representative of melodramatic music, with all the faults and virtues of such a style. In "Aida," his last work, the world remarked a striking change. The noble orchestration, the power and beauty of the choruses, the sustained dignity of treatment, the seriousness and pathos of the whole work, reveal how deeply new purposes and methods have been fermenting in the composer's development. Yet in the very prime of his powers, though no longer young, his next work ought to settle the value of the hopes raised by the last.

NOTE BY THE EDITOR.—In 1874 Verdi composed his "Requiem Mass." It is written in a popular style, and received unanimous praise from the Italian critics, and as thorough condemnation from those of Germany, in particular from Herr Hans von Bülow, the celebrated pianist. It was chance which induced the composer to attempt sacred music. On the death of Rossini, Verdi suggested that a "Requiem" should be written in memory of the dead master, by thirteen Italian composers in combination, and that the mass should be performed on every hundredth anniversary of the death in the cathedral of Bologna. The attempt naturally proved a complete failure, owing to the impossibility of unity in the method of such a composition. On the death, however, of Alessandro Manzoni at Milan, Verdi wrote for the anniversary of the great man's death a Requiem, into which he incorporated the movement *Libera me* which he had previously written for the Rossini Requiem.

In 1881 "Simon Boccanegra" was performed at Milan, with very partial success. It was a revival of an opera Verdi had written ten years previously, but which had failed owing to a confused libretto and a bad interpretation. It, however, in its present form, falls short in merit when compared with the composer's finest operas—"Rigoletto," "Il Trovatore," and "Aida."

Verdi's last work, "Otello," has been brought out since this volume went to press; its brilliant success at the theatre of La Scala, Milan, on the 5th of February, is a matter of such recent date that it is unnecessary to enlarge upon it at present. Verdi has accepted an invitation from the managers of the Grand Opera at Paris to produce "Otello" at their theatre in the course of the year; the libretto will be translated by M. du Loche, and a ballet will be introduced in the second act, according to the traditions of the French opera. In all probability it will also be performed in London, but as yet no public intimation on the subject has been made.

It is of course impossible at present for any definite decision to be pronounced on the merits of this latest work compared with the composer's other operas; the few following facts, however, concerning "Otello," excerpted from the reports of the musical critics of our leading journals, may prove of interest.

Verdi was first induced to undertake the composition of "Otello" on the occasion of the performance of his "Messa da Requiem," at the Scala, for the benefit of the sufferers by the inundations at Ferrara. The next day he gave a dinner to the four principal solo singers, at which were present several friends, among them Signor Faccio and Signor Ricordi. The latter laid siege to the *maestro*, trying to persuade him to undertake a new work. For a long time Verdi resisted, and his wife declared that probably only a Skakespearian subject could induce him to take up his pen again. A few hours later Faccio and Ricordi went to Boïto, who at once agreed to make the third in the generous conspiracy, and two days after sent to Verdi a complete sketch of the plan for the opera, following strictly the Shakespearian tragedy. Verdi approved of the sketch, and from that moment it fell to the part of Giulia Ricordi to urge on the composer and the poet by constant reminders. Every Christmas he sent to Verdi's house an "Othello" formed of chocolate, which, at first very small, grew larger as the opera progressed.

Rossini's famous opera on the same subject, in which Pasta and

Malibran won renown in their day, was produced in Naples in the autumn of 1816. How it impressed Lord Byron, who saw it in Venice soon afterwards, we learn from an amusing postscript to his letter to Samuel Rogers, wherein he says:—"They have been crucifying 'Othello' into an opera; the music good but lugubrious; but as for the words—all the real scenes with Iago cut out and the greatest nonsense instead. The handkerchief turned into a billet-doux, and the first singer would not black his face, for some exquisite reason assigned in the preface." In this curiously maimed and mangled version, Roderigo became of far more importance than the Moor's crafty lieutenant. Odder still was the modified French version played in 1823, when the leading tenor, David, thinking the final duet with Desdemona unsuited to his voice, substituted the soft and pretty duet, "Amor, possente nume," from Rossini's later opera "Armida." A contemporary French critic, who witnessed this curious performance, observes—"As it was impossible to kill Desdemona to such a tune, the Moor, after giving way to the most violent jealousy, sheathed his dagger, and began the duet in the most tender and graceful manner; after which he took Desdemona politely by the hand and retired, amidst the applause and bravos of the public, who seemed to think it quite natural that the piece should finish in this fashion."

Verdi, with that healthy horror of tiring the public which has always distinguished him, declined Signor Boïto's proposal to treat the subject in five acts; and, Shakespeare's introductory act being discarded, the first act of the opera corresponds with the second act of the tragedy. After that the musical drama marches scene by scene, and situation by situation, on parallel lines with the play, with this important exception only—namely, that the "Willow Song," as in Rossini's opera, is transferred from the last act but one to the last act. There are no symphonic pieces in "Othello," unless the brief orchestral presentation of the "Willow Song" before the fourth act can be so considered. The work is a drama set to music, in which there are no repetitions, no detached or detachable airs written specially for the singers, no passages of display, nothing whatever in the way of music but what is absolutely necessary for the elucidation of the piece. The influence of Wagner is perceptible here and there, but there are no leading motives, and the general style is that of Verdi at his best, as in "Aida."

"It is well for the Italians that, in hailing Verdi as a great man of genius, they are not honouring one who moves the profane world to compassion, scarcely distinguished from contempt, by weakness of character. His work is so good throughout, so full of method, so complete, because his nature is complete and his life methodical; for the same reason, no doubt, he has preserved to a ripe old age all the essential qualities of the genius of his manhood. The leaves that remain on the Autumnal trees are yet green, and the birds still sing among them. 'Otello' itself will, in some form or other, soon be heard in London; and it is pleasant to think that the subject is taken from one of the greatest works of the greatest of all literary Englishmen. The theme is noble, and so, apparently, is the treatment. Nor should we forget that so distinguished a composer as Signor Boïto has not disdained, nay, has elected, to compose the libretto for the old *maestro*. That is a form and sample of co-operation we can all admire. Will Italy One and Free continue to produce great and original musicians? Verdi is the product of other and more melancholy times. Be that as it may, better national freedom, civil activity, and personal dignity, than all the operas that were ever written."

CHERUBINI AND HIS PREDECESSORS.

I.

In France, as in Italy, the regular musical drama was preceded by mysteries, masks, and religious plays, which introduced short musical parts, as also action, mechanical effects, and dancing. The ballet, however, where dancing was the prominent feature, remained for a long time the favourite amusement of the French court until the advent of Jean Baptiste Lulli. The young Florentine, after having served in the king's band, was promoted to be its chief, and the composer of the music of the court ballets. Lulli, born in 1633, was bought of his parents by Chevalier de Guise, and sent to Paris as a present to Mdlle. de Montpensier, the king's niece. His capricious mistress, after a year or two, deposed the boy of fifteen from the position of page to that of scullion; but Count Nogent, accidentally hearing him sing and struck by his musical talent, influenced the princess to place him under the care of good masters. Lulli made such rapid progress that he soon commenced to compose music of a style superior to that before current in divertisements of the French court.

The name of Philippe Quinault is closely associated with the musical career of Lulli; for to the poet the musician was indebted for his best librettos. Born at Paris in 1636, Quinault's genius for poetry displayed itself at an early age. Before he was twenty he had written several successful comedies. Though he produced many plays, both tragedies and comedies, well known to readers of French poetry, his operatic poems are those which have rendered his memory illustrious. He died on November 29, 1688. It is said that during his last illness he was extremely penitent on account of the voluptuous tendency of his works. All his lyrical dramas are full of beauty, but "Atys," "Phaëton," "Isis," and "Armide" have been ranked the highest. "Armide" was the last of the poet's efforts, and Lulli was so much in love with the opera, when completed, that he had it performed over and over again for his own pleasure without any other auditor. When "Atys" was performed first in 1676, the eager throng began to pour in the theatre at ten o'clock in the morning, and by noon the building was filled. The King and the Count were charmed with the work in spite of the bitter dislike of Boileau, the Aristarchus of his age. "Put me in a place where I shall not be able to hear the words," said the latter to the box-keeper; "I like Lulli's music very much, but have a sovereign contempt for Quinault's words." Lulli obliged the poet to write "Armide" five times over, and the felicity of his treatment is proved by the fact that Gluck afterwards set the same poem to the music which is still occasionally sung in Germany.

Lulli in the course of his musical career became so great a favourite with the King that the originally obscure kitchen-boy was ennobled. He was made one of the King's secretaries in spite of the loud murmurs of this pampered fraternity against receiving into their body a player and a buffoon. The musician's wit and affability, however, finally dissipated these prejudices, especially as he was wealthy and of irreproachable character.

The King having had a severe illness in 1686, Lulli composed a "Te Deum" in honour of his recovery. When this was given, the musician, in beating time with great ardour, struck his toe with his baton. This brought on a mortification, and there was great grief when it was announced that he could not recover. The Princes de Vendôme lodged four thousand pistoles in the hands of a banker, to be paid to any physician who would cure him. Shortly before his death his confessor severely reproached him for the licentiousness of his operas, and refused to give him absolution unless he consented to burn the score of "Achille et Polyxène," which was ready for the stage. The manuscript was put into the flames, and the priest made the musician's peace with God. One of the young princes visited him a few days after, when he seemed a little better.

"What, Baptiste," the former said, "have you burned your opera? You were a fool for giving such credit to a gloomy confessor and burning good music."

"Hush, hush!" whispered Lulli, with a satirical smile on his lip. "I cheated the good father. I only burned a copy."

He died singing the words, "*Il faut mourir, pécheur, il faut maurir,*" to one of his own opera airs.

Lulli was not only a composer, but created his own orchestra, trained his artists in acting and singing, and was machinist as well as ballet-master and music-director. He was intimate with Corneille, Molière, La Fontaine, and Boileau; and these great men were proud to contribute the texts to which he set his music. He introduced female dancers into the ballet, disguised men having hitherto served in this capacity, and in many essential ways was the father of early French opera, though its foundation had been laid by Cardinal Mazarin. He had to fight against opposition and cabals, but his energy, tact, and persistence made him the victor, and won the friendship of the leading men of his time. Such of his music as still exists is of a pleasing and melodious character, full of vivacity and fire, and at times indicates a more deep and serious power than that of merely creating catching and tuneful airs. He was the inventor of the operatic overture, and introduced several new instruments into the orchestra. Apart from his splendid administrative faculty, he is entitled to rank as an original and gifted, if not a great composer.

A lively sketch of the French opera of this period is given by Addison in No. 29 of the *Spectator*. "The music of the French," he says, "is indeed very properly adapted to their pronunciation and accent, as their whole opera wonderfully favours the genius of such a gay, airy people. The chorus in which that opera abounds gives the parterre frequent opportunities of joining in concert with the stage. This inclination of the audience to sing along with the actors so prevails with them that I have sometimes known the performer on the stage to do no more in a celebrated song than the clerk of a parish church, who serves only to raise the psalm, and is afterwards drowned in the music of the congregation. Every actor that comes on the stage is a beau. The queens and heroines are so painted that they appear as ruddy and cherry-cheeked as milkmaids. The shepherds are all embroidered, and acquit themselves in a ball better than our English dancing-masters. I have seen a couple of rivers appear in red stockings; and Alpheus, instead of having his head covered with sedge and bulrushes, making love in a fair, full-bottomed periwig, and a plume of feathers; but with a voice so full of shakes and quavers, that I should have thought the murmur of a country brook the much more agreeable music. I remember the last opera I saw in that merry nation was the 'Rape of Proserpine,' where Pluto, to make the more tempting figure, puts himself in a French equipage, and brings Ascalaphus along with him as his *valet de chambre*. This is what we call folly and impertinence, but what the French look upon as gay and polite."

II.

The French musical drama continued without much change in the hands of the Lulli school (for the musician had several skilful imitators and successors) till the appearance of Jean Philippe Rameau, who inaugurated a new era.

This celebrated man was born in Auvergne in 1683, and was during his earlier life the organist of the Clermont cathedral church. Here he pursued the scientific researches in music which entitled him in the eyes of his admirers to be called the Newton of his art. He had reached the age of fifty without recognition as a dramatic composer, when the production of "Hippolyte et Aricie" excited a violent feud by creating a strong current of opposition to the music of Lulli. He produced works in rapid succession, and finally overcame all obstacles, and won for himself the name of being the greatest lyric composer which France up to that time had produced. His last opera, "Les Paladins," was given in 1760, the composer being then seventy-seven.

The bitterness of the art-feuds of that day, afterwards shown in the Gluck-Piccini contest, was foreshadowed in that waged by Rameau against Lulli, and finally against the Italian new-comers, who sought to take possession of the French stage. The matter became a national quarrel, and it was considered an insult to France to prefer the music of an Italian to that of a Frenchman—an insult which was often settled by the rapier point, when tongue and pen had failed as arbitrators. The subject was keenly debated by journalists and pamphleteers, and the press groaned with essays to prove that Rameau was the first musician in Europe, though his works were utterly unknown outside of France. Perhaps no more valuable testimony to the character of these operas can be adduced than that of Baron Grimm:—

"In his operas Rameau has overpowered all his predecessors by dint of harmony and quantity of notes. Some of his choruses are very fine. Lulli could only sustain his vocal psalmody by a simple bass; Rameau accompanied almost all his recitatives with the orchestra. These accompaniments are generally in bad taste; they drown the voice rather than support it, and force the singers to scream and howl in a manner which no ear of any delicacy can tolerate. We come away from an opera of Rameau's intoxicated with harmony and stupified with the noise of voice and instruments. His taste is always Gothic, and, whether his subject is light or forcible, his style is equally heavy. He was not destitute of ideas, but did not know what use to make of them. In his recitatives the sound is continually in opposition to the sense, though they occasionally contain happy declamatory passages. . . . If he had formed himself in some of the schools of Italy, and thus acquired a notion of musical style and habits of musical thought, he never would have said (as he did) that all poems were alike to him, and that he could set the *Gazette de France* to music."

From this it may be gathered that Rameau, though a scientific and learned musician, lacked imagination, good taste, and dramatic insight—qualities which in the modern lyric school of France have been so pre-eminent. It may be admitted, however, that he inspired a taste for sound musical science, and thus prepared the way for the great Gluck, who to all and more of Rameau's musical knowledge united the grand genius which makes him one of the giants of his art.

Though Rameau enjoyed supremacy over the serious opera, a great excitement was created in Paris by the arrival of an Italian company, who in 1752 obtained permission to perform Italian burlettas and intermezzi at the opera-house. The partisans of the French school took alarm, and the admirers of Lulli and Rameau forgot their bickerings to join forces against the foreign intruders. The battle-field was strewed with floods of ink, and the literati pelted each other with ferocious lampoons.

Among the literature of this controversy, one pamphlet has an imperishable place, Rousseau's famous "Lettre sur la Musique Française," in which the great sentimentalist espoused the cause of Italian music with an eloquence and acrimony rarely surpassed. The inconsistency of the author was as marked in this as in his private life. Not only did he at a later period become a great advocate of Gluck against Piccini, but, in spite of his argument that it was impossible to compose music to French words, that the language was quite unfit for it, that the French never had music and never would, he himself had composed a good deal of music to French words and produced a French opera, "Le Devin du Village." Diderot was also a warm partisan of the Italians. Pergolesi's beautiful music having been murdered by the French orchestra-players at the Grand Opera-House, Diderot proposed for it the following witty and laconic inscription:—"Hic Marsyas Apollinem." *

Rousseau's opera, "Le Devin du Village," was performed with considerable success, in spite of the repugnance of the orchestral performers, of whom Rousseau always spoke in terms of unmeasured contempt, to do justice to the music. They burned Rousseau in effigy for his scoffs. "Well," said the author of the *Confessions*, "I don't wonder that they should hang me now, after having so long put me to the torture."

The eloquence and abuse of the wits, however, did not long impair the supremacy of Rameau; for the Italian company returned to their own land, disheartened by their reception in the French capital. Though this composer commenced so late in life, he left thirty-six dramatic works. His greatest work was "Castor et Pollux." Thirty years later Grimm recognised its merits by admitting, in spite of the great faults of the composer, "It is the pivot on which the glory of French music turns." When Louis XIV. offered Rameau a title, he answered, touching his breast and forehead, "My nobility is here and here." This composer marked a step forward in French music, for he gave it more boldness and freedom, and was the first really scientific and well-equipped exponent of a national school. His choruses were full of energy and fire, his orchestral effects rich and massive. He died in 1764, and the mortuary music, composed by himself, was performed by a double orchestra and chorus from the Grand Opera.

* Here Marsyas flayed Apollo.

III.

A distinguished place in the records of French music must be assigned to ANDRÉ ERNEST GRÉTRY, born at Liége in 1741. His career covered the most important changes in the art as coloured and influenced by national tastes, and he is justly regarded as the father of comic opera in his adopted country. His childish life is one of much severe discipline and tribulation, for he was dedicated to music by his father, who was first violinist in the college of St. Denis, when he was only six years old. He afterwards wrote of this time in his *Essais sur la Musique*—"The hour for the lesson afforded the teacher an opportunity to exercise his cruelty. He made us sing each in turn, and woe to him who made the least mistake; he was beaten unmercifully, the youngest as well as the oldest. He seemed to take pleasure in inventing torture. At times he would place us on a short round stick, from which we fell head over heels if we made the least movement. But that which made us tremble with fear was to see him knock down a pupil and beat him; for then we were sure he would treat some others in the same manner, one victim being insufficient to gratify his ferocity. To maltreat his pupils was a sort of mania with him; and he seemed to feel that his duty was performed in proportion to the cries and sobs which he drew forth."

In 1759 Grétry went to Rome, where he studied counterpoint for five years. Some of his works were received favourably by the Roman public, and he was made a member of the Philharmonic Society of Bologna. Pressed by pecuniary necessity, Grétry determined to go to Paris; but he stopped at Geneva on the route to earn money by singing-lessons. Here he met Voltaire at Ferney. "You are a musician and have genius," said the great man; "it is a very rare thing, and I take much interest in you." In spite of this, however, Voltaire would not write him the text for an opera. The philosopher of Ferney feared to trust his reputation with an unknown musician. When

Grétry arrived in Paris he still found the same difficulty, as no distinguished poet was disposed to give him a libretto till he had made his powers recognised. After two years of starving and waiting, Marmontel gave him the text of "The Huron," which was brought out in 1769 and well received. Other successful works followed in rapid succession.

At this time Parisian frivolity thought it good taste to admire the rustic and naïve. The idyls of Gessner and the pastorals of Florian were the favourite reading, and Watteau the popular painter. Gentlefolks, steeped in artifice, vice, and intrigue, masked their empty lives under the assumption of Arcadian simplicity, and minced and ambled in the costumes of shepherds and shepherdesses. Marie Antoinette transformed her chalet of Petit Trianon into a farm, where she and her courtiers played at pastoral life—the farce preceding the tragedy of the Revolution. It was the effort of dazed society seeking change. Grétry followed the fashionable bent by composing pastoral comedies, and mounted on the wave of success.

In 1774 "Fausse Magie" was produced with the greatest applause Rousseau was present, and the composer waited on him in his box, meeting a most cordial reception. On their way home after the opera, Grétry offered his new friend his arm to help him over an obstruction. Rousseau with a burst of rage said, "Let me make use of my own powers," and henceforward the sentimental misanthrope refused to recognise the composer. About this time Grétry met the English humorist Hales, who afterwards furnished him with many of his comic texts. The two combined to produce the "Jugement de Midas," a satire on the old style of music, which met with remarkable popular favour, though it was not so well received by the court.

The crowning work of this composer's life was given to the world in 1785. This was "Richard Cœur de Lion," and it proved one of the great musical events of the period. Paris was in ecstasies, and the judgment of succeeding generations has confirmed the contemporary verdict, as it is still a favourite opera in France and Germany. The works afterwards composed by Grétry showed decadence in power. Singularly rich in fresh and sprightly ideas, he lacked depth and grandeur, and failed to suit the deeper and sounder taste which Cherubini and Méhul, great followers in the footsteps of Gluck, gratified by a series of noble masterpieces. Grétry's services to his art, however, by his production of comic operas full of lyric vivacity and sparkle, have never been forgotten nor underrated. His bust was placed in the opera-house during his lifetime, and he was made a member of the French Academy of Fine Arts and Inspector of the Conservatory. Grétry possessed qualities of heart which endeared him to all, and his death in 1813 was the occasion of a general outburst of lamentation. Deputations from the theatres and the Conservatory accompanied his remains to the cemetery, where Méhul pronounced an eloquent eulogium. In 1828 a nephew of Grétry caused the heart of him who was one of the glorious sons of Liége to be returned to his native city.

Grétry founded a school of musical composition in France which has since been cultivated with signal success—that of lyric comedy. The efforts of Lulli and Rameau had been turned in another direction. The former had done little more than set courtly pageants to music, though he had done this with great skill and tact, enriching them with a variety of concerted and orchestral pieces, and showing much fertility in the invention alike of pathetic and lively melodies. Rameau followed in the footsteps of Lulli, but expanded and crystallised his ideas into a more scientific form. He had indeed carried his love of form to a radical extreme. Jean Jacques Rousseau, who extended his taste for nature and simplicity to music, blamed him severely as one who neglected genuine natural tune for far-fetched harmonies, on the ground that "music is a child of nature, and has a language of its own for expressing emotional transports, which cannot be learned from thorough-bass rules." Again, Rousseau, in his forcible tract on French music, says of Rameau, from whose school Grétry's music was such a significant departure—

"One must confess that M. Rameau possesses very great talent, much fire and euphony, and a considerable knowledge of harmonious combinations and effects; one must also grant him the art of appropriating the ideas of others by changing their character, adorning and developing them, and turning them around in all manner of ways. On the other hand, he shows less facility in inventing new ones. Altogether he has more skill than fertility, more knowledge than genius, or rather genius smothered by knowledge, but always force, grace, and very often a beautiful *cantilena*. His recitative is not as natural but much more varied than that of Lulli; admirable in a few scenes, but bad as a rule." Rousseau continues to reproach Rameau with a too powerful instrumentation, compared with Italian simplicity, and sums up that nobody knew better than Rameau how to conceive the spirit of single passages and to produce artistic contrasts, but that he entirely failed to give his operas "a happy and much-to-be-desired unity." In another part of the quoted passage Rousseau says that Rameau stands far beneath Lulli in *esprit* and artistic tact, but that he is often superior to him in dramatic expression.

A clear understanding of the musical position of Rameau is necessary to fully appreciate the place of Grétry, his antithesis as a composer. For a short time the popularity of Rameau had been shaken by an Italian opera company, called by the French *Les Bouffons*, who had created a genuine sensation by their performance of airy and sparkling operettas, entirely removed in spirit from the ponderous productions of the prevailing school. Though the Italian comedians did not meet with permanent success, the suave charm of their music left behind it memories which became fruitful.* It furnished the point of departure for

---

* In its infancy Italian comic opera formed the *intermezzo* between the acts of a serious opera, and—similar to the Greek sylvan drama which followed the tragic trilogy—was frequently a parody on the piece which preceded it; though more frequently still (as in Pergolesi's

the lively and facile genius of Grétry, who laid the foundation stones for that lyric comedy which has flourished in France with so much luxuriance. From the outset merriment and humour were by no means the sole object of the French comic opera, as in the case of its Italian sister. Grétry did not neglect to turn the nobler emotions to account, and by a judicious admixture of sentiment he gave an ideal colouring to his works, which made them singularly fascinating and original. Around Grétry flourished several disciples and imitators, and for twenty years this charming hybrid between opera and vaudeville engrossed French musical talent, to the exclusion of other forms of composition. It was only when Gluck* appeared on the scene, and by his commanding genius restored serious opera to its supremacy, that Grétry's repute was overshadowed. From this decline in public favour he never fully recovered, for the master left behind him gifted disciples, who embodied his traditions, and were inspired by his lofty aims—pre-eminently so in the case of Cherubini, perhaps the greatest name in French music. While French comic opera, since the days of Grétry, has become modified in some of its forms, it preserves the spirit and colouring which he so happily imparted to it, and looks back to him as its founder and lawgiver.

IV.

One of the most accomplished of historians and critics, Oulibischeff, sums up the place of Cherubini in musical art in these words—"If on the one hand Gluck's calm and

"Serva Padrona") it was not a satire on any particular subject, but designed to heighten the ideal artistic effect of the serious opera by broad comedy. Having acquired a complete form on the boards of the small theatres, it was transferred to the larger stage. Though it lacked the external splendour and consummate vocalisation of the elder sister, its simpler forms endowed it with a more characteristic rendering of actual life.

* See article on "Gluck," in *The Great German Composers* (the first part of this work), in which his connection with French music is discussed.

plastic grandeur, and on the other the tender and voluptuous charm of the melodies of Piccini and Zacchini, had suited the circumstances of a state of society sunk in luxury and nourished with classical exhibitions, this could not satisfy a society shaken to the very foundations of its faith and organisation. The whole of the dramatic music of the eighteenth century must naturally have appeared cold and languid to men whose minds were profoundly moved with troubles and wars; and even at the present day the word languor best expresses that which no longer touches us in the operas of the last century, without even excepting those of Mozart himself. What we require for the pictures of dramatic music is larger frames, including more figures, more passionate and moving song, more sharply marked rhythms, greater fulness in the vocal masses, and more sonorous brilliancy in the instrumentation. All these qualities are to be found in 'Lodoïska' and 'Les Deux Journées;' and Cherubini may not only be regarded as the founder of the modern French opera, but also as that musician who, after Mozart, has exerted the greatest general influence on the tendency of the art. An Italian by birth and the excellence of his education, which was conducted by Sarti, the great teacher of composition; a German by his musical sympathies as well as by the variety and profundity of his knowledge; and a Frenchman by the school and principles to which we owe his finest dramatic works, Cherubini strikes me as being the most accomplished musician, if not the greatest genius, of the nineteenth century."

Again, the English composer, Macfarren, observes—"Cherubini's position is unique in the history of his art; actively before the world as a composer for threescore years and ten, his career spans over more vicissitudes in the progress of music than that of any other man. Beginning to write in the same year with Cimarosa, and even earlier than Mozart, and being the contemporary of Verdi and Wagner, he witnessed almost the origin of the two modern classical schools of France and Germany, their rise to perfection, and, if not their decline, the arrival of a time when criticism would usurp the place of creation, and when to propound new rules for art claims higher consideration than to act according to its ever unalterable principles. His artistic life indeed was a rainbow based on the two extremes of modern music which shed light and glory on the great art-cycle over which it arched. .... His excellence consists in his unswerving earnestness of purpose, in the individuality of his manner, in the vigour of his ideas, and in the purity of his harmony."

"Such," says M. Miel, "was Cherubini; a colossal and incommensurable genius, an existence full of days, of masterpieces, and of glory. Among his rivals he found his most sincere appreciators. The Chevalier Seyfried has recorded, in a notice on Beethoven, that that grand musician regarded Cherubini as the first of his contemporary composers. We will add nothing to this praise: the judgment of such a rival is, for Cherubini, the voice itself of posterity."

LUIGI CARLO ZANOBE SALVADORE MARIA CHERUBINI was born at Florence on September 14, 1760, the son of a harpsichord accompanist at the Pergola Theatre. Like so many other great composers, young Cherubini displayed signs of a fertile and powerful genius at an early age, mastering the difficulties of music as if by instinct. At the age of nine he was placed under the charge of Felici, one of the best Tuscan professors of the day; and four years afterwards he composed his first work, a mass. His creative instinct, thus awakened, remained active, and he produced a series of compositions which awakened no little admiration, so that he was pointed at in the streets of Florence as the young prodigy. When he was about sixteen the attention of the Grand Duke Leopold of Tuscany was directed to him, and through that prince's liberality he was enabled to become a pupil of the most celebrated Italian master of the age, Giuseppe Sarti, of whom he soon became the favourite pupil. Under the direction of Sarti, the young composer produced a series of operas, sonatas, and masses, and wrote much of the music which appeared under the *maestro's* own name—a practice then common in the music and painting schools of Italy. At the age of nineteen Cherubini was recognised as one of the most learned and accomplished musicians of the age, and his services were in active demand at the Italian theatres. In four years he produced thirteen operas, the names and character of which it is not necessary now to mention, as they are unknown except to the antiquary whose zeal prompts him to defy the dust of the Italian theatrical libraries. Halévy, whose admiration of his master led him to study these early compositions, speaks of them as full of striking beauties, and, though crude in many particulars, distinguished by those virile and daring conceptions which from the outset stamped the originality of the man.

Cherubini passed through Paris in 1784, while the Gluck-Piccini excitement was yet warm, and visited London as composer for the Royal Italian Opera. Here he became a constant visitor in courtly circles, and the Prince of Wales, the Duke of Queensbury, and other noble amateurs, conceived the warmest admiration for his character and abilities. For some reason, however, his operas written for England failed, and he quitted England in 1786, intending to return to Italy. But the fascinations of Paris held him, as they have done so many others, noticeably so among the great musicians; and what was designed as a flying visit became a life-long residence, with the exception of brief interruptions in Germany and Italy, whither he went to fill professional engagements.

Cherubini took up his residence with his friend Viotti, who introduced him to the Queen, Marie Antoinette, and the highest society of the capital, then as now the art-centre of the world. He became an intimate of the brilliant salons of Mdme. de Polignac, Mdme. d'Etioles, Mdme. de Richelieu, and of the various bright assemblies where the wit, rank, and beauty of Paris gathered in the days just prior to the Revolution. The poet Marmontel became his intimate friend, and gave him the opera story of

"Demophon" to set to music. It was at this period that Cherubini became acquainted with the works of Haydn, and learned from him how to unite depth with lightness, grace with power, jest with earnestness, and toying with dignity.

A short visit to Italy for the carnival of 1788 resulted in the production of the opera of "Ifigenia in Aulide" at La Scala, Milan. The success was great, and this work, the last written for his native country, was given also at Florence and Parma with no less delight and approbation on the part of the public. Had Cherubini died at this time, he would have left nothing but an obscure name for Fétis's immense dictionary. Unlike Mozart and Schubert, who at the same age had reached their highest development, this robust and massive genius ripened slowly. With him as with Gluck, with whom he had so many affinities, a short life would have been fatal to renown. His last opera showed a turning point in his development. Halévy, his great disciple, speaks of this period as follows:—"He is already more nervous; there peeps out I know not exactly how much of force and virility of which the Italian musicians of his day did not know or did not seek the secret. It is the dawn of a new day. Cherubini was preparing himself for the combat. Gluck had accustomed France to the sublime energy of his masterpieces. Mozart had just written 'Le Nozze di Figaro' and 'Don Giovanni.' He must not lag behind. He must not be conquered. In that career which he was about to dare to enter, he met two giants. Like the athlete who descends into the arena, he anointed his limbs and girded his loins for the fight."

v.

Marmontel had furnished the libretto of an opera to Cherubini, and the composer shortly after his return from Turin to Paris had it produced at the Royal Academy of Music. Vogel's opera on the same text, "Demophon," was also brought out, but neither one met with great success. Cherubini's work, though full of vigour and force, wanted colour and dramatic point. He was disgusted with his failure, and resolved to eschew dramatic music; so for the nonce he devoted himself to instrumental music and cantata. Two works of the latter class, "Amphion" and "Circe," composed at this time, were of such excellence as to retain a permanent hold on the French stage. Cherubini, too, became director of the Italian opera troupe, "Les Bouffons," organised under the patronage of Léonard, the Queen's performer, and exercised his taste for composition by interpolating airs of his own into the works of the Italian composers, which were then interesting the French public as against the operas of Rameau.

"At this time," we are told by Lafage, "Cherubini had two distinct styles, one of which was allied to Paisiello and Cimarosa by the grace, elegance, and purity of the melodic forms; the other, which attached itself to the school of Gluck and Mozart, more harmonic than melodious, rich in instrumental details." This manner was the then unappreciated type of a new school destined to change the forms of musical art.

In 1790 the Revolution broke out and rent the established order of things into fragments. For a time all the interests of art were swallowed up in the frightful turmoil which made Paris the centre of attention for astonished and alarmed Europe. Cherubini's connection had been with the aristocracy, and now they were fleeing in a mad panic or mounting the scaffold. His livelihood became precarious, and he suffered severely during the first five years of anarchy. His seclusion was passed in studying music, the physical sciences, drawing, and botany; and his acquaintance was wisely confined to a few musicians like himself. Once, indeed, his having learned the violin as a child was the means of saving his life. Independently venturing out at night, he was arrested by a roving band of drunken *Sansculottes*, who were seeking musicians to conduct their street chants. Somebody recognised Cherubini as a favourite of court circles, and, when he refused to lead their obscene music, the fatal cry, "The Royalist, the Royalist!" buzzed through the crowd. At this critical moment another kidnapped player thrust a violin in Cherubini's hands and persuaded him to yield. So the two musicians marched all day amid the hoarse yells of the drunken revolutionists. He was also enrolled in the National Guard, and obliged to accompany daily the march of the unfortunate throngs who shed their blood under the axe of the guillotine. Cherubini would have fled from these horrible surroundings, but it was difficult to evade the vigilance of the French officials; he had no money; and he would not leave the beautiful Cécile Tourette, to whom he was affianced.

One of the theatres opened during the revolutionary epoch was the Théâtre Feydeau. The second opera performed was Cherubini's "Lodoïska" (1791), at which he had been labouring for a long time, and which was received throughout Europe with the greatest enthusiasm and delight, not less in Germany than in France and Italy. The stirring times aroused a new taste in music, as well as in politics and literature. The dramas of Racine and the operas of Lulli were akin. No less did the stormy genius of Schiller find its counterpart in Beethoven and Cherubini. The production of "Lodoïska" was the point of departure from which the great French school of serious opera, which has given us "Robert le Diable," "Les Huguenots," and "Faust," got its primal value and significance. Two men of genius, Gluck and Grétry, had formed the tastes of the public in being faithful to the accents of nature. The idea of reconciling this taste, founded on strict truth, with the seductive charm of the Italian forms, to which the French were beginning to be sensible, suggested to Cherubini a system of lyric drama capable of satisfying both. Wagner himself even says, in his *Tendencies and Theories*, speaking of Cherubini and his great co-labourers, Méhul and Spontini—"It would be difficult to answer them, if they now perchance came among us and asked in what respect we had improved on their mode of musical procedure."

"Lodoïska," which cast the old Italian operas into permanent oblivion, and laid the foundation of the modern French dramatic school in music, has a libretto similar to that of "Fidelio" and Grétry's "Cœur de Lion" combined, and was taken from a romance of Faiblas by Fillette Loraux. The critics found only one objection: the music was all so beautiful that no breathing time was granted the listener. In one year the opera was performed two hundred times, and at short intervals two hundred more representations took place.

The Revolution culminated in the crisis of 1793, which sent the King to the scaffold. Cherubini found a retreat at La Chartreuse, near Rouen, the country-seat of his friend, the architect Louis. Here he lived in tranquillity, and composed several minor pieces and a three-act opera, never produced, but afterwards worked over into "Ali Baba" and "Faniska." In his Norman retreat Cherubini heard of the death of his father, and while suffering under this infliction, just before his return to Paris in 1794, he composed the opera of "Elisa." This work was received with much favour at the Feydeau theatre, though it did not arouse the admiration called out by "Lodoïska."

In 1795 the Paris Conservatory was founded, and Cherubini appointed one of the five inspectors, as well as professor of counterpoint, his associates being Lesueur, Grétry, Gossec, and Méhul. The same year also saw him united to Cécile Tourette, to whom he had been so long and devotedly attached. Absorbed in his duties at the Conservatory, he did not come before the public again till 1797, when the great tragic masterpiece of "Médée" was produced at the Feydeau theatre. "Lodoïska" had been somewhat gay; "Elisa," a work of graver import, followed; but in "Médée" was sustained the profound tragic power of Gluck and Beethoven. Hoffman's libretto was indeed unworthy of the great music, but this has not prevented its recognition by musicians as one of the noblest operas ever written. It has probably been one of the causes, however, why it is so rarely represented at the present time, its overture alone being well known to modern musical audiences. This opera has been compared by critics to Shakespeare's "King Lear," as being a great expression of anguish and despair in their more stormy phases. Chorley tells us that, when he first saw it, he was irresistibly reminded of the lines in Barry Cornwall's poem to Pasta —

"Now thou art like some wingèd thing that cries
  Above some city, flaming fast to death."

The poem which Chorley quotes from was inspired by the performance of the great Pasta in Simone Mayer's weak musical setting of the fable of the Colchian sorceress, which crowded the opera-houses of Europe. The life of the French classical tragedy, too, was powerfully assisted by Rachel. Though the poem on which Cherubini worked was unworthy of his genius, it could not be from this or from lack of interest in the theme alone that this great work is so rarely performed; it is because there have been not more than three or four actresses in the last hundred years combining the great tragic and vocal requirements exacted by the part. If the tragic genius of Pasta could have been united with the voice of a Catalania, made as it were of adamant and gold, Cherubini's sublime musical creation would have found an adequate interpreter. Mdlle. Tietjens, indeed, has been the only late dramatic singer who dared essay so difficult a task. Musical students rank the instrumental parts of this opera with the organ music of Bach, the choral fugues of Handel, and the symphonies of Beethoven, for beauty of form and originality of ideas.

On its first representation, on the 13th of March 1797, one of the journals, after praising its beauty, professed to discover imitations of Méhul's manner in it. The latter composer, in an indignant rejoinder, proclaimed himself and all others as overshadowed by Cherubini's genius: a singular example of artistic humility and justice. Three years after its performance in Paris, it was given at Berlin and Vienna, and stamped by the Germans as one of the world's great musical masterpieces. This work was a favourite one with

Schubert, Beethoven, and Weber, and there have been few great composers who have not put on record their admiration of it.

As great, however, as "Médée" is ranked, "Les Deux Journées,"* produced in 1800, is the opera on which Cherubini's fame as a dramatic composer chiefly rests. Three hundred consecutive performances did not satisfy Paris; and at Berlin and Frankfort, as well as in Italy, it was hailed with acclamation. Bouilly was the author of the opera-story, suggested by the generous action of a water-carrier towards a magistrate who was related to the author. The story is so interesting, so admirably written, that Goethe and Mendelssohn considered it the true model for a comic opera. The musical composition, too, is nearly faultless in form and replete with beauties. In this opera Cherubini anticipated the reforms of Wagner, for he dispensed with the old system which made the drama a web of beautiful melodies, and established his musical effects for the most part by the vigour and charm of the choruses and concerted pieces. It has been accepted as a model work by composers, and Beethoven was in the habit of keeping it by him on his writing-table for constant study and reference.

Spohr, in his autobiography, says, "I recollect, when the 'Deux Journées' was performed for the first time, how, intoxicated with delight and the powerful impression the work had made on me, I asked on that very evening to have the score given me, and sat over it the whole night; and that it was that opera chiefly that gave me my first impulse to composition." Weber, in a letter from Munich written in 1813, says, "Fancy my delight when I beheld lying upon the table of the hotel the play-bill with the magic name *Armand*. I was the first person in the theatre, and planted myself in the middle of the pit, where I waited most anxiously for the tones which I knew beforehand would elevate and inspire me. I think I may assert boldly that 'Les Deux Journées' is a really great dramatic and

* In German known as "Die Wasserträger," in English, "The Water-Carriers."

classical work. Everything is calculated so as to produce the greatest effect; all the various pieces are so much in their proper place that you can neither omit one nor make any addition to them. The opera displays a pleasing richness of melody, vigorous declamation, and all-striking truth in the treatment of situations, ever new, ever heard and retained with pleasure." Mendelssohn, too, writing to his father of a performance of this opera, speaks of the enthusiasm of the audience as extreme, as well as of his own pleasure as surpassing anything he had ever experienced in a theatre. Mendelssohn, who never completed an opera, because he did not find until shortly before his death a theme which properly inspired him to dramatic creation, corresponded with Planché, with the hope of getting from the latter a libretto which should unite the excellences of "Fidelio" with those of "Les Deux Journées." He found, at last, a libretto, which, if it did not wholly satisfy him, at least overcame some of his prejudices, in a story based on the Rhine myth of Lorelei. A fragment of it only was finished, and the finale of the first act is occasionally performed in England.

VI.

Before Napoleon became First Consul, he had been on familiar terms with Cherubini. The soldier and the composer were seated in the same box listening to an opera by the latter. Napoleon, whose tastes for music were for the suave and sensuous Italian style, turned to him and said, "My dear Cherubini, you are certainly an excellent musician; but really your music is so noisy and complicated that I can make nothing of it;" to which Cherubini replied, "My dear general, you are certainly an excellent soldier; but in regard to music you must excuse me if I don't think it necessary to adapt my music to your comprehension." This haughty reply was the beginning of an estrangement. Another illustration of Cherubini's sturdy pride and dignity was his rejoinder to Napoleon, when the latter was praising the works of the Italian composers, and covertly sneering at his own. "Citizen General," he replied, "occupy yourself with battles and victories, and allow me to treat according to my talent an art of which you are grossly ignorant." Even when Napoleon became Emperor, the proud composer never learned "to crook the pregnant hinges of his knee" to the man before whom Europe trembled.

On the 12th of December 1800, a grand performance of "The Creation" took place at Paris. Napoleon on his way to it narrowly escaped being killed by an infernal machine. Cherubini was one of the deputation, representing the various corporations and societies of Paris, who waited on the First Consul to congratulate him upon his escape. Cherubini kept in the background, when the sarcasm, "I do not see Monsieur Cherubini," pronounced in the French way, as if to indicate that Cherubini was not worthy of being ranked with the Italian composers, brought him promptly forward. "Well," said Napoleon, "the French are in Italy." "Where would they not go," answered Cherubini, "led by such a hero as you?" This pleased the First Consul, who, however, soon got to the old musical quarrel. "I tell you I like Paisiello's music immensely; it is soft and tranquil. You have much talent, but there is too much accompaniment." Said Cherubini, "Citizen Consul, I conform myself to French taste." "Your music," continued the other, "makes too much noise. Speak to me in that of Paisiello; that is what lulls me gently." "I understand," replied the composer; "you like music which doesn't stop you from thinking of state affairs." This witty rejoinder made the arrogant soldier frown, and the talk suddenly ceased.

As a result of this alienation Cherubini found himself persistently ignored and ill-treated by the First Consul. In spite of his having produced such great masterpieces, his income was very small, apart from his pay as Inspector of the Conservatory. The ill-will of the ruler of France was a steady check to his preferment. When Napoleon established his consular chapel in 1802, he invited Paisiello from Naples to become director at a salary of 12,000 francs a-year. It gave great umbrage to the Conservatory that its famous teachers should have been slighted for an Italian foreigner, and musical circles in Paris were shaken by petty contentions. Paisiello, however, found the public indifferent to his works, and soon wearied of a place where the admiration to which he had been accustomed no longer flattered his complacency. He resigned, and his position was offered to Méhul, who is said to have declined it because he regarded Cherubini as far more worthy of it, and to have accepted it only on condition that his friend could share the duties and emoluments with him. Cherubini, fretted and irritated by his condition, retired for a time from the pursuit of his art, and devoted himself to flowers. The opera of "Anacreon," a powerful but unequal work, which reflected the disturbance and agitation of his mind, was the sole fruit of his musical efforts for about four years.

While Cherubini was in the deepest depression—for he had a large family depending on him and small means with which to support them—a ray of sunshine came in 1805 in the shape of an invitation to compose for the managers of the opera at Vienna. His advent at the Austrian capital produced a profound sensation, and he received a right royal welcome from the great musicians of Germany. The aged Haydn, Hummel, and Beethoven became his warm friends with the generous freemasonry of genius, for his rank as a musician was recognised throughout Europe.

The war which broke out after our musician's departure from Paris between France and Austria ended shortly in the capitulation of Ulm, and the French Emperor took up his residence at Schönbrunn. Napoleon received Cherubini kindly when he came in answer to his summons, and it was arranged that a series of twelve concerts should be given alternately at Schönbrunn and Vienna. The pettiness which entered into the French Emperor's nature in spite of his greatness continued to be shown in his ebullitions of wrath because Cherubini persisted in holding his own musical views against the imperial opinion. Napoleon, however, on the eve of his return to France, urged him to accompany him, offering the long-coveted position of musical director; but Cherubini was under contract to remain a certain length of time at Vienna, and he would not break his pledge.

The winter of 1805 witnessed two remarkable musical events at the Austrian capital, the production of Beethoven's "Fidelio" and the last great opera written by Cherubini, "Faniska." Haydn and Beethoven were both present at the latter performance. The former embraced Cherubini and said to him "You are my son, worthy of my love." Beethoven cordially hailed him as "the first dramatic composer of the age." It is an interesting fact that two such important dramatic compositions should have been written at the same time, independently of each other; that both works should have been in advance of their age; that they should have displayed a striking similarity of style; and that both should have suffered from the reproach of the music being too learned for the public. The opera of "Faniska" is based on a Polish legend of great dramatic beauty, which, however, was not very artistically treated by the librettist. Mendelssohn in after years noted the striking resemblance between Beethoven and our composer in the conception and method of dramatic composition. In one of his letters to Edouard Devrient he says, speaking of "Fidelio," "On looking into the score, as well as on listening to the performance, I everywhere perceive Cherubini's dramatic style of composition. It is true that Beethoven did not ape that style, but it was before his mind as his most cherished pattern." The unity of idea and musical colour between "Faniska" and "Fidelio" seems to have been noted by many critics both of contemporary and succeeding times.

Cherubini would gladly have written more for the Viennese, by whom he had been so cordially treated; but the unsettled times and his home-sickness for Paris conspired to take him back to the city of his adoption. He exhausted many efforts to find Mozart's tomb in

Vienna, and desired to place a monument over his neglected remains, but failed to locate the resting-place of one he loved so much. Haydn, Beethoven, Hummel, Salieri, and the other leading composers reluctantly parted with him, and on April 1, 1806, his return to Paris was celebrated by a brilliant fête improvised for him at the Conservatory. Fate, however, had not done with her persecutions, for fate in France took the shape of Napoleon, whose hostility, easily aroused, was implacable; who aspired to rule the arts and letters as he did armies and state policy; who spared neither Cherubini nor Madame de Staël. Cherubini was neglected and insulted by authority, while honours were showered on Méhul, Grétry, Spontini, and Lesueur. He sank into a state of profound depression, and it was even reported in Vienna that he was dead. He forsook music and devoted himself to drawing and botany. Had he not been a great musician, it is probable he would have excelled in pictorial art. One day the great painter David entered the room where he was working in crayon on a landscape of the Salvator Rosa style. So pleased was the painter that he cried, "Truly admirable! Courage!" In 1808 Cherubini found complete rest in a visit to the country-seat of the Prince de Chimay in Belgium, whither he was accompanied by his friend and pupil, Auber.

VII.

With this period Cherubini closed his career practically as an operatic composer, though several dramatic works were produced subsequently, and entered on his no less great sphere of ecclesiastical composition. At Chimay for a while no one dared to mention music in his presence. Drawing and painting flowers seemed to be his sole pleasure. At last the president of the little music society at Chimay ventured to ask him to write a mass for St. Cecilia's feast-day. He curtly refused, but his hostess noticed that he was agitated by the incident, as if his slumbering instincts had started again into life. One day the Princess placed

music paper on his table, and Cherubini on returning from his walk instantly began to compose, as if he had never ceased it. It is recorded that he traced out in full score the "Kyrie" of his great mass in F during the intermission of a single game of billiards. Only a portion of the mass was completed in time for the festival, but, on Cherubini's return to Paris in 1809, it was publicly given by an admirable orchestra, and hailed with a great enthusiasm, that soon swept through Europe. It was perceived that Cherubini had struck out for himself a new path in church music. Fétis, the musical historian, records its reception as follows :—" All expressed an unreserved admiration for this composition of a new order, whereby Cherubini has placed himself above all musicians who have as yet written in the concerted style of church music. Superior to the masses of Haydn, Mozart, and Beethoven, and the masters of the Neapolitan school, that of Cherubini is as remarkable for originality of idea as for perfection in art." Picchiante, a distinguished critic, sums up the impressions made by this great work in the following eloquent and vigorous passage :—
" All the musical science of the good age of religious music, the sixteenth century of the Christian era, was summed up in Palestrina, who flourished at that time, and by its aid he put into form noble and sublime conceptions. With the grave Gregorian melody, learnedly elaborated in vigorous counterpoint and reduced to greater clearness and elegance without instrumental aid, Palestrina knew how to awaken among his hearers mysterious, grand, deep, vague sensations, that seemed caused by the objects of an unknown world, or by superior powers in the human imagination. With the same profound thoughtfulness of the old Catholic music, enriched by the perfection which art has attained in two centuries, and with all the means which a composer nowadays can make use of, Cherubini perfected another conception, and this consisted in utilising the style adapted to dramatic composition when narrating the church text, by which means he was able to succeed in depicting man in his various vicissitudes, now rising to the praises of

Divinity, now gazing on the Supreme Power, now suppliant and prostrate. So that, while Palestrina's music places God before man, that of Cherubini places man before God." Adolphe Adam puts the comparison more epigrammatically in saying "If Palestrina had lived in our own times, he would have been Cherubini." The masters of the old Roman school of church music had received it as an emanation of pure sentiment, with no tinge of human warmth and colour. Cherubini, on the contrary, aimed to make his music express the dramatic passion of the words, and in the realisation of this he brought to bear all the resources of a musical science unequalled except perhaps by Beethoven. The noble masses in F and D were also written in 1809, and stamped themselves on public judgment as no less powerful works of genius and knowledge.

Some of Cherubini's friends in 1809 tried to reconcile the composer with the Emperor, and in furtherance of this an opera was written anonymously, "Pimmalione." Napoleon was delighted, and even affected to tears. Instantly, however, that Cherubini's name was uttered, he became dumb and cold. Nevertheless, as if ashamed of his injustice, he sent Cherubini a large sum of money, and a commission to write the music for his marriage ode. Several fine works followed in the next two years, among them the Mass in D, regarded by some of his admirers as his ecclesiastical masterpiece. Miél claims that in largeness of design and complication of detail, sublimity of conception and dramatic intensity, two works only of its class approach it, Beethoven's Mass in D and Niedermeyer's Mass in D minor.

In 1811 Halévy, the future author of "La Juive," became Cherubini's pupil, and a devoted friendship ever continued between the two. The opera of "La Abencérages" was also produced, and it was pronounced nowise inferior to "Médée" and "Les Deux Journées." Mendelssohn, many years afterwards, writing to Moscheles in Paris, asked, "Has Onslow written anything new? And old Cherubini? There's a matchless fellow! I have got his 'Abencérages,' and can not sufficiently admire the sparkling fire, the clear original phrasing, the extraordinary delicacy and refinement with which it is written, or feel grateful enough to the grand old man for it. Besides, it is all so free and bold and spirited." The work would have had a greater immediate success, had not Paris been in profound gloom from the disastrous results of the Moscow campaign and the horrors of the French retreat, where famine and disease finished the work of bayonet and cannon-ball.

The unsettled and disheartening times disturbed all the relations of artists. There is but little record of Cherubini for several years. A significant passage in a letter written in 1814, speaking of several military marches written for a Prussian band, indicates the occupation of Paris by the allies and Napoleon's banishment in Elba. The period of "The Hundred Days" was spent by Cherubini in England; and the world's wonder, the battle of Waterloo, was fought, and the Bourbons were permanently restored, before he again set foot in Paris. The restored dynasty delighted to honour the man whom Napoleon had slighted, and gifts were showered on him alike by the Court and by the leading academies of Europe. The walls of his studio were covered with medals and diplomas; and his appointment as director of the King's chapel (which, however, he refused unless shared with Lesueur, the old incumbent) placed him above the daily demands of want. So, at the age of fifty-five, this great composer for the first time ceased to be anxious on the score of his livelihood. Thenceforward the life of Cherubini was destined to flow with a placid current, its chief incidents being the great works in church music, which he poured forth year after year, to the admiration and delight of the artistic world. These remarkable masses, by their dramatic power, greatness of design, and wealth of instrumentation, excited as much discussion and interest throughout Europe as the operas of other composers. That written in 1816, the C minor requiem mass, is pronounced by Berlioz to be the greatest work of this description ever composed.

VIII.

As a man Cherubini presented himself in many different aspects. Extremely nervous, *brusque*, irritable, and absolutely independent, he was apt to offend and repel. But under his stern reserve of character there beat a warm heart and generous sympathies. This is shown by the fact that, in spite of the unevenness of his temper, he was almost worshipped by those around him. Auber, Halévy, Berton, Boïeldieu, Méhul, Spontini, and Adam, who were so intimately associated with him, speak of him with words of the warmest affection. Halévy, indeed, rarely alluded to him without tears rushing to his eyes; and the slightest term of disrespect excited his warmest indignation. It is recorded that, after rebuking a pupil with sarcastic severity, his fine face would relax with a smile so affectionate and genial that his whilom victim could feel nothing but enthusiastic respect. Without one taint of envy in his nature, conscious of his own extraordinary powers, he was quick to recognise genius in others; and his hearty praise of the powers of his rivals shows how sound and generous the heart was under his irritability. His proneness to satire and power of epigram made him enemies, but even these yielded to the suavity and fascination which alternated with his bitter moods. His sympathies were peculiarly open for young musicians. Mendelssohn and Liszt were stimulated by his warm and encouraging praise when they first visited Paris; and even Berlioz, whose turbulent conduct in the Conservatory had so embittered him at various times, was heartily applauded when his first great mass was produced. Arnold gives us the following pleasant picture of Cherubini:—

"Cherubini in society was outwardly silent, modest, unassuming, pleasing, obliging, and possessed of the finest manners. At the same time, he who did not know that he was with Cherubini would think him stern and reserved, so well did the composer know how to conceal everything, if only to avoid ostentation. He truly shunned brag or speaking of himself. Cherubini's voice was feeble, probably from narrow-chestedness, and somewhat hoarse, but was otherwise soft and agreeable. His French was Italianised. ... His head was bent forward, his nose was large and aquiline; his eyebrows were thick, black, and somewhat bushy, overshadowing his eyes. His eyes were dark, and glittered with an extraordinary brilliancy that animated in a wonderful way the whole face. A thin lock of hair came over the centre of his forehead, and somehow gave to his countenance a peculiar softness."

The picture painted by Ingres, the great artist, now in the Luxembourg gallery, represents the composer with Polyhymnia in the background stretching out her hand over him. His face, framed in waving silvery hair, is full of majesty and brightness, and the eye of piercing lustre. Cherubini was so gratified by this effort of the painter that he sent him a beautiful canon set to words of his own. Thus his latter years were spent in the society of the great artists and wits of Paris, revered by all, and recognised, after Beethoven's death, as the musical giant of Europe. Rossini, Meyerbeer, Weber, Schumann—in a word, the representatives of the most diverse schools of composition—bowed equally before this great name. Rossini, who was his antipodes in genius and method, felt his loss bitterly, and after his death sent Cherubini's portrait to his widow with these touching words—" Here, my dear madam, is the portrait of a great man, who is as young in your heart as he is in my mind."

A mutual affection between Cherubini and Beethoven existed through life, as is shown by the touching letter written by the latter just before his death, but which Cherubini did not receive till after that event. The letter was as follows :—

VIENNA, March 15, 1823.

HIGHLY ESTEEMED SIR—I joyfully take advantage of the opportunity to address you.

I have done so often in spirit, as I prize your theatrical works beyond others. The artistic world has only to lament that in

Germany, at least, no new dramatic work of yours has appeared. Highly as all your works are valued by true connoisseurs, still it is a great loss to art not to possess any fresh production of your great genius for the theatre.

True art is imperishable, and the true artist feels heartfelt pleasure in grand works of genius, and that is what enchants me when I hear a new composition of yours; in fact, I take greater interest in it than in my own; in short, I love and honour you. Were it not that my continued bad health stops my coming to see you in Paris, with what exceeding delight would I discuss questions of art with you! Do not think that this is meant merely to serve as an introduction to the favour I am about to ask of you. I hope and feel sure that you do not for a moment suspect me of such base sentiments. I recently completed a grand solemn Mass, and have resolved to offer it to the various European courts, as it is not my intention to publish it at present. I have therefore asked the King of France, through the French embassy here, to subscribe to this work, and I feel certain that his Majesty would at your recommendation agree to do so.

My critical situation demands that I should not solely fix my eyes upon heaven, as is my wont; on the contrary, it would have me fix them also upon earth, here below, for the necessities of life.

Whatever may be the fate of my request to you, I shall for ever continue to love and esteem you; and you for ever remain of all my contemporaries that one whom I esteem the most.

If you should wish to do me a very great favour, you would effect this by writing to me a few lines, which would solace me much. Art unites all; how much more, then, true artists! and perhaps you may deem me worthy of being included in that number.

With the highest esteem, your friend and servant,

LUDWIG VAN BEETHOVEN.

LUDWIG CHERUBINI.

Cherubini's admiration of the great German is indicated in an anecdote told by Professor Ella. The master rebuked a pupil who, in referring to a performance of a Beethoven symphony, dwelt mostly on the executive excellence—" Young man, let your sympathies be first wedded to the creation, and be you less fastidious of the execution; accept the interpretation, and think more of the creation of these musical works which are written for all time and all nations, models for imitation, and above all criticism."

Actively engaged as Director of the Conservatory, which he governed with consummate ability, his old age was further employed in producing that series of great masses which rank with the symphonies of Beethoven. His creative instinct and the fire of his imagination remained unimpaired to the time of his death. Mendelssohn, in a letter to Moscheles, speaks of him as "that truly wonderful old man, whose genius seems bathed in immortal youth." His opera of "Ali Baba," composed at seventy-six, though inferior to his other dramatic works, is full of beautiful and original music, and was immediately produced in several of the principal capitals of Europe; and the second Requiem mass, written in his eightieth year, is one of his masterpieces.

On the 12th of March 1842 the old composer died, surrounded by his affectionate family and friends. His fatal illness had been brought on in part by grief for the death of his son-in-law, M. Turcas, to whom he was most tenderly attached. His funeral was one of great military and civic magnificence, and royalty itself could not have been honoured with more splendid obsequies. The congregation of men great in arms and state, in music, painting, and literature, who did honour to the occasion, has rarely been equalled. His own noble Requiem mass, composed the year before his death, was given at the funeral services in the church of St. Roch by the finest orchestra and voices in Europe. Similar services were held throughout Europe, and everywhere the opera-houses were draped in black. Perhaps the death of no musician ever called forth such universal exhibitions of sorrow and reverence.

Cherubini's life extended from the early part of the reign of Louis XVI. to that of Louis Philippe, and was contemporaneous with many of the most remarkable events in modern history. The energy and passion which convulsed society during his youth and early manhood undoubtedly had much to do in stimulating that robust and virile quality in his mind which gave such character to his compositions. The fecundity of his intellect is shown in the fact that he produced four hundred and thirty works, out of which only eighty have been published. In this catalogue there are twenty-five operas and eleven masses.

As an operatic composer he laid the foundation of the modern French school. Uniting the melody of the Italian with the science of the German, his conceptions had a dramatic fire and passion which were, however, free from anything appertaining to the sensational and meretricious. His forms were indeed classically severe, and his style is defined by Adolphe Adam as the resurrection of the old Italian school, enriched by the discoveries of modern harmony. Though he was the creator of French opera as we know it now, he was free from its vagaries and extravagances. He set its model in the dramatic vigour and picturesqueness, the clean-cut forms, and the noble instrumentation which mark such masterpieces as "Faniska," "Médée," "Les Deux Journées," and "Lodoïska." The purity, classicism, and wealth of ideas in these works have always caused them to be cited as standards of ideal excellence. The reforms in opera of which Gluck was the protagonist, and Wagner the extreme modern exponent, characterise the dramatic works of Cherubini, though he keeps them within that artistic limit which a proper regard for melodic beauty prescribes. In the power and propriety of musical declamation his operas are conceded to be without a superior. His overtures hold their place in classical music as ranking with the best ever written, and show a richness of resource and knowledge of form in treating the orchestra which his contemporaries admitted were only equalled by Beethoven.

Cherubini's place in ecclesiastical music is that by which he is best known to the musical public of to-day; for his operas, owing to the immense demands they make on the dramatic and vocal resources of the artist, are but rarely presented in France, Germany, and England, and never in America. They are only given where music is loved on account of its noble traditions, and not for the mere sake of idle and luxurious amusement. As a composer of masses, however, Cherubini's genius is familiar to all who frequent the services of the Roman Church. His relation to the music of Catholicism accords with that of Sebastian Bach to the music of Protestantism. Haydn, Mozart, and even Beethoven, are held by the best critics to be his inferiors in this form of composition. His richness of melody, sense of dramatic colour, and great command of orchestral effects, gave him commanding power in the interpretation of religious sentiments; while an ardent faith inspired with passion, sweetness, and devotion what Place styles his "sublime visions." Miel, one of his most competent critics, writes of him in this eloquent strain—" If he represents the passion and death of Christ, the heart feels itself wounded with the most sublime emotion; and when he recounts the 'Last Judgment' the blood freezes with dread at the redoubled and menacing calls of the exterminating angel. All those admirable pictures that the Raphaels and Michael Angelos have painted with colours and the brush, Cherubini brings forth with the voice and orchestra."

In brief, if Cherubini is the founder of a later school of opera, and the model which his successors have always honoured and studied if they have not always followed, no less is he the chief of a later, and by common consent the greatest, school of modern church music.

MEHUL, SPONTINI, AND HALEVY.

I.

THE influence of Gluck was not confined to Cherubini, but was hardly less manifest in moulding the style and conceptions of Méhul and Spontini,* who held prominent places in the history of the French opera. HENRI ETIENNE MEHUL was the son of a French soldier stationed at the

---

* It is a little singular that some of the most distinguished names in the annals of French music were foreigners. Thus Gluck was a German, as also was Meyerbeer, while Cherubini and Spontini were Italians.

Givet barracks, where he was born June 24, 1763. His early love of music secured for him instructions from the blind organist of the Franciscan church at that garrison town, under whom he made astonishing progress. He soon found he had outstripped the attainments of his teacher, and contrived to place himself under the tuition of the celebrated Wilhelm Hemser, who was organist at a' neighbouring monastery. Here Méhul spent a number of happy and useful years, studying composition with Hemser and literature with the kind monks, who hoped to persuade their young charge to devote himself to ecclesiastical life.

Méhul's advent in Paris, whither he went at the age of sixteen, soon opened his eyes to his true vocation, that of a dramatic composer. The excitement over the contest between Gluck and Piccini was then at its height, and the youthful musician was not long in espousing the side of Gluck with enthusiasm. He made the acquaintance of Gluck accidentally, the great chevalier interposing one night to prevent his being ejected from the theatre, into one of whose boxes Méhul had slipped without buying a ticket. Thenceforward the youth had free access to the opera, and the friendship and tuition of one of the master minds of the age.

An opera, "Cora et Alonzo," had been composed at the age of twenty and accepted at the opera; but it was not till 1790 that he got a hearing in the comic opera of "Euphrasque et Coradin," composed under the direction of Gluck. This work was brilliantly successful, and "Stratonice," which appeared two years afterwards, established his reputation. The French critics describe both these early works as being equally admirable in melody, orchestral accompaniment, and dramatic effect. The stormiest year of the revolution was not favourable to operatic composition, and Méhul wrote but little music except pieces for republican festivities, much to his own disgust, for he was by no means a warm friend of the republic.

In 1797 he produced his "La Jeune Henri," which nearly caused a riot in the theatre. The story displeased the republican audience, who hissed and hooted till the turmoil compelled the fall of the curtain. They insisted, however, on the overture, which is one of great beauty, being performed over and over again, a compliment which has rarely been accorded to any composer. Méhul's appointment as inspector and professor in the newly organised Conservatory, at the same time with Cherubini, left him but little leisure for musical composition; but he found time to write the spectacular opera "Adrian," which was fiercely condemned by a republican audience, not as a musical failure, but because their alert and suspicious tempers suspected in it covert allusions to the dead monarchy. Even David, the painter, said he would set the torch to the opera-house rather than witness the triumph of a king. In 1806 Méhul produced the opera "Uthal," a work of striking vigour founded on an Ossianic theme, in which he made the innovation of banishing the violins from the orchestra, substituting therefor the violas.

It was in "Joseph," however, composed in 1807, that this composer vindicated his right to be called a musician of great genius, and entered fully into a species of composition befitting his grand style. Most of his contemporaries were incapable of appreciating the greatness of the work, though his gifted rival Cherubini gave it the warmest praise. In Germany it met with instant and extended success, and it is one of the few French operas of the old school which still continue to be given on the German stage. In England it is now frequently sung as an oratorio. It is on this remarkable work that Méhul's lasting reputation as a composer rests outside of his own nation. The construction of the opera of "Joseph" is characterised by admirable symmetry of form, dramatic power, and majesty of the choral and concerted passages, while the sustained beauty of the orchestration is such as to challenge comparison with the greatest works of his contemporaries. Such at least is the verdict of Fétis, who was by no means inclined to be over-indulgent in criticising Méhul. The fault in this opera, as in all of Méhul's works, appears to have been a lack of bright and graceful melody, though in the modern tendencies of music this defect is rapidly being elevated into a virtue.

The last eight years of Méhul's life were depressed by melancholy and suffering, proceeding from pulmonary disease. He resigned his place in the Conservatory, and retired to a pleasant little estate near Paris, where he devoted himself to raising flowers, and found some solace in the society of his musical friends and former pupils, who were assiduous in their attentions. Finally becoming dangerously ill, he went to the island of Hyères to find a more genial climate. But here he pined for Paris and the old companionships, and suffered more perhaps by fretting for the intellectual cheer of his old life than he gained by balmy air and sunshine. He writes to one of his friends after a short stay at Hyères—"I have broken up all my habits; I am deprived of all my old friends; I am alone at the end of the world, surrounded by people whose language I scarcely understand; and all this sacrifice to obtain a little more sun. The air which best agrees with me is that which I breathe among you." He returned to Paris for a few weeks only, to breathe his last on October 18, 1817, aged fifty-four.

Méhul was a high-minded and benevolent man, wrapped up in his art, and singularly childlike in the practical affairs of life. Abhorring intrigue, he was above all petty jealousies, and even sacrificed the situation of chapel-master under Napoleon, because he believed it should have been given to the greatest of his rivals, Cherubini. When he died Paris recognised his goodness as a man as well as greatness as a musician by a touching and spontaneous expression of grief, and funeral honours were given him throughout Europe. In 1822 his statue was crowned on the stage of the Grand Opera, at a performance of his "Valentine de Rohan." Notwithstanding his early death, he composed forty-two operas, and modern musicians and critics give him a notable place among those who were prominent in building up a national stage. A pupil and disciple of Gluck, a cordial co-worker with Cherubini, he contributed largely to the glory of French music, not only by his genius as a composer, but by his important labours in the reorganisation of the Conservatory, that nursery which has fed so much of the highest musical talent of the world.

II.

LUIGI GASPARDO PACIFICO SPONTINI, born of peasant parents at Majolati, Italy, November 14, 1774, displayed his musical passion at an early age. Designed for holy orders from childhood, his priestly tutors could not make him study; but he delighted in the service of the church, with its organ and choir effects, for here his true vocation asserted itself. He was wont, too, to hide in the belfry, and revel in the roaring orchestra of metal, when the chimes were rung. On one occasion a stroke of lightning precipitated him from his dangerous perch to the floor below, and the history of music nearly lost one of its great lights. The bias of his nature was intractable, and he was at last permitted to study music, at first under the charge of his uncle Joseph, the curé of Jesi, and finally at the Naples Conservatory, where he was entered at the age of sixteen.

His first opera, "I Puntigli delle Donne," was composed at the age of twenty-one, and performed at Rome, where it was kindly received. The French invasion unsettled the affairs of Italy, and Spontini wandered somewhat aimlessly, unable to exercise his talents to advantage till he went to Paris in 1803, where he found a large number of brother Italian musicians, and a cordial reception, though himself an obscure and untried youth. He produced several minor works on the French stage, noticeably among them the one-act opera of "Milton," in which he stepped boldly out of his Italian mannerism, and entered on that path afterwards pursued with such brilliancy and boldness. Yet, though his talents began to be recognised, life was a trying struggle, and it is doubtful if he could have overcome the difficulties in his way when he was ready to produce "La Vestale," had he not enlisted the sympathies of the Empress Josephine, who loved music, and played the part of patroness as gracefully as she did all others.

By Napoleon's order "La Vestale" was rehearsed against the wish of the manager and critics of the Academy of Music, and produced December 15, 1807. Previous to this some parts of it had been performed privately at the Tuileries, and the Emperor had said, "M. Spontini, your opera abounds in fine airs and effective duets. The march to the place of execution is admirable. You will certainly have the great success you so well deserve." The imperial prediction was justified by consecutive performances of one hundred nights. His next work, "Fernand Cortez," sustained the impression of genius earned for him by its predecessor. The scene of the revolt is pronounced by competent critics to be one of the finest dramatic conceptions in operatic music.

In 1809 Spontini married the niece of Erard, the great pianoforte-maker, and was called to the direction of the Italian opera; but he retained this position only two years, from the disagreeable conditions he had to contend with, and the cabals that were formed against him. The year 1814 witnessed the production of "Pélage," and two years later "Les Dieux Rivaux" was composed, in conjunction with Persuis, Berton, and Kreutzer; but neither work attracted much attention. The opera of "Olympie," worked out on the plan of "La Vestale" and "Cortez," was produced in 1819. Spontini was embittered by its poor success, for he had built many hopes on it, and wrought long and patiently. That he was not in his best vein, and like many other men of genius was not always able to estimate justly his own work, is undeniable; for Spontini, contrary to the opinion of his contemporaries and of posterity, regarded this as his best opera. His acceptance of the Prussian King's offer to become musical director at Berlin was the result of his chagrin. Here he remained for twenty years. "Olympie" succeeded better at Berlin, though the boisterousness of the music seems to have called out some sharp strictures even among the Berlinese, whose penchant for noisy operatic effects was then as now a butt for the satire of the musical wits. Apropos of the long run of "Olympie" at Berlin, an amusing anecdote is told on the authority of Castel-Blaze. A wealthy amateur had become deaf, and suffered much from his deprivation of the enjoyment of his favourite art. After trying many physicians, he was treated in a novel fashion by his latest doctor. "Come with me to the opera this evening," wrote down the doctor. "What's the use? I can't hear a note," was the impatient rejoiner. "Never mind," said the other; "come, and you will see something at all events." So the twain repaired to the theatre to hear Spontini's "Olympie." All went well till one of the overwhelming finales, which happened to be played that evening more *fortissimo* than usual. The patient turned around beaming with delight, exclaiming, "Doctor, I can hear." As there was no reply, the happy patient again said, "Doctor, I tell you, you have cured me." A blank stare alone met him, and he found that the doctor was as deaf as a post, having fallen a victim to his own prescription. The German wits had a similar joke afterwards at Halévy's expense. The *Punch* of Vienna said that Halévy made the brass play so loudly that the French horn was actually blown quite straight.

Among the works produced at Berlin were "Nurmahal," in 1825; "Alcidor," the same year; and 1829, "Agnes von Hohenstaufen." Various other new works were given from time to time, but none achieved more than a brief hearing. Spontini's stiff-necked and arrogant will kept him in continual trouble, and the Berlin press aimed its arrows at him with incessant virulence: a war which the composer fed by his bitter and witty rejoinders, for he was an adept in the art of invective. Had he not been singularly adroit, he would have been obliged to leave his post. But he gloried in the disturbance he created, and was proof against the assaults of his numerous enemies, made so largely by his having come of the French school, then as now an all-sufficient cause of Teutonic dislike. Spontini's unbending intolerance, however, at last undermined his musical supremacy, so long held good with an iron hand; and an intrigue headed by Count Brühl, intendant of the Royal Theatre, at last obliged him to resign after a rule of a score of years. His influence on the lyric theatre of Berlin, however, had been valuable, and he had the glory of forming singers among the Prussians, who until his time had thought more of cornet-playing than of beautiful and true vocalisation. The Prussian King allowed him on his departure a pension of 16,000 francs.

When Spontini returned to Paris, though he was appointed member of the Academy of Fine Arts, he was received with some coldness by the musical world. He had no little difficulty in getting a production of his operas; only the Conservatory remained faithful to him, and in their hall large audiences gathered to hear compositions to which the opera-house denied its stage. New idols attracted the public, and Spontini, though burdened with all the orders of Europe, was obliged to rest in the traditions of his earlier career. A passionate desire to see his native land before death made him leave Paris in 1850, and he went to Majolati, the town of his birth, where he died after a residence of a few months in 1851. His cradle was his tomb.

III.

A well-known musical critic sums up his judgment of Halévy in these words—"If in France a contemporary of Louis XIV., an admirer of Racine, could return to us, and, full of the remembrance of his earthly career under that renowned monarch, he should wish to find the nobly pathetic, the elevated inspiration, the majestic arrangements of the olden times upon a modern stage, we would not take him to the Théâtre Français, but to the Opera on the day in which one of Halévy's works was given."

Unlike Méhul and Spontini, with whom in point of style

and method Halévy must be associated, he was not in any direct sense a disciple of Gluck, but inherited the influence of the latter through his great successor Cherubini, of whom Halévy was the favourite pupil and the intimate friend. FORMENTAL HALÉVY, a scion of the Hebrew race, which has furnished so many geniuses to the art world, left a deep impress on his times, not simply by his genius and musical knowledge, which was profound, varied, and accurate, but by the elevation and nobility which lifted his mark up to a higher level than that which we accord to mere musical gifts, be they ever so rich and fertile. The motive that inspired his life is suggested in his devout saying that music is an art that God has given us, in which the voices of all nations may unite their prayers in one harmonious rhythm.

Halévy was a native of Paris, born May 27, 1799. He entered the Conservatory at the age of eleven years, where he soon attracted the particular attention of Cherubini. When he was twenty the Institute awarded him the grand prize for the composition of a cantata; and he also received a government pension which enabled him to dwell at Rome for two years, assiduously cultivating his talents in composition. Halévy returned to Paris, but it was not till 1827 that he succeeded in having an opera produced. This portion of his life was full of disappointment and chilled ambitions; for, in spite of the warm friendship of Cherubini, who did everything to advance his interests, he seemed to make but slow progress in popular estimation, though a number of operas were produced.

Halévy's full recognition, however, was found in the great work of "La Juive," produced February 23, 1835, with lavish magnificence. It is said that the managers of the Opera expended 150,000 francs in putting it on the stage. This opera, which surpasses all his others in passion, strength, and dignity of treatment, was interpreted by the greatest singers in Europe, and the public reception at once assured the composer that his place in music was fixed. Many envious critics, however, declaimed against him, asserting that success was not the legitimate desert of the opera, but of its magnificent presentation. Halévy answered his detractors by giving the world a delightful comic opera, "L'Éclair," which at once testified to the genuineness of his musical inspiration and the versatility of his powers, and was received by the public with even more pleasure than " La Juive."

Halévy's next brilliant stroke (three unsuccessful works in the meanwhile having been written) was "La Reine de Chypre," produced in 1841. A somewhat singular fact occurred during the performance of this opera. One of the singers, every time he came to the passage,

> " Ce mortel qu'on remarque
> Tient-il
> Plus que nous de la Parque
> Le fil?"

was in the habit of fixing his eyes on a certain proscenium box wherein were wont to sit certain notabilities in politics and finance. As several of these died during the first run of the work, superstitious people thought the box was bewitched, and no one cared to occupy it. Two fine works, "Charles VI." and "Le Val d'Andorre," succeeded at intervals of a few years; and in 1849 the noble music to Æschylus's "Prometheus Bound" was written with an idea of reproducing the supposed effects of the enharmonic style of the Greeks.

Halévy's opera of "The Tempest," written for London, and produced in 1850, rivalled the success of "La Juive." Balfe led the orchestra, and its popularity caused the basso Lablache to write the following epigram:—

> " The 'Tempest' of Halévy
> Differs from other tempests.
> These rain hail,
> That rains gold."

The Academy of Fine Arts elected the composer secretary in 1854, and in the exercise of his duties, which involved considerable literary composition, Halévy showed the same elegance of style and good taste which marked his musical writings. He did not, however, neglect his own proper work, and a succession of operas, which were cordially received, proved how unimpaired and vigorous his intellectual faculties remained.

The composer's death occurred at Nice, whither he had gone on account of failing strength, March 17, 1862. His last moments were cheered by the attentions of his family and the consolations of philosophy and literature, which he dearly loved to discuss with his friends. His ruling passion displayed itself shortly before his end in characteristic fashion. Trying in vain to reach a book on the table, he said, "Can I do nothing now in time?" On the morning of his death, wishing to be turned on his bed, he said to his daughter, "Lay me down like a gamut," at each movement repeating, with a soft smile, "*Do, re, mi,*" etc., until the change was made. These were his last words.

The celebrated French critic Sainte-Beuve pays a charming tribute to Halévy, whom he knew and loved well:—

"Halévy had a natural talent for writing, which he cultivated and perfected by study, by a taste for reading which he always gratified in the intervals of labour, in his study, in public conveyances—everywhere, in fine, when he had a minute to spare. He could isolate himself completely in the midst of the various noises of his family, or the conversation of the drawing-room if he had no part in it. He wrote music, poetry, and prose, and he read with imperturbable attention while people around him talked.

"He possessed the instinct of languages, was familiar with German, Italian, English, and Latin, knew something of Hebrew and Greek. He was conversant with etymology, and had a perfect passion for dictionaries. It was often difficult for him to find a word; for on opening the dictionary somewhere near the word for which he was looking, if his eye chanced to fall on some other, no matter what, he stopped to read that, then another and another, until he sometimes forgot the word he sought. It is singular that this estimable man, so fully occupied, should at times have nourished some secret sadness. Whatever the hidden wound might be, none, not even his most intimate friends, knew what it was. He never made any complaint. Halévy's nature was rich, open, and communicative. He was well organised, accessible to the sweets of sociability and family joys. In fine, he had, as one may say, too many strings to his bow to be very unhappy for any length of time. To define him practically, I would say he was a bee that had not lodged himself completely in his hive, but was seeking to make honey elsewhere too."

IV.

Méhul laboured successfully in adapting the noble and severe style of Gluck to the changing requirements of the French stage. The turmoil and passions of the revolution had stirred men's souls to the very roots, and this influence was perpetuated and crystallised in the new forms given to French thought by Napoleon's wonderful career. Méhul's musical conceptions, which culminated in the opera of "Joseph," were characterised by a stir, a vigour, and largeness of dramatic movement, which came close to the familiar life of that remarkable period. His great rival, Cherubini, on the other hand, though no less truly dramatic in fitting musical expression to thought and passion, was so austere and rigid in his ideals, so dominated by musical form and an accurate science which would concede nothing to popular prejudice and ignorance, that he won his laurels, not by force of the natural flow of popular sympathy, but by the sheer might of his genius. Cherubini's severe works made them models and foundation-stones for his successors in French music; but Méhul familiarised his audiences with strains dignified yet popular, full of massive effects and brilliant combinations. The people felt the tramp of the Napoleonic armies in the vigour and movement of his measures.

Spontini embodied the same influences and characteristics in still larger degree, for his musical genius was organised on a more massive plan. Deficient in pure, graceful melody alike with Méhul, he delighted in great masses of tone and vivid orchestral colouring. His music was full of the military fire of his age, and dealt for the most part with the peculiar tastes and passions engendered by a condition of chronic warfare. Therefore dramatic movement in his operas was always of the heroic order, and never touched the more subtile and complex elements of life. Spontini added to the majestic repose and ideality of the Gluck music-drama (to use a name now naturalised in art by Wagner) the keenest dramatic vigour. Though he had a strong command of effects by his power of delineation and delicacy of detail, his prevalent tastes led him to encumber his music too often with overpowering military effects, alike tonal and scenic. Riehl, a great German critic, says—"He is more successful in the delineation of masses and groups than in the pourtrayal of emotional scenes; his rendering of the national struggle between the Spaniards and Mexicans in 'Cortez' is, for example, admirable. He is likewise most successful in the management of large masses in the instrumentation. In this respect he was, like Napoleon, a great tactician." In "La Vestale" Spontini attained his *chef-d'œuvre*. Schlüter, in his *History of Music*, gives it the following encomium—"His pourtrayal of character and truthful delineation of passionate emotion in this opera are masterly indeed. The subject of 'La Vestale' (which resembles that of 'Norma,' but how differently treated!) is tragic and sublime as well as intensely emotional. Julia, the heroine, a prey to guilty passion; the severe but kindly high priestess; Licinius, the adventurous lover, and his faithful friend Cinna; pious vestals, cruel priests, bold warriors, and haughty Romans, are represented with statuesque relief and finish. Both these works, 'La Vestale' (1807) and 'Cortez' (1809), are among the finest that have been written for the stage; they are remarkable for naturalness and sublimeness, qualities lost sight of in the noisy instrumentation of his later works."

Halévy, trained under the influences of Cherubini, was largely inspired by that great master's musical purism and reverence for the higher laws of his art. Halévy's powerful sense of the dramatic always influenced his methods and sympathies. Not being a composer of creative imagination, however, the melodramatic element is more prominent than the purely tragic or comic. His music shows remarkable resources in the production of brilliant and captivating, though always tasteful, effects, which rather please the senses and the fancy than stir the heart and imagination. Here and there scattered through his works, notably so in "La Juive," are touches of emotion and grandeur; but Halévy must be characterised as a composer who is rather distinguished for the brilliancy, vigour, and completeness of his art than for the higher creative power, which belongs in such pre-eminent degree to men like Rossini and Weber, or even to Auber, Meyerbeer, and Gounod. It is nevertheless true that Halévy composed works which will retain a high rank in French art "La Juive," "Guido," "La Reine de Chypre," and "Charles VI." are noble lyric dramas, full of beauties, though it is said they can never be seen to the best advantage off the French stage. Halévy's genius and taste in music bear much the same relation to the French stage as do those of Verdi to the Italian stage; though the former composer is conceded by critics to be a greater purist in musical form, if he rarely equals the Italian composer in the splendid bursts of musical passion with which the latter redeems so much that is meretricious and false, and the charming melody which Verdi shares with his countrymen.

BOIELDIEU AND AUBER.

I.

THE French school of light opera, founded by Grétry, reached its greatest perfection in the authors of "La Dame Blanche" and "Fra Diavolo," though to the former of these composers must be accorded the peculiar distinction of having given the most perfect example of this style of composition. FRANCOIS ADRIEN BOIELDIEU, the scion of a Norman family, was born at Rouen, December 16, 1775. He received his early musical training at the hands of Broche, a great musician and the cathedral organist, but a drunkard and brutal taskmaster. At the age of sixteen he had become a good pianist and knew something of composition. At all events, his passionate love of the theatre prompted him to try his hand at an opera, which was actually performed at Rouen. The revolution which made such havoc with the clergy and their dependants ruined the Boïeldieu family (the elder Boïeldieu had been secretary of the archiepiscopal diocese), and young François, at the age of nineteen, was set adrift on the world, his heart full of hope and his ambition bent on Paris, whither he set his feet. Paris, however, proved a stern stepmother at the outset, as she always has been to the struggling and unsuccessful. He was obliged to tune pianos for his living, and was glad to sell his brilliant *chansons*, which afterwards made a fortune for his publisher, for a few francs apiece.

Several years of hard work and bitter privation finally culminated in the acceptance of an opera, "La Famille Suisse," at the Théâtre Faydeau in 1796, where it was given on alternate nights with Cherubini's "Médée." Other operas followed in rapid succession, among which may be mentioned "La Dot de Suzette" (1798) and "Le Calife de Bagdad" (1800). The latter of these was remarkably popular, and drew from the severe Cherubini the following rebuke—"Malheureux! Are you not ashamed of such undeserved triumph?" Boïeldieu took the brusque criticism meekly and preferred a request for further instruction from Cherubini—a proof of modesty and good sense quite remarkable in one who had attained recognition as a favourite with the musical public. Boïeldieu's three years' studies under the great Italian master were of much service, for his next work, "Ma Tante Aurore," produced in 1803, showed noticeable artistic progress.

It was during this year that Boïeldieu, goaded by domestic misery (for he had married the danseuse Clotilde Mafleuray, whose notorious infidelity made his name a bye-word), exiled himself to Russia, even then looked on as an El Dorado for the musician, where he spent eight years as conductor and composer of the Imperial Opera. This was all but a total eclipse in his art-life, for he did little of note during the period of his St. Petersburg career.

He returned to Paris in 1811, where he found great changes. Méhul and Cherubini, disgusted with the public, kept an obstinate silence; and Nicolo was not a dangerous rival. He set to work with fresh zeal, and one of his most charming works, "Jean de Paris," produced in 1812, was received with a storm of delight. This and "La Dame Blanche" are the two masterpieces of the composer in refined humour, masterly delineation, and sustained power both of melody and construction. The fourteen years which elapsed before Boïeldieu's genius took a still higher flight were occupied in writing works of little value except as names in a catalogue. The long-expected opera "La Dame Blanche" saw the light in 1825, and it is to-day a stock opera in Europe, one Parisian theatre alone having given it nearly two thousand times. Boïeldieu's latter years were uneventful and unfruitful. He died in 1834 of pulmonary disease, the germs of which were planted by St. Petersburg winters. "Jean de Paris" and "La Dame Blanche" are the two works, out of nearly thirty operas, which the world cherishes as masterpieces.

II.

DANIEL FRANCOIS ESPRIT AUBER was born at Caen, Normandy, January 29, 1784. He was destined by his parents for a mercantile career, and was articled to a French firm in London to perfect himself in commercial training. As a child he showed his passion and genius for music, a fact so noticeable in the lives of most of the great musicians. He composed ballads and romances at the age of eleven, and during his London life was much sought after as a musical prodigy alike in composition and execution. In consequence of the breach of the treaty of Amiens in 1804, he was obliged to return to Paris, and we hear no more of the counting-room as a part of his life. His resetting of an old libretto in 1811 attracted the attention of Cherubini, who impressed himself so powerfully on French music and musicians, and the master offered to superintend his further studies, a chance eagerly seized by Auber. To the instruction of Cherubini Auber owed his mastery over the technical difficulties of his art. Among the pieces written at this time was a mass for the Prince of Chimay, of which the prayer was afterwards transferred to "Masaniello." The comic opera "Le Séjour Militaire," produced in 1813, when Auber was thirty, was really his début as a composer. It was coldly received, and it was not till the loss of private fortune set a sharp spur to his creative activity that he set himself to serious work. "La Bergère Châtelaine," produced in 1820, was his first genuine success, and equal fortune attended "Emma" in the following season.

The duration and climax of Auber's musical career were founded on his friendship and artistic alliance with Scribe, one of the most fertile librettists and playwrights of modern times. To this union, which lasted till Scribe's death, a great number of operas, comic and serious, owe their existence: not all of equal value, but all evincing the apparently inexhaustible productive genius of the joint authors. The works on which Auber's claims to musical greatness rest are as follows:—"Leicester," 1822; "Le Maçon," 1825, the composer's *chef-d'œuvre* in comic opera; "La Muette de Portici," otherwise "Masaniello," 1828; "Fra Diavolo," 1830; "Lestocq," 1835; "Le Cheval de Bronze," 1835; "L'Ambassadrice," 1836; "Le Domino Noir," 1837; "Les Diamants de la Couronne," 1841; "Carlo Braschi," 1842; "Haydée," 1847; "L'Enfant Prodigue," 1850; "Zerline," 1851, written for Madame Alboni; "Manon Lescaut," 1856; "La Fiancée du Roi de

Garbe," 1867; "Le Premier Jour de Bonheur," 1868; and "Le Rêve d'Amour," 1869. The last two works were composed after Auber had passed his eightieth year.

The indifference of this Anacreon of music to renown is worthy of remark. He never attended the performance of his own pieces, and disdained applause. The highest and most valued distinctions were showered on him; orders, jewelled swords, diamond snuff-boxes, were poured in from all the courts of Europe. Innumerable invitations urged him to visit other capitals, and receive honour from imperial hands. But Auber was a true Parisian, and could not be induced to leave his beloved city. He was a Member of the Institute, Commander of the Legion of Honour, and Cherubini's successor as Director of the Conservatory. He enjoyed perfect health up to the day of his death in 1871. Assiduous in his duties at the Conservatory, and active in his social relations, which took him into the most brilliant circles of an extended period, covering the reigns of Napoleon I., Charles X., Louis Philippe, and Napoleon III., he yet always found time to devote several hours a day to composition. Auber was a small, delicate man, yet distinguished in appearance, and noted for wit. His *bons mots* were celebrated. While directing a musical *soirée* when over eighty, a gentleman having taken a white hair from his shoulder, he said, laughingly, "This hair must belong to some old fellow who passed near me."

A good anecdote is told à *propos* of an interview of Auber with Charles X. in 1830. "Masaniello," a bold and revolutionary work, had just been produced, and stirred up a powerful popular ferment. "Ah, M. Auber," said the King, "you have no idea of the good your work has done me." "How, sire?" "All revolutions resemble each other. To sing one is to provoke one. What can I do to please you?" "Ah, sire! I am not ambitious." "I am disposed to name you director of the court concerts. Be sure that I shall remember you. But," added he, taking the artist's arm with a cordial and confidential air, "from this day forth you understand me well, M. Auber, I expect you to bring out the 'Muette' but *very seldom*." It is well known that the Brussels riots of 1830, which resulted in driving the Dutch out of the country, occurred immediately after a performance of this opera, which thus acted the part of "Lillibulero" in English political annals. It is a striking coincidence that the death of the author of this revolutionary inspiration, May 13, 1871, was partly caused by the terrors of the Paris Commune.

III.

Boïeldieu and Auber are by far the most brilliant representatives of the French school of Opéra Comique. The work of the former which shows his genius at its best is "La Dame Blanche." It possesses in a remarkable degree dramatic *verve*, piquancy of rhythm, and beauty of structure. Mr. Franz Hueffer speaks of this opera as follows :—

"Peculiar to Boïeldieu is a certain homely sweetness of melody which proves its kinship to that source of all truly national music, the popular song. The 'Dame Blanche' might be considered as the artistic continuation of the *chanson*, in the same sense as Weber's 'Der Freischütz' has been called a dramatised *Volkslied*. With regard to Boïeldieu's work, this remark indicates at the same time a strong development of what has been described as the 'amalgamating force of French art and culture;' for it must be borne in mind that the subject treated is Scotch. The plot is a compound of two of Scott's novels—the 'Monastery' and 'Guy Mannering.' Julian, *alias* George Brown, comes to his paternal castle unknown to himself. He hears the songs of his childhood, which awaken old memories in him; but he seems doomed to misery and disappointment, for on the day of his return his hall and his broad acres are to become the property of a villain, the unfaithful steward of his own family. Here is a situation full of gloom and sad foreboding. But Scribe and Boïeldieu knew better. Their hero is a dashing cavalry officer, who

makes love to every pretty woman he comes across, the
'White Lady of Avenel' among the number. Yet no one
who has witnessed the impersonation of George Brown by
the great Roger can have failed to be impressed with the
grace and noble gallantry of the character."

The tune of "Robin Adair," introduced by Boïeldieu
and described as "le chant ordinaire de la tribu d'Avenel,"
would hardly be recognised by a genuine Scotchman; but
what it loses in homely vigour it has gained in sweetness.
The musician's taste is always gratified in Boïeldieu's two
great comic operas by the grace and finish of the instrumentation, and the carefully composed *ensembles*, while the
public is delighted with the charming ballads and songs.
The airs of "La Dame Blanche" are more popular in
classic Germany than those of any other opera. Boïeldieu
may then be characterised as the composer who carried the
French operetta to its highest development, and endowed it
in the fullest sense with all the grace, sparkle, dramatic
symmetry, and gamesome touch so essentially the heritage
of the nation.

Auber's position in art may be defined as that of the last
great representative of French comic opera, the legitimate
successor of Boïeldieu, whom he surpasses in refinement
and brilliancy of individual effects, while he is inferior in
simplicity, breadth, and that firm grasp of details which
enables the composer to blend all the parts into a perfect
whole. In spite of the fact that "La Muette," Auber's
greatest opera, is a romantic and serious work, full of bold
strokes of genius that astonish no less than they please, he
must be held to be essentially a master in the field of
operatic comedy. In the great opera to which allusion has
been made, the passions of excited public feeling have their
fullest sway, and heroic sentiments of love and devotion are
expressed in a manner alike grand and original. The
traditional forms of the opera are made to expand with the
force of the feeling bursting through them. But this was
the sole flight of Auber into the higher regions of his art,
the offspring of the thoroughly revolutionised feeling of the

time (1828), which within two years shook Europe with such force. Aside from this outcome of his Berserker mood, Auber is a charming exponent of the grace, brightness, and piquancy of French society and civilisation. If rarely deep, he is never dull, and no composer has given the world more elegant and graceful melodies of the kind which charm the drawing-room and furnish a good excuse for young-lady pianism.

The following sprightly and judicious estimate of Auber by one of the ablest of modern critics, Henry Chorley, in the main fixes him in his right place:—

"He falls short of his mark in situations of profound pathos (save perhaps in his sleep-song of 'Masaniello'). He is greatly behind his Italian brethren in those mad scenes which they so largely affect. He is always light and piquant for voices, delicious in his treatment of the orchestra, and at this moment of writing—though I believe the patriarch of opera-writers (born, it is said, in 1784), having begun to compose at an age when other men have died exhausted by precocious labour—is perhaps the lightest-hearted, lightest-handed man still pouring out fragments of pearl and spangles of pure gold on the stage. . . . With all this it is remarkable as it is unfair, that among musicians—when talk is going around, and this person praises that portentous piece of counterpoint, and the other analyses some new chord the ugliness of which has led to its being neglected by former composers—the name of this brilliant man is hardly if ever heard at all. His is the next name among the composers belonging to the last thirty years which should be heard after that of Rossini, the number and extent of the works produced by him taken into account, and with these the beauties which they contain."

MEYERBEER.

I.

Few great names in art have been the occasion of such diversity of judgment as Giacomo Meyerbeer, whose works fill so large a place in French music. By one school of critics he is lauded beyond all measure as one "whose scientific skill and gorgeous orchestration are only equalled by his richness of melody and genius for dramatic and scenic effects; by far the greatest composer of recent years;" by another class we hear him stigmatised as "the very caricature of the universal Mozart ... the Cosmopolitan Jew, who hawks his wares among all nations indifferently, and does his best to please customers of every kind." The truth lies between the two, as is wont to be the case in such extremes of opinion. Meyerbeer's remarkable talent so nearly approaches genius as to make the distinction a difficult one. He cannot be numbered among those great creative artists who by force of individuality have moulded musical epochs and left an undying imprint on their own and succeeding ages. On the other hand, his remarkable power of combining the resources of the lyric stage in a grand mosaic of all that can charm the eye and ear, of wedding rich and gorgeous music with splendid spectacle, gives him an unique place in music; for, unlike Wagner, whose ideas of stage necessities are no less exacting, Meyerbeer aims at no reforms in lyric music, but only to develop the old forms to their highest degree of effect, under conditions that shall gratify the general artistic sense. To accomplish this, he spares no means either in or out of music. Though a German, there is but little of the Teutonic *genre* in the music of Weber's fellow-pupil. When at the outset he wrote for Italy, he showed but little of that easy assumption of the genius of Italian art which many other foreign composers have attained. It was not till he formed his celebrated art partnership with Scribe, the greatest of librettists, and succeeded in opening the gates of the Grand Opera of Paris with all its resources, more vast than exist anywhere else, that Meyerbeer found his true vocation, the production of elaborate dramas in music of the eclectic school. He inaugurated no clearly defined tendencies in his art; he distinctively belongs to no national school of music; but his long and important connection with the French lyric stage classifies him unmistakably with the composers of this nation.

The subject of this sketch belonged to a family of marked ability. Jacob Beer was a rich Jewish banker of Berlin, highly honoured for his robust intellect and scholarly culture, as well as his wealth. William, one of the sons, became a distinguished astronomer; another, Michael, achieved distinction as a dramatic poet; while the eldest, Jacob, was the composer, who gained his renown under the Italianised name of Giacomo Meyerbeer, a part of the surname having been adopted from that of the rich banker Meyer, who left the musician a great fortune.

MEYERBEER was born at Berlin, September 5, 1791, and was a musical prodigy from his earliest years. When only four years old he would repeat on the piano the airs he heard from the hand-organs, composing his own accompaniment. At five he took lessons of Lanska, a pupil of Clementi, and at six he made his appearance at a concert. Three years afterwards the critics spoke of him as one of the best pianists in Berlin. He studied successively under the greatest masters of the time, Clementi, Bernhard Anslem Weber, and Abbé Vogler. While in the latter's school at Darmstadt, he had for fellow-pupils Carl von Weber, Winter, and Gansbacher. Every morning the abbé called together his pupils after mass, gave them some theoretical instruction, then assigned each one a theme for composition. There was great emulation and friendship between Meyerbeer and Weber, which afterwards cooled, however, owing to Weber's disgust at Meyerbeer's lavish catering to an extravagant taste. Weber's severe and bitter criticisms were not forgiven by the Franco-German composer.

Meyerbeer's first work was the oratorio "Gott und die Natur," which was performed before the Grand Duke with such success as to gain for him the appointment of court composer. Meyerbeer's concerts at Darmstadt and Berlin were brilliant exhibitions; and Moscheles, no mean judge, has told us that if Meyerbeer had devoted himself to the piano, no performer in Europe could have surpassed him. By advice of Salieri, whom Meyerbeer met in Vienna, he proceeded to Italy to study the cultivation of the voice; for he seems in early life to have clearly recognised how necessary it is for the operatic composer to understand this, though, in after-years, he treated the voice as ruthlessly in many of his most important arias and scenas as he would a brass instrument. He arrived in Vienna just as the Rossini madness was at its height, and his own blood was fired to compose operas à la Rossini for the Italian theatres. So he proceeded with prodigious industry to turn out operas. In 1818 he wrote "Romilda e Costanza" for Padua; in 1819, "Semiramide" for Turin; in 1820, "Emma di Resburgo" for Venice; in 1822, "Margherita d'Anjou" for Milan; and in 1823, "L'Esule di Granata," also for Milan. These works of the composer's 'prentice hand met with the usual fate of the production of the thousand and one musicians who pour forth operas in unremitting flow for the Italian theatres; but they were excellent drill for the future author of "Robert le Diable" and "Les Huguenots." On returning to Germany Meyerbeer was very sarcastically criticised on the one side as a fugitive from the ranks of German music, on the other as an imitator of Rossini.

Meyerbeer returned to Venice, and in 1824 brought out "Il Crociato in Egitto" in that city, an opera which made the tour of Europe, and established a reputation for the author as the coming rival of Rossini, no one suspecting from what Meyerbeer had then accomplished that he was about to strike boldly out in a new direction. "Il

Crociato" was produced in Paris in 1825, and the same year in London. In the latter city, Veluti, the last of the male sopranists, was one of the principal singers in the opera; and it was said by some of the ill-natured critics that curiosity to see and hear this singer of a peculiar kind, of whom it was said, "Non vir sed Veluti," had as much to do with the success of the opera as its merits. Lord Mount-Edgcumbe, however, an excellent critic, wrote of it "as quite of the new school, but not copied from its founder, Rossini; original, odd, flighty, and it might be termed fantastic, but at times beautiful. Here and there most delightful melodies and harmonies occurred, but it was unequal, solos being as rare as in all the modern operas." This was the last of Meyerbeer's operas written in the Italian style.

In 1827 the composer married, and for several years lived a quiet, secluded life. The loss of his first two children so saddened him as to concentrate his attention for a while on church music. During this period he composed only a "Stabat," a "Miserere," a "Te Deum," and eight of Klopstock's songs. But he was preparing for that new departure on which his reputation as a great composer now rests, and which called forth such bitter condemnation on the one hand, such thunders of eulogy on the other. His old fellow-pupil, Weber, wrote of him in after-years— "He prostituted his profound, admirable, and serious German talent for the applause of the crowd which he ought to have despised." And Mendelssohn wrote to his father in words of still more angry disgust—"When in 'Robert le Diable' nuns appear one after the other and endeavour to seduce the hero, till at length the lady abbess succeeds; when the hero, aided by a magic branch, gains access to the sleeping apartment of his lady, and throws her down, forming a tableau which is applauded here, and will perhaps be applauded in Germany; and when, after that, she implores for mercy in an aria; when, in another opera, a girl undresses herself, singing all the while that she will be married to-morrow, it may be effective, but I find no music in it. For it is vulgar, and if such is the taste of the day, and therefore necessary, I prefer writing sacred music."

II.

"Robert le Diable" was produced at the Académie Royale in 1831, and inaugurated the brilliant reign of Dr. Véron as manager. The bold innovations, the powerful situations, the daring methods of the composer, astonished and delighted Paris, and the work was performed more than a hundred consecutive times. The history of "Robert le Diable" is in some respects curious. It was originally written for the Ventadour Theatre, devoted to comic opera; but the company were found unable to sing the difficult music. Meyerbeer was inspired by Weber's "Der Freischütz" to attempt a romantic, semi-fantastic legendary opera, and trod very closely in the footsteps of his model. It was determined to so alter the libretto and extend and elaborate the music as to fit it for the stage of the Grand Opera. MM. Scribe and Delavigne, the librettists, and Meyerbeer, devoted busy days and nights to hurrying on the work. The whole opera was remodelled, recitative substituted for dialogue, and one of the most important characters, Raimbaud, cut out in the fourth and fifth acts— a suppression which is claimed to have befogged a very clear and intelligible plot. Highly suggestive in its present state of Weber's opera, the opera of "Robert le Diable" is said to have been marvellously similar to "Der Freischütz" in the original form, though inferior in dignity of motive.

Paris was all agog with interest at the first production. The critics had attended the rehearsals, and it was understood that the libretto, the music, and the ballet were full of striking interest. Nourrit played the part of Robert; Levasseur, Bertram; Mdme. Cinti Damoreau, Isabelle; and Mdlle. Dorus, Alice. The greatest dancers of the age were in the ballet, and the brilliant Taglioni led the band of resuscitated nuns. Habeneck was conductor, and everything had been done in the way of scenery and costumes. The success was a remarkable one, and Meyerbeer's name became famous throughout Europe.

Dr. Véron, in his *Mémoires d'un Bourgeois de Paris*, describes a thrilling yet ludicrous accident that occurred on the first night's performance. After the admirable trio, which is the *dénoûment* of the work, Levasseur, who personated Bertram, sprang through the trap to rejoin the kingdom of the dead, whence he came so mysteriously. Robert, on the other hand, had to remain on the earth, a converted man, and destined to happiness in marriage with his princess, Isabelle. Nourrit, the Robert of the performance, misled by the situation and the fervour of his own feelings, threw himself into the trap, which was not properly set. Fortunately the mattresses beneath had not all been removed, or the tenor would have been killed, a doom which those on the stage who saw the accident expected. The audience supposed it was part of the opera, and the people on the stage were full of terror and lamentation, when Nourrit appeared to calm their fears. Mdlle. Dorus burst into tears of joy, and the audience, recognising the situation, broke into shouts of applause.

The opera was brought out in London the same year, with nearly the same cast, but did not excite so much enthusiasm as in Paris. Lord Mount-Edgcumbe, who represented the connoisseurs of the old school, expressed the then current opinion of London audiences—"Never did I see a more disagreeable or disgusting performance. The sight of the resurrection of a whole convent of nuns, who rise from their graves and begin dancing like so many bacchantes, is revolting; and a sacred service in a church, accompanied by an organ on the stage, not very decorous. Neither does the music of Meyerbeer compensate for a fable which is a tissue of nonsense and improbability."*

M. Véron was so delighted with the great success of "Robert" that he made a contract with Meyerbeer for

---

* Yet Lord Mount-Edgcumbe is inconsistent enough to be an ardent admirer of Mozart's "Zauberflöte."

another grand opera, "Les Huguenots," to be completed by a certain date. Meanwhile, the failing health of Mdme. Meyerbeer obliged the composer to go to Italy, and work on the opera was deferred, thus causing him to lose thirty thousand francs as the penalty of his broken contract. At length, after twenty-eight rehearsals, and an expense of more than one hundred and sixty thousand francs in preparation, "Les Huguenots" was given to the public, February 26, 1836. Though this great work excited transports of enthusiasm in Paris, it was interdicted in many of the cities of Southern Europe on account of the subject being a disagreeable one to ardent and bigoted Catholics. In London it has always been the most popular of Meyerbeer's three great operas, owing perhaps partly to the singing of Mario and Grisi, and more lately of Titiens and Giuglini.

When Spontini resigned his place as chapel-master at the Court of Berlin, in 1832, Meyerbeer succeeded him. He wrote much music of an accidental character in his new position, but a slumber seems to have fallen on his greater creative faculties. The German atmosphere was not favourable to the fruitfulness of Meyerbeer's genius. He seems to have needed the volatile and sparkling life of Paris to excite him into full activity. Or perhaps he was not willing to produce one of his operas, with their large dependence on elaborate splendour of production, away from the Paris Grand Opera. During Meyerbeer's stay in Berlin he introduced Jenny Lind to the Berlin public, as he afterwards did indeed to Paris, her *début* there being made in the opening performance of "Das Feldlager in Schlesien," afterwards remodelled into "L'Etoile du Nord."

Meyerbeer returned to Paris in 1849, to present the third of his great operas, "La Prophète." It was given with Roger, Viardot-Garcia, and Castellan in the principal characters. Mdme. Viardot-Garcia achieved one of her greatest dramatic triumphs in the difficult part of Fides. In London the opera also met with splendid success, having, as Chorley tells us, a great advantage over the Paris presentation in "the remarkable personal beauty of Signor Mario, whose appearance in his coronation robes reminded one of some bishop-saint in a picture by Van Eyck or Dürer, and who could bring to bear a play of feature without grimace into the scene of false fascination, entirely beyond the reach of the clever French artist Roger, who originated the character."

"L'Etoile du Nord" was given to the public February 16, 1854. Up to this time the opera of "Robert" had been sung three hundred and thirty-three times, "Les Huguenots" two hundred and twenty-two, and "Le Prophète" a hundred and twelve. The "Pardon de Ploërmel," also known as "Dinorah," was offered to the world of Paris April 4, 1859. Both these operas, though beautiful, are inferior to his other works.

III.

Meyerbeer, a man of handsome private fortune, like Mendelssohn, made large sums by his operas, and was probably the wealthiest of the great composers. He lived a life of luxurious ease, and yet laboured with intense zeal a certain number of hours each day. A friend one day begged him to take more rest, and he answered smilingly, "If I should leave work, I should rob myself of my greatest pleasure; for I am so accustomed to work that it has become a necessity." Probably few composers have been more splendidly rewarded by contemporary fame and wealth, or been more idolised by their admirers. No less may it be said that few have been the object of more severe criticism. His youth was spent amid the severest classic influences of German music, and the spirit of romanticism and nationality, which blossomed into such beautiful and characteristic works as those composed by his friend and fellow-pupil Weber, also found in his heart an eloquent echo. But Meyerbeer resolutely disenthralled himself from what he appeared to have regarded as trammels, and followed out an ambition to be a cosmopolitan composer.

In pursuit of this purpose he divested himself of that fine flavour of individuality and devotion to art for its own sake which marks the highest labours of genius. He can not be exempted from the criticism that he regarded success and the immediate plaudits of the public as the only satisfactory rewards of his art. He had but little of the lofty content which shines out through the vexed and clouded lives of such souls as Beethoven and Gluck in music, of Bacon and Milton in literature, who looked forward to immortality of fame as the best vindication of their work. A marked characteristic of the man was a secret dissatisfaction with all that he accomplished, making him restless and unhappy, and extremely sensitive to criticism. With this was united a tendency at times to oscillate to the other extreme of vain-gloriousness. An example of this was a reply to Rossini one night at the opera when they were listening to "Robert le Diable." The "Swan of Pesaro" was a warm admirer of Meyerbeer, though the latter was a formidable rival, and his works had largely replaced those of the other in popular repute. Sitting together in the same box, Rossini, in his delight at one portion of the opera, cried out in his impulsive Italian way, "If you can write anything to surpass this, I will undertake to dance upon my head." "Well, then," said Meyerbeer, "you had better soon commence practising, for I have just commenced the fourth act of 'Les Huguenots.'" Well might he make this boast, for into the fourth act of his musical setting of the terrible St. Bartholomew tragedy he put the finest inspirations of his life.

Singular to say, though he himself represented the very opposite pole of art spirit and method, Mozart was to him the greatest of his predecessors. Perhaps it was this very fact, however, which was at the root of his sentiment of admiration for the composer of "Don Giovanni" and "Le Nozze di Figaro." A story is told to the effect that Meyerbeer was once dining with some friends, when a discussion arose respecting Mozart's position in the musical hierarchy. Suddenly one of the guests suggested that "certain beauties of Mozart's music had become stale with age. I defy you," he continued, "to listen to 'Don Giovanni' after the fourth act of the 'Huguenots.'" "So much the worse, then, for the fourth act of the 'Huguenots,'" said Meyerbeer, furious at the clumsy compliment paid to his own work at the expense of his idol.

Critics wedded to the strict German school of music never forgave Meyerbeer for his dereliction from the spirit and influences of his nation, and the prominence which he gave to melodramatic effects and spectacular show in his operas. Not without some show of reason, they cite this fact as proof of poverty of musical invention. Mendelssohn, who was habitually generous in his judgment, wrote to the poet Immermann from Paris of "Robert le Diable"—"The subject is of the romantic order; *i.e.*, the devil appears in it (which suffices the Parisians for romance and imagination). Nevertheless, it is very bad, and, were it not for two brilliant seduction scenes, there would not even be effect. . . . The opera does not please me; it is devoid of sentiment and feeling. . . . People admire the music, but where there is no warmth and truth, I cannot even form a standard of criticism."

Schlüter, the historian of music, speaks even more bitterly of Meyerbeer's irreverence and theatric sensationalism— "'Les Huguenots' and the far weaker production 'Le Prophète' are, we think, all the more reprehensible (nowadays especially, when too much stress is laid on the subject of a work, and consequently on the libretto of an opera), because the Jew has in these pieces ruthlessly dragged before the footlights two of the darkest pictures in the annals of Catholicism, nor has he scrupled to bring high mass and chorale on the boards."

Wagner, the last of the great German composers, cannot find words too scathing and bitter to mark his condemnation of Meyerbeer. Perhaps his extreme aversion finds its psychological reason in the circumstance that his own early efforts were in the sphere of Meyerbeer and Halévy, and from his present point of view he looks back with disgust on what he regards as the sins of his youth. The fairest of the German estimates of the composer, who not only cast aside the national spirit and methods, but offended his countrymen by devoting himself to the French stage, is that of Vischer, an eminent writer on æsthetics—"Notwithstanding the composer's remarkable talent for musical drama, his operas contain sometimes too much, sometimes too little—too much in the subject-matter, external adornment, and effective 'situations'—too little in the absence of poetry, ideality, and sentiment (which are essential to a work of art), as well as in the unnatural and constrained combinations of the plot."

But despite the fact that Meyerbeer's operas contain such strange scenes as phantom nuns dancing, girls bathing, sunrise, skating, gunpowder explosions, a king playing the flute, and the prima donna leading a goat, dramatic music owes to him new accents of genuine pathos and an addition to its resources of rendering passionate emotions. Though much that is merely showy and meretricious there come frequent bursts of genuine musical power and energy, which give him a high and unmistakable rank, though he has had less permanent influence in moulding and directing the development of musical art than any other composer who has had so large a place in the annals of his time.

The last twelve years of Meyerbeer's life were spent, with the exception of brief residences in Germany and Italy, in Paris, the city of his adoption, where all who were distinguished in art and letters paid their court to him. When he was seized with his fatal illness he was hard at work on "L'Africaine," for which Scribe had also furnished the libretto. His heart was set on its completion, and his daily prayer was that his life might be spared to finish it. But it was not to be. He died May 2, 1864. The same morning Rossini called to inquire after the health of the sick man, equally his friend and rival. When he heard the sad news he sank into a fit of profound despondency and grief, from which he did not soon recover. All Paris mourned with him, and even Germany forgot its critical dislike to join in regret at the loss of one who, with all his defects, was so great an artist and so good a man.

Meyerbeer seems to have been greatly afraid of being buried alive. In his pocket-book after his death was found a paper giving directions that small bells should be attached to his hands and feet, and that his body should be carefully watched for four days, after which it should be sent to Berlin to be interred by the side of his mother, to whom he had been most tenderly attached.

The composer was the intimate friend of most of the celebrities of his time in art and literature. Victor Hugo, Lamartine, George Sand, Balzac, Alfred de Musset, Delacroix, Jules Janin, and Théophile Gautier were his familiar intimates; and the reunions between these and other gifted men, who then made Paris so intellectually brilliant, are charmingly described by Liszt and Moscheles. Meyerbeer's correspondence, which was extensive, deserves publication, as it displays marked literary faculty, and is full of bright sympathetic thought, vigorous criticism, and playful fancy. The following letter to Jules Janin, written from Berlin a few years before his death, gives some pleasant insight into his character:—

"Your last letter was addressed to me at Königsberg; but I was in Berlin working—working away like a young man, despite my seventy years, which somehow certain people, with a peculiar generosity, try to put upon me. As I am not at Königsberg, where I am to arrange for the Court concert for the eighteenth of this month, I have now leisure to answer your letter, and will immediately confess to you how greatly I was disappointed that you were so little interested in Rameau; and yet Rameau was always the bright star of your French opera, as well as your master in the music. He remained to you after Lulli, and it was he who prepared the way for the Chevalier Gluck: therefore his family have a right to expect assistance from the Parisians, who on several occasions have cared for the descendants of Racine and the grandchildren of the great Corneille. If I had been in Paris, I certainly would have given two hundred francs for a seat; and I take this opportunity to beg you to hand that sum to the poor family, who cannot fail to be unhappy in their disappointment. At the same time I send you a power of attorney for M. Guyot, by which I renounce all claims to the parts of my operas which may be represented at the benefit for the celebrated and unfortunate Rameau family. Why will you not come to Königsberg at the festival? Why, in other words, are you not in Berlin? What splendid music we have in preparation! As to myself, it is not only a source of pleasure to me, but I feel it a duty, in the position I hold, to compose a grand march, to be performed at Königsberg while the royal procession passes from the castle into the church, where the ceremony of crowning is to take place. I will even compose a hymn, to be executed on the day that our king and master returns to his good Berlin. Besides, I have promised to write an overture for the great concert of the four nations, which the directors of the London exhibition intend to give at the opening of the same, next spring, in the Crystal Palace. All this keeps me back: it has robbed me of my autumn, and will also take a good part of next spring; but with the help of God, dear friend, I hope we shall see each other again next year, free from all cares, in the charming little town of Spa, listening to the babbling of its waters and the rustling of its old grey oaks.

"Truly your friend,

"MEYERBEER."

IV.

Meyerbeer's operas are so intricate in their elements, and travel so far out of the beaten track of precedent and rule, that it is difficult to clearly describe their characteristics in a few words. His original flow of melody could not have been very rich, for none of his tunes have become household words, and his excessive use of that element of opera which has nothing to do with music, as in the case of Wagner, can have but one explanation. It is in the treatment of the orchestra that he has added most largely to the genuine treasures of music. His command of colour in tone-painting and power of dramatic suggestion have rarely been equalled, and never surpassed. His genius for musical rhythm is the most marked element in his power. This is specially noticeable in his dance music, which is very bold, brilliant, and voluptuous. The vivacity and grace of the ballets in his operas save more than one act which otherwise would be insufferably heavy and tedious. It is not too much to say that the most spontaneous side of his creative fancy is found in these affluent, vigorous, and stirring measures.

Meyerbeer appears always to have been uncertain of

himself and his work. There was little of that masterly prevision of effect in his mind which is one of the attributes of the higher imagination. His operas, though most elaborately constructed, were often entirely modified and changed in rehearsal, and some of the finest scenes, both in the dramatic and musical sense, were the outcome of some happy accidental suggestion at the very last moment. "Robert," "Les Huguenots," "Le Prophète," in the forms we have them, are quite different from those in which they were first cast. These operas have therefore been called "the most magnificent patchwork in the history of art," though this is a harsh phrasing of the fact, which somewhat outrides justice. Certain it is, however, that Meyerbeer was largely indebted to the chapter of accidents.

The testimony of Dr. Véron, who was manager of the Grand Opera during the most of the composer's brilliant career, is of great interest, as illustrating this trait of Meyerbeer's composition. He tells us in his *Mémoires*, before alluded to, that "Robert" was made and remade before its final production. The ghastly but effective colour of the resuscitation scene in the graveyard of the ruined convent was a change wrought by a stage manager, who was disgusted with the chorus of simpering women in the original. This led Meyerbeer to compose the weird ballet music which is such a characteristic feature of "Robert le Diable." So, too, we are told on the same authority, the fourth act of "Les Huguenots," which is the most powerful single act in Meyerbeer's operas, owes its present shape to Nourrit, the most intellectual and creative tenor singer of whom we have record. It was originally designed that the St. Bartholomew massacre should be organised by Queen Marguerite, but Nourrit pointed out that the interest centering in the heroine, Valentine, as an involuntary and horrified witness, would be impaired by the predominance of another female character. So the plot was largely reconstructed, and fresh music written. Another still more striking attraction was the addition of the great duet with which the act now closes—a duet which critics have cited as an evidence of unequalled power, coming as it does at the very heels of such an astounding chorus as "The Blessing of the Swords." Nourrit felt that the parting of the two lovers at such a time and place demanded such an outburst and confession as would be wrung from them by the agony of the situation. Meyerbeer acted on the suggestion with such felicity and force as to make it the crowning beauty of the work. Similar changes are understood to have been made in "Le Prophète" by advice of Nourrit, whose poetical insight seems to have been unerring. It was left to Duprez, Nourrit's successor, however, to be the first exponent of John of Leyden.

These instances suffice to show how uncertain and how unequal was the grasp of Meyerbeer's genius, and to explain in part why he was so prone to gorgeous effects, aside from that tendency of the Israelitish nature which delights in show and glitter. We see something in it akin to the trick of the rhetorician, who seeks to hide poverty of thought under glittering phrases. Yet Meyerbeer rose to occasions with a force that was something gigantic. Once his work was clearly defined in a mind not powerfully creative, he expressed it in music with such vigour, energy, and warmth of colour as cannot be easily surpassed. With this composer there was but little spontaneous flow of musical thought, clothing itself in forms of unconscious and perfect beauty, as in the case of Mozart, Beethoven, Cherubini, Rossini, and others who could be cited. The constitution of his mind demanded some external power to bring forth the gush of musical energy.

The operas of Meyerbeer may be best described as highly artistic and finished mosaic work, containing much that is precious with much that is false. There are parts of all his operas which cannot be surpassed for beauty of music, dramatic energy, and fascination of effect. In addition, the strength and richness of his orchestration, which contains original strokes not found in other composers, give him a lasting claim on the admiration of the lovers of music. No other composer has united so many glaring defects with such splendid power; and were it not that Meyerbeer strained his ingenuity to tax the resources of the singer in every possible way, not even the mechanical difficulty of producing these operas in a fashion commensurate with their plan would prevent their taking a high place among popular operas.

GOUNOD.

I.

MOSCHELES, one of the severe classical pianists of the German school, writes as follows, in 1861, in a letter to a friend—" In Gounod I hail a real composer. I have heard his 'Faust' both at Leipsic and Dresden, and am charmed with that refined, piquant music. Critics may rave if they like against the mutilation of Goethe's masterpiece; the opera is sure to attract, for it is a fresh, interesting work, with a copious flow of melody and lovely instrumentation."

Henry Chorley in his *Thirty Years' Musical Recollections*, writing of the year 1851, says—" To a few hearers, since then grown into a European public, neither the warmest welcome nor the most bleak indifference could alter the conviction that among the composers who have appeared during the last twenty-five years, M. Gounod was the most promising one, as showing the greatest combination of sterling science, beauty of idea, freshness of fancy, and individuality. Before a note of 'Sappho' was written, certain sacred Roman Catholic compositions and some exquisite settings of French verse had made it clear to some of the acutest judges and profoundest musicians living, that in him at last something true and new had come—may I not say, the most poetical of French musicians that has till now written?" The same genial and acute critic, in further discussing the envy, jealousy, and prejudice that Gounod awakened in certain musical quarters, writes in still more decided strains—"The fact has to be swallowed and digested that already the composer of 'Sappho,' the choruses to 'Ulysse,' 'Le Médecin malgré lui,' 'Faust,' 'Philemon et Baucis,' a superb Cecilian mass, two excellent symphonies, and half a hundred songs and romances, which may be ranged not far from Schubert's and above any others existing in France, is one of the very few individuals left to whom musical Europe is now looking for its pleasure." Surely it is enough praise for a great musician that, in the domain of opera, church music, symphony, and song, he has risen above all others of his time in one direction, and in all been surpassed by none.

It was not till "Faust" was produced that Gounod's genius evinced its highest capacity. For nineteen years the exquisite melodies of this great work have rung in the ears of civilisation without losing one whit of the power with which they first fascinated the lovers of music. The verdict which the aged Moscheles passed in his Leipsic home—Moscheles, the friend of Beethoven, Weber, Schumann, and Mendelssohn; which was re-echoed by the patriarchal Rossini, who came from his Passy retirement to offer his congratulations; which Auber took up again, as with tears of joy in his eyes he led Gounod, the ex-pupil of the Conservatory, through the halls wherein had been laid the foundation of his musical skill—that verdict has been affirmed over and over again by the world. For in "Faust" we recognise not only some of the most noble music ever written, but a highly dramatic expression of spiritual truth. It is hardly a question that Gounod has succeeded in an unrivalled degree in expressing the characters and symbolisms of "Mephistopheles," "Faust," and "Gretchen" in music not merely beautiful, but spiritual, humorous, subtile, and voluptuous, accordingly as the varied meanings of Goethe's masterpiece demand.

Visitors at Paris, while the American civil war was at its height, might frequently have observed at the beautiful

Théâtre Lyrique, afterwards burned by the Vandals of the Commune, a noticeable-looking man, of blonde complexion and tawny beard, clear-cut features, and large, bright, almost sombre-looking eyes. As the opera of "Faust" progresses, his features eloquently express his varying emotions, now of approval, now of annoyance at different parts of the performance. M. Gounod is criticising the interpretation of the great opera, which suddenly lifted him into fame as perhaps the most imaginative and creative of late composers.

An aggressive disposition, an energy and faith that accepted no rebuffs, and the power of "toiling terribly," had enabled Gounod to battle his way into the front rank. Unlike Rossini and Auber, he disdained social recreation, and was so rarely seen in the fashionable quarters of Paris and London that only an occasional musical announcement kept him before the eyes of the public. Gounod seems to have devoted himself to the strict sphere of his art-life with an exclusive devotion quite foreign to the general temperament of the musician, into which something luxurious and pleasure-loving is so apt to enter. This composer, standing in the very front rank of his fellows, has injected into the veins of the French school to which he belongs a seriousness, depth, and imaginative vigour, which prove to us how much he is indebted to German inspiration and German models.

CHARLES GOUNOD, born in Paris, June 17, 1818, betrayed so much passion for music during tender years, that his father gave him every opportunity to gratify and improve this marked bias. He studied under Reicha and Le Sueur, and finally under Halévy, completing under the latter the preparation which fitted him for entrance into the Conservatory. The talents he displayed there were such as to fix on him the attention of his most distinguished masters. He carried off the second prize at nineteen, and at twenty-one received the grand prize for musical composition awarded by the French Institute. His first published work was a mass performed at the Church of St. Eustache, which, while not specially successful, was sufficiently encouraging to both the young composer and his friends.

Gounod now proceeded to Rome, where there seems to have been some inclination on his part to study for holy orders. But music was not destined to be cheated of so gifted a votary. In 1841 he wrote a second mass, which was so well thought of in the papal capital as to gain for the young composer the appointment of an honorary chapel-master for life. This recognition of his genius settled his final conviction that music was his true life-work, though the religious sentiment, or rather a sympathy with mysticism, is strikingly apparent in all of his compositions. The next goal in the composer's art pilgrimage was the music-loving city of Vienna, the home of Haydn, Mozart, Beethoven, and Schubert, though its people waited till the last three great geniuses were dead before it accorded them the loving homage which they have since so freely rendered. The reception given by the capricious Viennese to a requiem and a Lenten mass (for as yet Gounod only thought of sacred music as his vocation) was not such as to encourage a residence. Paris, the queen of the world, towards which every French exile ever looks with longing eyes, seemed to beckon him back; so at the age of twenty-five he turned his steps again to his beloved Lutetia. His education was finished; he had completed his "Wanderjahre;" and he was eager to enter on the serious work of life.

He was appointed chapel-master at the Church of Foreign Missions, in which office he remained for six years, in the meanwhile marrying a charming woman, the daughter of Herr Zimmermann, the celebrated theologian and orator. In 1849 he composed his third mass, which made a powerful impression on musicians and critics, though Gounod's ambition, which seems to have been powerfully stimulated by his marriage, began to realise that it was in the field of lyric drama only that his powers would find their full development. He had been an ardent student in literature and art as well as in music; his style had been formed on the most noble and serious German models, and his tastes, awakened into full activity, carried him with great zeal into the loftier field of operatic composition.

The dominating influence of Gluck, so potent in shaping the tastes and methods of the more serious French composers, asserted itself from the beginning in the work of Gounod, and no modern composer has been so brilliant and effective a disciple in carrying out the formulas of that great master. More free, flexible, and melodious than Spontini and Halévy, measuring his work by a conception of art more lofty and ideal than that of Meyerbeer, and in creative power and originality by far their superior, Gounod's genius, as shown in the one opera of "Faust," suffices to stamp his great mastership.

But he had many years of struggle yet before this end was to be achieved. His early lyric compositions fell dead. Score after score was rejected by the managers. No one cared to hazard the risk of producing an opera by this unknown composer. His first essay was a pastoral opera, "Philemon and Baucis," and it did not escape from the manuscript for many a long year, though it has in more recent times been received by critical German audiences with great applause. A catalogue of Gounod's failures would have no significance except as showing that his industry and energy were not relaxed by public neglect. His first decided encouragement came in 1851, when "Sappho" was produced at the French Opera through the influence of Madame Pauline Viardot, the sister of Malibran, who had a generous belief in the composer's future, and such a position in the musical world of Paris as to make her requests almost mandatory. This opera, based on the fine poem of Emile Augier, was well received, and cheered Gounod's heart to make fresh efforts. In 1852 he composed the choruses for Poussard's classical tragedy of "Ulysse," performed at the Théâtre Français. The growing recognition of the world was evidenced in his appointment as director of the Normal Singing School of Paris, the primary school of the Conservatory. In 1854 a five-act opera, with a libretto from the legend of the "Bleeding Nun," was completed and produced, and Gounod was further gratified to see that musical authorities were willing to grant him a distinct place in the ranks of art, though as yet not a very high one.

For years Gounod's serious and elevated mind had been pondering on Goethe's great poem as the subject of an opera, and there is reason to conjecture that parts of it were composed and arranged, if not fully elaborated, long prior to its final crystallisation. But he was not yet quite ready to enter seriously on the composition of the masterpiece. He must still try his hand on lesser themes. Occasional pieces for the orchestra or choruses strengthened his hold on these important elements of lyric composition, and in 1858 he produced "Le Médecin malgré lui," based on Molière's comedy, afterwards performed as an English opera under the title of "The Mock Doctor." Gounod's genius seems to have had no affinity for the graceful and sparkling measures of comic music, and his attempt to rival Rossini and Auber in the field where they were pre-eminent was decidedly unsuccessful, though the opera contained much fine music.

II.

The year of his triumph had at last arrived. He had waited and toiled for years over "Faust," and it was now ready to flash on the world with an electric brightness that was to make his name instantly famous. One day saw him an obscure, third-rate composer, the next one of the brilliant names in art. "Faust," first performed 19th March 1859, fairly took the world by storm. Gounod's warmest friends were amazed by the beauty of the masterpiece, in which exquisite melody, great orchestration, and a dramatic passion never surpassed in operatic art, were combined with a scientific skill and precision which would vie with that of the great masters of harmony. Carvalho, the manager of the Théâtre Lyrique, had predicted that the work would have a magnificent reception by the art world, and lavished on it every stage resource. Madame Miolan-Carvalho, his brilliant wife, one of the leading sopranos of the day, sang the rôle of the heroine, though five years afterwards she was succeeded by Nilsson, who invested the part with a poetry and tenderness which have never been quite equalled.

"Faust" was received at Berlin, Vienna, Milan, St. Petersburg, and London, with an enthusiasm not less than that which greeted its Parisian début. The clamour of dispute between the different schools was for the moment hushed in the delight with which the musical critics and public of universal Europe listened to the magical measures of an opera which to classical chasteness and severity of form and elevation of motive united such dramatic passion, richness of melody, and warmth of orchestral colour. From that day to the present "Faust" has retained its place as not only the greatest but the most popular of modern operas. The proof of the composer's skill and sense of symmetry in the composition of "Faust" is shown in the fact that each part is so nearly necessary to the work, that but few "cuts" can be made in presentation without essentially marring the beauty of the work; and it is therefore given with close faithfulness to the author's score.

After the immense success of "Faust," the doors of the Academy were opened wide to Gounod. On February 28, 1862, the "Reine de Saba" was produced, but was only a *succès d'estime*, the libretto by Gérard de Nerval not being fitted for a lyric tragedy.* Many numbers of this fine work, however, are still favourites on concert programmes, and it has been given in English under the name of "Irene." Gounod's love of romantic themes, and the interest in France which Lamartine's glowing eulogies had excited about "Mireio," the beautiful national poem of the Provençal, M. Frédéric Mistral, led the former to compose an opera on a

---

* It has been a matter of frequent comment by the ablest musical critics that many noble operas, now never heard, would have retained their place in the repertoires of modern dramatic music, had it not been for the utter rubbish to which the music has been set.

libretto from this work, which was given at the Théâtre Lyrique, March 19, 1864, under the name of "Mireille." The music, however, was rather descriptive and lyric than dramatic, as befitted this lovely ideal of early French provincial life; and in spite of its containing some of the most captivating airs ever written, and the fine interpretation of the heroine by Miolan-Carvalho, it was accepted with reservations. It has since become more popular in its three-act form to which it was abridged. It is a tribute to the essential beauty of Gounod's music that, however unsuccessful as operas certain of his works have been, they have all contributed charming *morceaux* for the enjoyment of concert audiences. Not only did the airs of "Mireille" become public favourites, but its overture is frequently given as a distinct orchestral work.

The opera of "La Colombe," known in English as "The Pet Dove," followed in 1866; and the next year was produced the five-act opera of "Roméo et Juliette," of which the principal part was again taken by Madame Miolan-Carvalho. The favourite pieces in this work, which is a highly poetic rendering of Shakespeare's romantic tragedy, are the song of *Queen Mab*, the garden duet, a short chorus in the second act, and the duel scene in the third act. For some occult reason, "Roméo et Juliette," though recognised as a work of exceptional beauty and merit, and still occasionally performed, has no permanent hold on the operatic public of to-day.

The evils that fell on France from the German war and the horrors of the Commune drove Gounod to reside in London, unlike Auber, who resolutely refused to forsake the city of his love, in spite of the suffering and privation which he foresaw, and which were the indirect cause of the veteran composer's death. Gounod remained several years in England, and lived a retired life, seemingly as if he shrank from public notice and disdained public applause. His principal appearances were at the Philharmonic, the Crystal Palace, and at Mrs. Weldon's concerts, where he directed the performances of his own compositions. The circumstances of his London residence seem to have cast a cloud over Gounod's life and to have strangely unsettled his mind. Patriotic grief probably had something to do with this at the outset. But even more than this as a source of permanent irritation may be reckoned the spell cast over Gounod's mind by a beautiful adventuress, who was ambitious to attain social and musical recognition through the *éclat* of the great composer's friendship. Though newspaper report may be credited with swelling and distorting the naked facts, enough appears to be known to make it sure that the evil genius of Gounod's London life was a woman, who traded recklessly with her own reputation and the French composer's fame.

However untoward the surroundings of Gounod, his genius did not lie altogether dormant during this period of friction and fretfulness, conditions so repressive to the best imaginative work. He composed several masses and other church music; a "Stabat Mater" with orchestra; the oratorio of "Tobie"; "Gallia," a lamentation for France; incidental music for Legouvé's tragedy of "Les Deux Reines," and for Jules Barbier's "Jeanne d'Arc;" a large number of songs and romances, both sacred and secular, such as "Nazareth," and "There is a Green Hill;" and orchestral works, "Saltcrello in A," and the "Funeral March of a Marionette."

At last he broke loose from the bonds of Delilah, and, remembering that he had been elected to fill the place of Clapisson in the Institute, he returned to Paris in 1876 to resume the position which his genius so richly deserved. On the 5th of March of the following year his "Cinq-Mars" was brought out at the Théâtre de l'Opéra Comique; but it showed the traces of the haste and carelessness with which it was written, and therefore commanded little more than a respectful hearing. His last opera, "Polyeucte," produced at the Grand Opera, October 7, 1878, though credited with much beautiful music, and nobly orchestrated, is not regarded by the French critics as likely to add anything to the reputation of the composer of "Faust."

Gounod, now at the age of sixty, if we judge him by the prolonged fertility of so many of the great composers, may be regarded as not having largely passed the prime of his powers. The world still has a right to expect much from his genius. Conceded even by his opponents to be a great musician and a thorough master of the orchestra, more generous critics in the main agree to rank Gounod as the most remarkable contemporary composer, with the possible exception of Richard Wagner. The distinctive trait of his dramatic conceptions seems to be an imagination hovering between sensuous images and mystic dreams. Originally inspired by the severe Greek sculpture of Gluck's music, he has applied that master's laws in the creation of tone-pictures full of voluptuous colour, but yet solemnised at times by an exaltation which recalls the time when as a youth he thought of the spiritual dignity of priesthood. The use he makes of his religious reminiscences is familiarly illustrated in "Faust." The contrast between two opposing principles is marked in all of Gounod's dramatic works, and in "Faust" this struggle of "a soul which invades mysticism and which still seeks to express voluptuousness" not only colours the music with a novel fascination, but amounts to an interesting psychological problem.

III.

Gounod's genius fills too large a space in contemporary music to be passed over without a brief special study. In pursuit of this no better method suggests itself than an examination of the opera of "Faust," into which the composer poured the finest inspirations of his life, even as Goethe embodied the sum and flower of his long career, which had garnered so many experiences, in his poetic masterpiece.

The story of "Faust" has tempted many composers. Prince Radziwill tried it, and then Spohr set a version of the theme at once coarse and cruel, full of vulgar witch-work and love-making only fit for a chambermaid. Since then Schumann, Liszt, Wagner, and Berlioz have treated the story orchestrally with more or less success. Gounod's treatment of the poem is by far the most intelligible, poetic, and dramatic ever attempted, and there is no opera since the days of Gluck with so little weak music, except Beethoven's " Fidelio."

In the introduction the restless gloom of the old philosopher and the contrasted joys of youth engaged in rustic revelry outside are expressed with graphic force ; and the Kirmes music in the next act is so quaint and original, as well as melodious, as to give the sense of delightful comedy. When Marguerite enters on the scene, we have a waltz and chorus of such beauty and piquancy as would have done honour to Mozart. Indeed, in the dramatic use of dance music Gounod hardly yields in skill and originality to Meyerbeer himself, though the latter composer specially distinguished himself in this direction. The third and fourth acts develop all the tenderness and passion of Marguerite's character, all the tragedy of her doom.

After Faust's beautiful monologue in the garden come the song of the "King of Thule" and Marguerite's delight at finding the jewels, which conjoined express the artless vanity of the child in a manner alike full of grace and pathos. The quartet that follows is one of great beauty, the music of each character being thoroughly in keeping, while the admirable science of the composer blends all into thorough artistic unity. It is hardly too much to assert that the love scene which closes this act has nothing to surpass it for fire, passion, and tenderness, seizing the mind of the hearer with absorbing force by its suggestion and imagery, while the almost cloying sweetness of the melody is such as Rossini and Schubert only could equal. The full confession of the enamoured pair contained in the brief *adagio* throbs with such rapture as to find its most suggestive parallel in the ardent words commencing

" Gallop apace, ye fiery-footed steeds,"

placed by Shakespeare in the mouth of the expectant Juliet.

Beauties succeed each other in swift and picturesque succession, fitting the dramatic order with a nicety which forces the highest praise of the critic. The march and the chorus marking the return of Valentine's regiment beat with a fire and enthusiasm to which the tramp of victorious squadrons might well keep step. The wicked music of Mephistopheles in the sarcastic serenade, the powerful duel trio, and Valentine's curse are of the highest order of expression; while the church scene, where the fiend whispers his taunts in the ear of the disgraced Marguerite, as the gloomy musical hymn and peals of the organ menace her with an irreversible doom, is a weird and thrilling picture of despair, agony, and devilish exultation.

Gounod has been blamed for violating the reverence due to sacred things, employing portions of the church service in this scene, instead of writing music for it. But this is the last resort of critical hostility, seeking a peg on which to hang objection. Meyerbeer's splendid introduction of Luther's great hymn, "Ein' feste Burg," in "Les Huguenots," called forth a similar criticism from his German assailants. Some of the most dramatic effects in music have been created by this species of musical quotation, so rich in its appeal to memory and association. Who that has once heard can forget the thrilling power of "La Marseillaise" in Schumann's setting of Heinrich Heine's poem of "The Two Grenadiers?" The two French soldiers, weary and broken-hearted after the Russian campaign, approach the German frontier. The veterans are moved to tears as they think of their humiliated Emperor. Up speaks one suffering with a deadly hurt to the other, "Friend, when I am dead, bury me in my native France, with my cross of honour on my breast, and my musket in my hand, and lay my good sword by my side." Until this time the melody has been a slow and dirge-like stave in the minor key. The old soldier declares his belief that he will rise again from the clods when he hears the victorious tramp of his Emperor's squadrons passing over his grave, and the minor breaks into a weird setting of the

"Marseillaise" in the major key. Suddenly it closes with a few solemn chords, and, instead of the smoke of battle and the march of the phantom host, the imagination sees the lonely plain with its green mounds and mouldering crosses.

Readers will pardon this digression illustrating an artistic law, of which Gounod has made such effective use in the church scene of his "Faust" in heightening its tragic solemnity. The wild goblin symphony in the fifth act has added some new effects to the gamut of deviltry in music, and shows that Weber in the "Wolf's Glen" and Meyerbeer in the "Cloisters of St. Rosalie" did not exhaust the somewhat limited field. The whole of this part of the act, sadly mutilated and abridged often in representation, is singularly picturesque and striking as a musical conception, and is a fitting companion to the tragic prison scene. The despair of the poor crazed Marguerite; her delirious joy in recognising Faust; the temptation to fly; the final outburst of faith and hope, as the sense of Divine pardon sinks into her soul—all these are touched with the fire of genius, and the passion sweeps with an unfaltering force to its climax. These references to the details of a work so familiar as "Faust," conveying of course no fresh information to the reader, have been made to illustrate the peculiarities of Gounod's musical temperament, which sways in such fascinating contrast between the voluptuous and the spiritual. But whether his accents belong to the one or the other, they bespeak a mood flushed with earnestness and fervour, and a mind which recoils from the frivolous, however graceful it may be.

In the Franco-German school, of which Gounod is so high an exponent, the orchestra is busy throughout developing the history of the emotions, and in "Faust" especially it is as busy a factor in expressing the passions of the characters as the vocal parts. Not even in the "garden scene" does the singing reduce the instruments to a secondary importance. The difference between Gounod and Wagner, who professes to elaborate the importance of the orchestra in dramatic music, is that the former has a skill in writing for the voice which the other lacks. The one lifts the voice by the orchestration, the other submerges it. Gounod's affluence of lovely melody can only be compared with that of Mozart and Rossini, and his skill and ingenuity in treating the orchestra have wrung reluctant praise from his bitterest opponents.

The special power which makes Gounod unique in his art, aside from those elements before alluded to as derived from temperament, is his unerring sense of dramatic fitness, which weds such highly suggestive music to each varying phase of character and action. To this perhaps one exception may be made. While he possesses a certain airy playfulness, he fails in rich broad humour utterly, and situations of comedy are by no means so well handled as the more serious scenes. A good illustration of this may be found in the "Le Médecin malgré lui," in the couplets given to the drunken "Sganarelle." They are beautiful music, but utterly unflavoured with the *vis comica*.

Had Gounod written only "Faust," it should stamp him as one of the most highly-gifted composers of his age. Noticeably in his other works, pre-eminently in this, he has shown a melodic freshness and fertility, a mastery of musical form, a power of orchestration, and a dramatic energy, which are combined to the same degree in no one of his rivals. Therefore it is just to place him in the first rank of contemporary composers.

NOTE BY THE EDITOR.—Gounod is a strongly religious man, and more than once has been on the point of entering the Church. It is, therefore, not surprising that he should have in his later life turned his attention to the finest form of sacred music, the oratorio. His first and greatest work of this class is his "Redemption," produced at the Birmingham Festival of 1882, and conducted by himself. It was well received, and has met with success at all subsequent performances. It is intended to illustrate "three great facts (to quote the composer's words in his prefatory commentary) on which the existence of the Christian Church depends. . . The Passion and death of the

Saviour, His glorious life on earth from His resurrection to His Ascension, and finally the spread of Christianity in the world through the mission of the apostles. These three parts of the present trilogy are preceded by a Prologue on the Creation and Fall of our first parents, and the promise of the Redeemer." In this work Gounod has discarded the polyphonic method of the previous school of Italian and German sacred music, and adopted the dramatic treatment. A competent critic has written of this work in the following words:—" The 'Redemption' may be classed among its author's noblest productions. It is a work of high aim, written regardless of immediate popularity, and therefore all the more likely to take rank among the permanent additions which sacred music owes to modern music." In 1885 the oratorio of "Mors et Vita" was produced at the Birmingham Festival, conducted by Herr Richter. Though well received, it did not make as great an impression as its predecessor, to which it stands in the light of a sequel. It consists of four parts—a short Prologue, a Requiem Mass, the Last Judgment, and Judex (or the Celestial City). In the Prologue a special *leitmotive* accompanying the words " Horrendum est in incidere in Manus Dei" signifies the Death, not only of the body, but of the unredeemed soul. A gleam of hope, however, pierces the darkness, and a beautiful theme is heard frequently throughout the work expressive of "the idea of justice tempered with mercy, and finally the happiness of the blessed. The two opposing forces of the design, *Mors* and *Vita*, are thus well defined." The work, however, is unequal; the Requiem Mass, in particular, does not rise in importance when compared with the many fine examples of the Italian and German sacred music which preceded it. "Compared with that truly inspired work, 'Redemption,' partly written, it should be remembered, more than ten years previously, Gounod's new effort shows a distinct decline, especially as regards unity of style and genuine inspiration."

BERLIOZ.

I.

IN the long list of brilliant names which have illustrated the fine arts, there is none attached to a personality more interesting and impressive than that of Hector Berlioz. He stands solitary, a colossus in music, with but few admirers and fewer followers. Original, puissant in faculties, fiercely dogmatic and intolerant, bizarre, his influence has impressed itself profoundly on the musical world both for good and evil, but has failed to make disciples or to rear a school. Notwithstanding the defects and extravagances of Berlioz, it is safe to assert that no art or philosophy can boast of an example of more perfect devotion to an ideal. The startling originality of Berlioz as a musician rests on a mental and emotional organisation different from and in some respects superior to that of any other eminent master. He possessed an ardent temperament; a gorgeous imagination, that knew no rest in its working, and at times became heated to the verge of madness; a most subtile sense of hearing; an intellect of the keenest analytic turn; a most arrogant will, full of enterprise and daring, which clung to its purpose with unrelenting tenacity; and passions of such heat and fervour that they rarely failed when aroused to carry him beyond all bounds of reason. His genius was unique, his character cast in the mould of a Titan, his life a tragedy. Says Blaze de Bussy—"Art has its martyrs, its forerunners crying in the wilderness, and feeding on roots. It has also its spoiled children sated with bonbons and dainties." Berlioz belongs to the former of these classes, and, if ever a prophet lifted up his voice with a vehement and incessant outcry, it was he.

HECTOR BERLIOZ was born on December 11, 1803, at Côte Saint André, a small town between Grenoble and Lyons. His father was an excellent physician of more than ordinary attainments, and he superintended his son's studies with great zeal, in the hope that the lad would also become an ornament of the healing profession. But young Hector, though an excellent scholar in other branches, developed a special aptitude for music, and at twelve he could sing at sight, and play difficult concertos on the flute. The elder regarded music only as a graceful ornament to life, and in nowise encouraged his son in thinking of music as a profession. So it was not long before Hector found his attention directed to anatomy, physiology, osteology, etc. In his father's library he had already read of Gluck, Haydn, Mozart, etc., and had found a manuscript score of an opera which he had committed to memory. His soul revolted more and more from the path cut out for him. "Become a physician!" he cried, "study anatomy; dissect; take part in horrible operations? No! no! That would be a total subversion of the natural course of my life."

But parental resolution carried the day, and, after he had finished the preliminary course of study, he was ordered up to Paris to join the army of medical students. So at the age of nineteen we find him lodged in the Quartier Latin. His first introduction to medical studies had been unfortunate. On entering a dissecting-room he had been so convulsed with horror as to leap from the window, and rush to his lodgings in an agony of dread and disgust, whence he did not emerge for twenty-four hours. At last, however, by dint of habit he became somewhat used to the disagreeable facts of his new life, and, to use his own words, "bade fair to add one more to the army of bad physicians," when he went to the opera one night and heard "Les Danaïdes," Salieri's opera, performed with all the splendid completeness of the Académie Royale. This awakened into fresh life an unquenchable thirst for music, and he neglected his medical studies for the library of the Conservatoire, where he learned by heart the scores of Gluck and Rameau. At last, on coming out one night from a performance of "Iphigénie," he swore that henceforth music should have her divine rights of him, in spite of all and everything. Henceforth hospital, dissecting-room, and professor's lectures knew him no more.

But to get admission to the Conservatoire was now the problem; Berlioz set to work on a cantata with orchestral accompaniments, and in the meantime sent the most imploring letters home asking his father's sanction for this change of life. The inexorable parent replied by cutting off his son's allowance, saying that he would not help him to become one of the miserable herd of unsuccessful musicians. The young enthusiast's cantata gained him admission to the classes of Le Sueur and Reicha at the Conservatoire, but alas! dire poverty stared him in the face. The history of his shifts and privations for some months is a sad one. He slept in an old, unfurnished garret, and shivered under insufficient bed-clothing, ate his bread and grapes on the Pont Neuf, and sometimes debated whether a plunge into the Seine would not be the easiest way out of it all. No mongrel cur in the capital but had a sweeter bone to crunch than he. But the young fellow for all this stuck to his work with dogged tenacity, managed to get a mass performed at St. Roch church, and soon finished the score of an opera, "Les Francs Juges." Flesh and blood would have given way at last under this hard diet, if he had not obtained a position in the chorus of the Théâtre des Noveauteaus. Berlioz gives an amusing account of his going to compete with the horde of applicants—butchers, bakers, shop-apprentices, etc.—each one with his roll of music under his arm.

The manager scanned the raw-boned starveling with a look of wonder. "Where's your music?" quoth the tyrant of a third-class theatre. "I don't want any, I can sing anything you can give me at sight," was the answer. "The devil!" rejoined the manager; "but we haven't any music here." "Well, what do you want?" said Berlioz. "I sing every note of all the operas of Gluck, Piccini, Salieri, Rameau, Spontini, Grétry, Mozart, and Cimarosa, from memory." At hearing this amazing declaration, the rest of the competitors slunk away abashed, and Berlioz, after singing an aria from Spontini, was accorded the place, which guaranteed him fifty francs per month—a pittance, indeed, and yet a substantial addition to his resources. This pot-boiling connection of Berlioz was never known to the public till after he became a distinguished man, though he was accustomed to speak in vague terms of his early dramatic career as if it were a matter of romantic importance.

At last, however, he was relieved of the necessity of singing on the stage to amuse the Paris *bourgeoisie*, and in a singular fashion. He had been put to great straits to get his first work, which had won him his way into the Conservatoire, performed. An application to the great Chateaubriand, who was noted for benevolence, had failed, for the author of *La Génie de Christianisme* was then almost as poor as Berlioz. At last a young friend, De Pons, advanced him twelve hundred francs. Part of this Berlioz had repaid, but the creditor, put to it for money, wrote to Berlioz *père*, demanding a full settlement of the debt. The father was thus brought again into communication with his son, whom he found nearly sick unto death with a fever. His heart relented, and the old allowance was resumed again, enabling the young musician to give his whole time to his beloved art, instantly he convalesced from his illness.

The eccentric ways and heretical notions of Berlioz made him no favourite with the dons of the Conservatoire, and by the irritable and autocratic Cherubini he was positively hated. The young man took no pains to placate this resentment, but on the other hand elaborated methods of making himself doubly offensive. His power of stinging repartee stood him in good stead, and he never put a button on his foil. Had it been in old Cherubini's power to expel this bold pupil from the Conservatoire, no scruple would have held him back. But the genius and industry of Berlioz were undeniable, and there was no excuse for such extreme measures. Prejudiced as were his judges, he successively took several important prizes.

II.

Berlioz's happiest evenings were at the Grand Opéra, for which he prepared himself by solemn meditation. At the head of a band of students and amateurs, he took on himself the right of the most outspoken criticism, and led the enthusiasm or the condemnation of the audience. At this time Beethoven was barely tolerated in Paris, and the great symphonist was ruthlessly clipped and shorn to suit the French taste, which pronounced him "bizarre, incoherent, diffuse, bustling with rough modulations and wild harmonies, destitute of melody, forced in expression, noisy, and fearfully difficult," even as England at the same time frowned down his immortal works as "obstreperous roarings of modern frenzy." Berlioz's clear, stern voice would often be heard, when liberties were taken with the score, loud above the din of the instruments. "What wretch has dared to tamper with the great Beethoven?" "Who has taken upon him to revise Gluck?" This self-appointed arbiter became the dread of the operatic management, for, as a pupil of the Conservatoire, he had some rights which could not be infringed.

Berlioz composed some remarkable works while at the Conservatoire, amongst which were the "Ouverture des Francs Juges," and the symphonic "Fantastique," and in many ways indicated that the bent of his genius had fully declared itself. His decided and indomitable nature disdained to wear a mask, and he never sugar-coated his opinion, however unpalatable to others. He was already in a state of fierce revolt against the conventional forms of the music of his day, and no trumpet-tones of protest were too loud for him. He had now begun to write for the journals, though oftentimes his articles were refused on account of their fierce assaults. "Your hands are too full of stones, and there are too many glass windows about," was the excuse of one editor, softening the return of a manuscript. But Berlioz did not fully know himself or appreciate the tendencies fermenting within him until in 1830 he became the victim of a grand Shakespearean passion. The great English dramatist wrought most powerfully on Victor Hugo and Hector Berlioz, and had much to do with their artistic development. Berlioz gives a very interesting account of his Shakespearean enthusiasm, which also involved one of the catastrophes of his own personal life. "An English company gave some plays of Shakespeare, at that time wholly unknown to the French public. I went to the first performance of 'Hamlet' at the Odéon. I saw, in the part of Ophelia, Harriet Smithson, who became my wife five years afterwards. The effect of her prodigious talent, or rather of her dramatic genius, upon my heart and imagination, is only comparable to the complete overturning which the poet, whose worthy interpreter she was, caused in me. Shakespeare, thus coming on me suddenly, struck me as with a thunderbolt. His lightning opened the heaven of art to me with a sublime crash, and lighted up its farthest depths. I recognised true dramatic grandeur, beauty, and truth. I measured at the same time the boundless inanity of the notions of Shakespeare in France, spread abroad by Voltaire.

'. . . ce singe de génie,
Chez l'homme en mission par le diable envoyé—'

('that ape of genius, an emissary from the devil to man'), and the pitiful poverty of our old poetry of pedagogues and ragged-school teachers. I saw, I understood, I felt that I was alive and must arise and walk." Of the influence of "Romeo and Juliet" on him, he says, "Exposing myself to the burning sun and balmy nights of Italy, seeing this love as quick and sudden as thought, burning like lava, imperious, irresistible, boundless, and pure and beautiful as the smile of angels, those furious scenes of vengeance, those distracted embraces, those struggles between love and death, was too much. After the melancholy, the gnawing anguish, the tearful love, the cruel irony, the sombre meditations, the heart-rackings, the madness, tears, mourning, the calamities [and sharp cleverness of Hamlet; after the grey clouds and icy winds of Denmark; after the third act, hardly breathing, in pain as if a hand of iron were squeezing at my heart, I said to myself with the fullest conviction, 'Ah! I am lost.' I must add that I did not at that time know a word of English, that I only caught glimpses of Shakespeare through the fog of Letourneur's translation, and that I consequently could not perceive the poetic web that surrounds his marvellous creations like a net of gold. I have the misfortune to be very nearly in the same sad case to-day. It is much harder for a Frenchman to sound the depths of Shakespeare than for an Englishman to feel the delicacy and originality of La Fontaine or Molière. Our two poets are rich continents; Shakespeare is a world. But the play of the actors, above all of the actress, the succession of the scenes, the pantomime and the accent of the voices, meant more to me, and filled me a thousand times more with Shakespearean ideas and passion than the text of my colourless and unfaithful translation. An English critic said last winter in the *Illustrated London News*, that, after seeing Miss Smithson in Juliet, I had cried out, 'I will marry that woman and write my grandest symphony on this play.' I did both, but never said anything of the sort."

The beautiful Miss Smithson became the rage, the inspiration of poets and painters, the idol of the hour, at whose feet knelt all the *roués* and rich idlers of the town. Delacroix painted her as the Ophelia of his celebrated picture, and the English company made nearly as much sensation in Paris as the Comédie Française recently aroused in London. Berlioz's mind, perturbed and inflamed with the mighty images of the Shakespearean world, swept with wide, powerful passion towards Shakespeare's interpreter. He raged and stormed with his accustomed vehemence, made no secret of his infatuation, and walked the streets at night, calling aloud the name of the enchantress, and cooling his heated brows with many a sigh. He, too, would prove that he was a great artist, and his idol should know that she had no unworthy lover. He would give a concert, and Miss Smithson should be present by hook or by crook. He went to Cherubini and asked permission to use the great hall of the Conservatoire, but was churlishly refused. Berlioz, however, managed to secure the concession over the head of Cherubini, and advertised his concert. He went to large expense in copyists, orchestra, solo-singers, and chorus, and, when the night came, was almost fevered with expectation. But the concert was a failure, and the adored one was not there; she had not even heard of it! The disappointment nearly laid the young composer on a bed of sickness; but, if he oscillated between deliriums of hope and despair, his powerful will was also full of elasticity, and not for long did he even rave in the utter ebb of disappointment. Throughout the whole of his life, Berlioz displayed this swiftness of recoil; one moment crazed with grief and depression, the next he would bend to his labour with a cool, steady fixedness of purpose, which would sweep all interferences aside like cobwebs. But still, night after night, he would haunt the Odéon, and drink in the sights and sounds of the magic world of Shakespeare, getting fresh inspiration nightly for his genius and love. If he paid dearly for this rich intellectual acquaintance by his passion for La Belle Smithson, he yet gained impulses and suggestions for his imagination, ravenous of new impressions, which wrought deeply and permanently. Had Berlioz known the outcome, he would not have bartered for immunity by losing the jewels and ingots of the Shakespeare treasure-house.

The year 1830 was for Berlioz one of alternate exaltation and misery; of struggle, privation, disappointment; of all manner of torments inseparable from such a volcanic temperament and restless brain. But he had one consolation which gratified his vanity. He gained the Prix de Rome by his cantata of "Sardanapalus." This honour had a practical value also. It secured him an annuity of three thousand francs for a period of five years, and two years' residence in Italy. Berlioz would never let "well enough" alone, however. He insisted on adding an orchestral part to the completed score, describing the grand conflagration of the palace of Sardanapalus. When the work was produced, it was received with a howl of sarcastic derision, owing to the latest whim of the composer. So Berlioz started for Italy, smarting with rage and pain, as if the Furies were lashing him with their scorpion whips.

III.

The pensioners of the Conservatoire lived at Rome in the Villa Medici, and the illustrious painter, Horace Vernet, was the director, though he exercised but little supervision over the studies of the young men under his nominal charge. Berlioz did very much as he pleased—studied little or much as the whim seized him, visited the churches, studios, and picture-galleries, and spent no little of his time by starlight and sunlight roaming about the country adjacent to the Holy City in search of adventures. He had soon come to the conclusion that he had not much to learn of Italian music; that he could teach rather than be taught. He speaks of Roman art with the bitterest scorn, and Wagner himself never made a more savage indictment of Italian music than does Berlioz in his *Mémoires*. At the theatres he found the orchestra, dramatic unity, and common sense all sacrificed to mere vocal display. At St. Peter's and the Sistine Chapel religious earnestness and dignity were frittered away in pretty part-singing, in mere frivolity and meretricious show. The word "symphony" was not known except to indicate an indescribable noise before the rising of the curtain. Nobody had heard of Weber and Beethoven, and Mozart, dead more than a score of years, was mentioned by a well-known musical connoisseur as a young man of great promise! Such surroundings as these were a species of purgatory to Berlioz, against whose bounds he fretted and raged without intermission. The director's receptions were signalised by the performance of insipid cavatinas, and from these, as from his companions' revels, in which he would sometimes indulge with the maddest debauchery as if to kill his own thoughts, he would escape to wander in the majestic ruins of the Coliseum and see the magic Italian moonlight shimmer through its broken arches, or stroll on the lonely Campagna till his clothes were drenched with dew. No fear of the deadly Roman malaria could check his restless excursions, for, like a fiery horse, he was irritated to madness by the inaction of his life. To him the *dolce far niente* was a meaningless phrase. His comrades scoffed at him and called him "*Père la Joie,*" in derision of the fierce melancholy which despised them, their pursuits and pleasures.

At the end of the year he was obliged to present something before the Institute as a mark of his musical advancement, and he sent on a fragment of his "Mass" heard years before at St. Roch, in which the wise judges professed to find the "evidences of material advancement, and the total abandonment of his former reprehensible tendencies." One can fancy the scornful laughter of Berlioz at hearing this verdict. But his Italian life was not altogether purposeless. He revised his "Symphonie Fantastique," and wrote its sequel, "Lelio," a lyrical monologue, in which he aimed to express the memories of his passion for the beautiful Miss Smithson. These two parts comprised what Berlioz named "An Episode in the Life of an Artist." Our composer managed to get the last six months of his Italian exile remitted, and his return to Paris was hastened by one of those furious paroxysms of rage to which such ill-regulated minds are subject. He had adored Miss Smithson as a celestial divinity, a lovely ideal of art and beauty, but this had not prevented him from basking in the rays of the earthly Venus. Before leaving Paris he had had an intrigue with a certain Mdlle. M———, a somewhat frivolous and unscrupulous beauty, who had bled his not overfilled purse with the avidity of a leech. Berlioz heard just before returning to Paris that the coquette was about to marry, a conclusion one would fancy which would have rejoiced his mind. But, no! he was worked to a dreadful rage by what he considered such perfidy! His one thought was to avenge himself. He provided himself with three loaded pistols—one for the faithless one, one for his rival, and one for himself—and was so impatient to start that he could not wait for passports. He attempted to cross the frontier in women's clothes, and was arrested. A variety of *contretemps* occurred before he got to Paris, and by that time his rage had so cooled, his sense of the absurdity of the whole thing grown so keen, that he was rather willing to send Mdlle. M——— his blessing than his curse.

About the time of Berlioz's arrival, Miss Smithson also returned to Paris after a long absence, with the intent of undertaking the management of an English theatre. It was a necessity of our composer's nature to be in love, and the flames of his ardour, fed with fresh fuel, blazed up again from their old ashes. Berlioz gave a concert, in which his "Episode in the Life of an Artist" was interpreted in connection with the recitations of the text. The explanations of "Lelio" so unmistakably pointed to the feeling of the composer for herself, that Miss Smithson, who by chance was present, could not be deceived, though she never yet had seen Berlioz. A few days afterwards a benefit concert was arranged, in which Miss Smithson's troupe was to take part, as well as Berlioz, who was to direct a symphony of his own composition. At the rehearsal the looks of Berlioz followed Miss Smithson with such an intent stare, that she said to some one, "Who is that man whose eyes bode me no good?" This was the first occasion of their personal meeting, and it may be fancied that Berlioz followed up the introduction with his accustomed vehemence and pertinacity, though without immediate effect, for Miss Smithson was more inclined to fear than to love him.

The young directress soon found out that the rage for Shakespeare, which had swept the public mind under the influence of the romanticism led by Victor Hugo, Dumas, Théophile Gautier, Balzac, and others, was spurious. The wave had been frothing but shallow, and it ebbed away, leaving the English actress and her enterprise gasping for life. With no deeper tap-root than the Gallic love of novelty and the infectious enthusiasm of a few men of great genius, the Shakespearean mania had a short life, and Frenchmen shrugged their shoulders over their own folly, in temporarily preferring the English barbarian to Racine, Corneille, and Molière. The letters of Berlioz, in which he scourges the fickleness of his countrymen in returning again to their "false gods," are masterpieces of pointed invective.

Miss Smithson was speedily involved in great pecuniary difficulty, and, to add to her misfortunes, she fell down stairs and broke her leg, thus precluding her own appearance on the stage. Affairs were in this desperate condition, when Berlioz came to the fore with a delicate and manly chivalry worthy of the highest praise. He offered to pay Miss Smithson's debts, though a poor man himself, and to marry her without delay. The ceremony took place immediately, and thus commenced a connection which hampered and retarded Berlioz's career, as well as caused him no little personal unhappiness. He speedily discovered that his wife was a woman of fretful, imperious temper, jealous of mere shadows (though Berlioz was a man to give her substantial cause), and totally lacking in sympathy with his high-art ideals. When Mdme. Berlioz recovered, it was to find herself unable longer to act, as her leg was stiff and her movements unsuited to the exigencies of the stage. Poor Berlioz was crushed by the weight of the obligations he had assumed, and, as the years went on, the peevish plaints of an invalid wife, who had lost her beauty and power of charming, withered the affection which had once been so fervid and passionate. Berlioz finally separated from his once beautiful and worshipped Harriet Smithson, but to the very last supplied her wants as fully as he could out of the meagre earnings of his literary work and of musical compositions, which the Paris public, for the most part, did not care to listen to. For his son, Louis, the only offspring of this union, Berlioz felt a devoted affection, and his loss at sea in after-years was a blow that nearly broke his heart.

IV.

Owing to the unrelenting hostility of Cherubini, Berlioz failed to secure a professorship at the Conservatoire, a place to which he was nobly entitled, and was fain to take up with the position of librarian instead. The paltry wage he eked out by journalistic writing, for the most part as musical critic of the *Journal des Débats*, by occasional concerts, revising proofs, in a word anything which a versatile and desperate Bohemian could turn his hand to. In fact, for many years the main subsistence of Berlioz was derived from feuilleton-writing and the labours of a critic. His prose is so witty, brilliant, fresh, and epigrammatic, that he would have been known to posterity as a clever *littérateur*, had he not preferred to remain merely a great musician. Dramatic, picturesque, and subtile, with an admirable sense of art-form, he could have become a powerful dramatist, perhaps a great novelist. But his soul, all whose aspirations set towards one goal, revolted from the labours of literature, still more from the daily grind of journalistic drudgery. In that remarkable book, *Mémoires de Hector Berlioz*, he has made known his misery, and thus recounts one of his experiences:—" I stood at the window gazing into the gardens, at the heights of Montmartre, at the setting sun; reverie bore me a thousand leagues from my accursed comic opera. And when, on turning, my eyes fell upon the accursed title at the head of the accursed sheet, blank still, and obstinately awaiting my word, despair seized upon me. My guitar rested against the table; with a kick I crushed its side. Two pistols on the mantel stared at me with great round eyes. I regarded them for some time, then beat my forehead with clinched hand. At last I wept furiously, like a school-boy unable to do his theme. The bitter tears were a relief. I turned the pistols towards the wall; I pitied my innocent guitar, and sought a few chords, which were given without resentment. Just then my son of six years knocked at the door [the little Louis whose death, years after, was the last bitter drop in the composer's cup of life]; owing to my ill-humour, I had unjustly scolded him that morning. 'Papa,' he cried, 'wilt thou be friends?' 'I *will* be friends; come on, my boy;' and I ran to open the door. I took him on my knee, and, with his blonde head on my breast, we slept together. . . . Fifteen years since then, and my torment still endures. Oh, to be always there!— scores to write, orchestras to lead, rehearsals to direct. Let me stand all day with *bâton* in hand, training a chorus, singing their parts myself, and beating the measure until I spit blood, and cramp seizes my arm; let me carry desks, double basses, harps, remove platforms, nail planks like a porter or a carpenter, and then spend the night in rectifying the errors of engravers or copyists. I have done, do, and will do it. That belongs to my musical life, and I bear it without thinking of it, as the hunter bears the thousand fatigues of the chase. But to scribble eternally for a livelihood—— !"

It may be fancied that such a man as Berlioz did not spare the lash, once he gripped the whip-handle, and, though no man was more generous than he in recognising and encouraging genuine merit, there was none more relentless in scourging incompetency, pretentious commonplace, and the blind conservatism which rests all its faith in what has been. Our composer made more than one powerful enemy by this recklessness in telling the truth, where a more politic man would have gained friends strong to help in time of need. But Berlioz was too bitter and reckless, as well as too proud, to debate consequences.

In 1838 Berlioz completed his "Benvenuto Cellini," his only attempt at opera since "Les Francs Juges," and, wonderful to say, managed to get it done at the opera, though the director, Duponchel, laughed at him as a lunatic, and the whole company already regarded the work as damned in advance. The result was a most disastrous and *éclatant* failure, and it would have crushed any man whose moral backbone was not forged of thrice-tempered steel. With all these back-sets Hector Berlioz was not without encouragement. The brilliant Franz Liszt, one of the musical idols of the age, had bowed before him and called him master, the great musical protagonist. Spontini, one of the most successful composers of the time, held him in affectionate admiration, and always bade him be of good cheer. Paganini, the greatest of violinists, had hailed him as equal to Beethoven.

On the night of the failure of "Benvenuto Cellini," a strange-looking man with dishevelled black hair and eyes of piercing brilliancy had forced his way around into the green-room, and, seeking out Berlioz, had fallen on his knees before him and kissed his hand passionately. Then he threw his arms around him and hailed the astonished composer as the master-spirit of the age in terms of glowing eulogium. The next morning, while Berlioz was in bed, there was a tap at the door, and Paganini's son, Achille, entered with a note, saying his father was sick, or he would have come to pay his respects in person. On opening the note Berlioz found a most complimentary letter, and a more substantial evidence of admiration, a check on Baron Rothschild for twenty thousand francs! Paganini also gave Berlioz a commission to write a concerto for his Stradivarius viola, which resulted in a grand symphony, "Harold en Italie," founded on Byron's "Childe Harold," but still more an inspiration of his own Italian adventures, which had had a strong flavour of personal if they lacked artistic interest.

The generous gift of Paganini raised Berlioz from the slough of necessity so far that he could give his whole time to music. Instantly he set about his "Romeo and Juliet" symphony, which will always remain one of his masterpieces—a beautifully chiselled work, from the hands of one inspired by gratitude, unfettered imagination, and the sense of blessed repose. Our composer's first musical journey was an extensive tour in Germany in 1841, of which he gives charming memorials in his letters to Liszt, Heine, Ernst, and others. His reception was as generous and sympathetic as it had been cold and scornful in France. Everywhere he was honoured and praised as one of the great men of the age. Mendelssohn exchanged *bâtons* with him at Leipsic, notwithstanding the former only half understood this stalwart Berserker of music. Spohr called him one of the greatest artists living, though his own direct antithesis, and Schumann wrote glowingly in the *Neue Zeitschrift* —"For myself, Berlioz is as clear as the blue sky above. I really think there is a new time in music coming." Berlioz wrote joyfully to Heine—"I came to Germany as the men of ancient Greece went to the oracle at Delphi, and the response has been in the highest degree encouraging." But his Germanic laurels did him no good in France. The Parisians would have none of him except as a writer of *feuilletons*, who pleased them by the vigour with which he handled the knout, and tickled the levity of the million, who laughed while they saw the half-dozen or more victims flayed by merciless satire. Berlioz wept tears of blood because he had to do such executioner's work, but did it none the less vigorously for all that.

The composer made another musical journey in Austria and Hungary in 1844–45, where he was again received with the most enthusiastic praise and pleasure. It was in Hungary, especially, that the warmth of his audiences overran all bounds. One night, at Pesth, where he played the "Rackoczy Indulé," an orchestral setting of the martial hymn of the Magyar race, the people were worked into a positive frenzy, and they would have flung themselves before him that he might walk over their prostrate bodies. Vienna, Pesth, and Prague led the way, and the other cities followed in the wake of an enthusiasm which has been accorded to not many artists. The French heard these stories with amazement, for they could not understand how this musical demigod could be the same as he who was little better than a witty buffoon. During this absence Berlioz wrote the greater portion of his "Damnation de Faust," and, as he had made some money, he obeyed the strong instinct which always ruled him, the hope of winning the suffrages of his own countrymen.

An eminent French critic claims that this great work, of which we shall speak further on, contains that which Gounod's "Faust" lacks—insight into the spiritual significance of Goethe's drama. Berlioz exhausted all his resources in producing it at the Opéra Comique in 1846, but again he was disappointed by its falling still-born on the public interest. Berlioz was utterly ruined, and he fled from France in the dead of winter as from a pestilence.

The genius of this great man was recognised in Holland, Russia, Austria, and Germany, but among his own countrymen, for the most part, his name was a laughing-stock and a by-word. He offended the pedants and the formalists by his daring originality, he had secured the hate of rival musicians by the vigour and keenness of his criticisms. Berlioz was in the very heat of the artistic controversy between the classicists and romanticists, and was associated with Victor Hugo, Alexandre Dumas, Delacroix, Liszt, Chopin, and others, in fighting that acrimonious art-battle. While he did not stand formally with the ranks, he yet secured a still more bitter portion of hostility from their powerful opponents, for, to opposition in principle, Berlioz united a caustic and vigorous mode of expression. His name was a target for the wits. "A physician who plays on the guitar and fancies himself a composer," was the scoff of malignant gossips. The journals poured on him a flood of abuse without stint. French malignity is the most venomous and unscrupulous in the world, and Berlioz was selected as a choice victim for its most vigorous exercise, none the less willingly that he had shown so much skill and zest in impaling the victims of his own artistic and personal dislike.

V.

To continue the record of Berlioz's life in consecutive narrative would be without significance, for it contains but little for many years except the same indomitable battle against circumstance and enmity, never yielding an inch, and always keeping his eyes bent on his own lofty ideal. In all of art history is there no more masterful heroic struggle than Berlioz waged for thirty-five years, firm in his belief that some time, if not during his own life, his principles would be triumphant, and his name ranked among the immortals. But what of the meanwhile? This problem Berlioz solved, in his later as in earlier years, by doing the distasteful work of the literary scrub. But never did he cease composing; though no one would then have his works, his clear eye perceived the coming time when his genius would not be denied, when an apotheosis should comfort his spirit wandering in Hades.

Among Berlioz's later works was an opera of which he had composed both words and music, consisting of two parts, "The Taking of Troy," and "The Trojans at Carthage," the latter of which at last secured a few representations at a minor theatre in 1863. The plan of this work required that it should be carried out under the most perfect conditions. "In order," says Berlioz, "to properly produce such a work as 'Les Trojans,' I must be absolute master of the theatre, as of the orchestra in directing a symphony. I must have the good-will of all, be obeyed by all, from prima-donna to scene-shifter. A lyrical theatre, as I conceive it, is a great instrument of music, which, if I am to play, must be placed unreservedly in my hands." Wagner found a King of Bavaria to help him carry out a similar colossal scheme at Bayreuth, but ill luck followed a man no less great through life. His grand "Trojans" was mutilated, tinkered, patched, and belittled, to suit the Théatre Lyrique. It was a butchery of the work, but still it yielded the composer enough to justify his retirement from the *Journal des Débats*, after thirty years of slavery.

Berlioz was now sixty years old, a lonely man, frail in body, embittered in soul by the terrible sense of failure. His wife, with whom he had lived on terms of alienation, was dead; his only son far away, cruising on a man-of-war. His courage and ambition were gone. To one who remarked that his music belonged to the future, he replied that he doubted if it ever belonged to the past. His life seemed to have been a mistake, so utterly had he failed to impress himself on the public. Yet there were times when audiences felt themselves moved by the power of his music out of the ruts of preconceived opinion into a prophecy of his coming greatness. There is an interesting anecdote told by a French writer:—

"Some years ago M. Pasdeloup gave the *septuor* from the 'Trojans' at a benefit concert. The best places were occupied by the people of the world, but the *élite intelligente* were ranged upon the highest seats of the Cirque. The programme was superb, and those who were there neither for Fashion's nor Charity's sake, but for love of what was best in art, were enthusiastic in view of all those masterpieces. The worthless overture of the 'Prophète,' disfiguring this fine *ensemble*, had been hissed by some students of the Conservatoire, and, accustomed as I was to the blindness of the general public, knowing its implacable prejudices, I trembled for the fate of the magnificent *septuor* about to follow. My fears were strangely ill-founded; no sooner had ceased this hymn of infinite love and peace, than these same students, and the whole assemblage with them, burst into such a tempest of applause as I never heard before. Berlioz was hidden in the further ranks, and, the instant he was discovered, the work was forgotten for the man; his name flew from mouth to mouth, and four thousand people were standing upright, with their arms stretched towards him. Chance had placed me near him, and never shall I forget the scene. That name, apparently ignored by the crowd, it had learned all at once, and was repeating as that of one of its heroes. Overcome as by the strongest emotion of his life, his head upon his breast, he listened to this tumultuous cry of 'Vive Berlioz!' and when, on looking up, he saw all eyes upon him and all arms extended towards him, he could not withstand the sight; he trembled, tried to smile, and broke into sobbing."

Berlioz's supremacy in the field of orchestral composition, his knowledge of technique, his novel combination, his insight into the resources of instruments, his skill in grouping, his rich sense of colour, are incontestably without a parallel, except by Beethoven and Wagner. He describes his own method of study as follows:—

"I carried with me to the opera the score of whatever work was on the bill, and read during the performance. In this way I began to familiarise myself with orchestral methods, and to learn the voice and quality of the various instruments, if not their range and mechanism. By this attentive comparison of the effect with the means employed to produce it, I found the hidden link uniting musical expression to the special art of instrumentation. The study of Beethoven, Weber, and Spontini, the impartial examination both of the *customs* of orchestration and of *unusual* forms and combinations, the visits I made to *virtuosi*, the trials I led them to make upon their respective instruments, and a little instinct, did for me the rest."

The principal symphonies of Berlioz are works of colossal character and richness of treatment, some of them requiring several orchestras. Contrasting with these are such marvels of delicacy as "Queen Mab," of which it has been said that the "confessions of roses and the complaints of violets were noisy in comparison." A man of magnificent genius and knowledge, he was but little understood during his life, and it was only when his uneasy spirit was at rest that the world recognised his greatness. Paris, that stoned him when he was living, now listens to his grand music with enthusiasm. Hector Berlioz to the last never lost faith in himself, though this man of genius, in his much suffering from depression and melancholy, gave good witness to the truth of Goethe's lines :—

> " Who never ate with tears his bread,
> Nor, weeping through the night's long hours,
> Lay restlessly tossing on his bed—
> He knows ye not, ye heavenly Powers."

A man utterly without reticence, who, Gallic fashion, would shout his wrongs and sufferings to the uttermost ends of the earth, yet without a smack of Gallic posing and affectation, Berlioz talks much about himself, and dares to estimate himself boldly. There was no small vanity about this colossal spirit. He speaks of himself with outspoken frankness, as he would discuss another. We cannot do better than to quote one of these self-measurements :—" My style is in general very daring, but it has not the slightest tendency to destroy any of the constructive elements of art. On the contrary, I seek to increase the number of these elements. I have never dreamed, as has foolishly been supposed in France, of writing music without melody. That school exists to-day in Germany, and I have a horror of it. It is easy for any one to convince himself that, without confining myself to taking a very short melody for a theme, as the very greatest masters have, I have always taken care to invest my compositions with a real wealth of melody. The value of these melodies, their distinction, their novelty, and charm, can be very well contested; it is not for me to appraise them. But to deny their existence is either bad faith or stupidity; only as these melodies are often of very large dimensions, infantile and short-sighted minds do not clearly distinguish their form; or else they are wedded to other secondary melodies which veil their outlines from those same infantile minds; or, upon the whole, these melodies are so dissimilar to the little waggeries that the musical *plebs* call melodies that they cannot make up their minds to give the same name to both. The dominant qualities of my music are passionate expression, internal fire, rhythmic animation, and unexpected changes."

Heinrich Heine, the German poet, who was Berlioz's friend, called him a "colossal nightingale, a lark of eagle-size, such as they tell us existed in the primeval world." The poet goes on to say—"Berlioz's music, in general, has in it something primeval if not antediluvian to my mind; it makes me think of gigantic species of extinct animals, of fabulous empires full of fabulous sins, of heaped-up impossibilities; his magical accents call to our minds Babylon, the hanging gardens, the wonders of Nineveh, the daring edifices of Mizraim, as we see them in the pictures of the Englishman Martin." Shortly after the publication of "Lutetia," in which this bold characterisation was expressed, the first performance of Berlioz's "Enfance du Christ" was given, and the poet, who was on his sick-bed, wrote a penitential letter to his friend for not having given him justice. "I hear on all sides," he says, "that you have just plucked a nosegay of the sweetest melodious flowers, and that your oratorio is throughout a masterpiece of *naïveté*. I shall never forgive myself for having been so unjust to a friend."

Berlioz died at the age of sixty-five. His funeral services were held at the Church of the Trinity, a few days after those of Rossini. The discourse at the grave was pronounced by Gounod, and many eloquent things were said of him, among them a quotation of the epitaph of Marshal Trivulce, "*Hic tandem quiescit qui nunquam quievit*" (Here he is quiet, at last, who never was quiet before). Soon after his death appeared his *Mémoires*, and his bones had hardly got cold when the performance of his music at the Conservatoire, the Cirque, and the Chatelet began to be heard with the most hearty enthusiasm.

VI.

Théophile Gautier says that no one will deny to Berlioz a great character, though, the world being given to controversies, it may be argued whether or not he was a great genius. The world of to-day has but one opinion on both these questions. The force of Berlioz's character was phenomenal. His vitality was so passionate and active that brain and nerve quivered with it, and made him reach out towards experience at every facet of his nature. Quietude was torture, rest a sin, for this daring temperament. His eager and subtile intelligence pierced every sham, and his imagination knew no bounds to its sweep, oftentimes even disdaining the bounds of art in its audacity and impatience. This big, virile nature, thwarted and embittered by opposition, became hardened into violent self-assertion; this naturally resolute will settled back into fierce obstinacy; this fine nature, sensitive and sincere, got torn and ragged with passion under the stress of his unfortunate life. But, at one breath of true sympathy how quickly the nobility of the man asserted itself! All his cynicism and hatred melted away, and left only sweetness, truth, and genial kindness.

When Berlioz entered on his studies, he had reached an age at which Mozart, Schubert, Mendelssohn, Rossini, and others, had already done some of the best work of their lives. Yet it took only a few years to achieve a development that produced such a great work as the "Symphonie Fantastique," the prototype of modern programme music.

From first to last it was the ambition of Berlioz to widen the domain of his art. He strove to attain a more intimate connection between instrumental music and poetry in the portrayal of intense passions, and the suggestion of well-defined dramatic situations. In spite of the fact that he frequently overshot his mark, it does not make his works one whit less astonishing. An uncompromising champion of what has been dubbed "programme" music, he thought it legitimate to force the imagination of the hearer to dwell on exterior scenes during the progress of the music, and to distress the mind in its attempt to find an exact relation between the text and the music. The most perfect specimens of the works of Berlioz, however, are those in which the music speaks for itself, such as the "Scène aux Champs," and the "Marche au Supplice," in the "Symphonie Fantastique," the "Marche des Pèlerins," in "Harold;" the overtures to "King Lear," "Benvenuto Cellini," "Carnaval Romain," "Le Corsaire," "Les Francs Juges," etc.

As a master of the orchestra, no one has been the equal of Berlioz in the whole history of music, not even Beethoven or Wagner. He treats the orchestra with the absolute daring and mastery exercised by Paganini over the violin, and by Liszt over the piano. No one has showed so deep an insight into the individuality of each instrument, its resources, the extent to which its capabilities could be carried. Between the phrase and the instrument, or group of instruments, the equality is perfect; and independent of this power, made up equally of instinct and knowledge, this composer shows a sense of orchestral colour in combining single instruments so as to form groups, or in the combination of several separate groups of instruments by which he has produced the most novel and beautiful effects—effects not found in other composers. The originality and variety of his rhythms, the perfection of his instrumentation, have never been disputed even by his opponents. In many of his works, especially those of a religious character, there is a Cyclopean bigness of instrumental means used, entirely beyond parallel in art. Like the Titans of old, he would scale the very heavens in his daring. In one of his works he does not hesitate to use three orchestras, three choruses (all of full dimensions), four organs, and a triple quartet. The conceptions of Berlioz were so grandiose that he sometimes disdained detail, and the result was that more than one of his compositions have rugged grandeur at the expense of symmetry and balance of form.

Yet, when he chose, Berlioz could write the most exquisite and dainty lyrics possible. What could be more exquisitely tender than many of his songs and romances, and various of the airs and choral pieces from "Beatrice et Benedict," from "Nuits dE'té," "Irlande," and from "L'Enfance du Christ?"

Berlioz in his entirety, as man and composer, was a most extraordinary being, to whom the ordinary scale of measure can hardly be applied. Though he founded no new school, he pushed to a fuller development the possibilities to which Beethoven reached out in the Ninth Symphony. He was the great *virtuoso* on the orchestra, and on this Briarean instrument he played with the most amazing skill. Others have surpassed him in the richness of the musical substance out of which their tone-pictures are woven, in symmetry of form, in finish of detail; but no one has ever equalled him in that absolute mastery over instruments, by which a hundred become as plastic and flexible as one, and are made to embody every phase of the composer's thought with that warmth of colour and precision of form long believed to be necessarily confined to the sister arts.

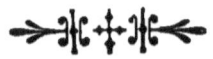

APPENDIX.

CHRONOLOGICAL TABLE.

1520—1594	*Palestrina.*
1633—1687	*Lulli.*
1658—1695	*Purcell.*
1659—1725	*A. Scarlatti.*
1685—1750	*S. Bach.*
1685—1759	*Handel.*
1710—1736	*Pergolesi.*
1714—1787	*Glück.*
1728—1800	*Piccini.*
1732—1809	*Haydn.*
1741—1816	*Paisiello.*
1741—1813	*Grétry.*
1749—1801	*Cimarosa.*
1756—1791	*Mozart.*
1760—1842	*Cerubini.*
1763—1817	*Méhul.*
1770—1802	*Beethoven.*
1774—1851	*Spontini.*
1775—1834	*Boieldieu.*
1782—1871	*Auber.*
1786—1826	*Weber.*
1791—1864	*Meyerbeer.*
1792—1868	*Rossini.*
1797—1828	*Schubert.*
1798—1848	*Donizetti.*
1799—1862	*Halévy.*
1802—1835	*Bellini.*
1803—1869	*Berlioz.*
1809—1847	*Mendelssohn.*
1809—1849	*Chopin.*
1810—1856	*Schumann.*
1813—1883	*Wagner.*
1813	*Verdi.*
1818	*Gounod.*

www.ingramcontent.com/pod-product-compliance
Lightning Source LLC
Chambersburg PA
CBHW031432230426
43668CB00007B/502